FOOD LOVERS' SERIES

FOOD LOVERS'
GUIDE TO
VERMONT &
NEW HAMPSHIRE

The Best Restaurants, Markets & Local Culinary Offerings

1st Edit

Patricia Harris & David Lyon

gpp

Guilford, Connecticut

Editor: Amy Lyons
Project Editor: Lynn Zelem
Layout Artist: Mary Ballachino
Text Design: Sheryl Kober
Illustrations by Jill Butler with additional art by Carleen Moira Powell and MaryAnn Dubé
Maps: Ryan Mitchell © Morris Book Publishing, LLC

ISBN 978-0-7627-7949-9

Printed in the United States of America
10 9 8 7 6 5 4 3 2 1

All the information in this guidebook is subject to change. We recommend that you call ahead to obtain current information before traveling.

Contents

New Hampshire, 185

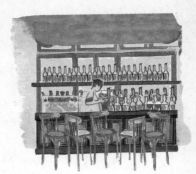

Recipes, 343

Appendices, 367

About the Authors

Patricia Harris and **David Lyon** met over ratatouille made from fresh garden vegetables and courted over fudge-topped brownies. Decades later, they're still cooking, still traveling, and still writing about it for their Hungry Travelers food and travel blog (hungry travelers.com). They are coauthors of Globe Pequot Press's *The Meaning of Food, Food Lovers' Guide to Massachusetts,* and *Food Lovers' Guide to Montreal,* and the forthcoming *Food Lovers' Guide to Boston*. Based in Cambridge, Massachusetts, they have written about Vermont cheese, Belgian beer, Tahitian *poisson cru,* New Hampshire hot dogs, Neapolitan pizza, Maine lobster, and Spanish elvers for such publications as the *Boston Globe, The Robb Report,* and *Cooking Light*. They have made every effort, however, to bring those tastes of travel back home and hope you do the same.

Dedication

This book is dedicated to hungry travelers everywhere.

Acknowledgments

We would like to acknowledge the Vermont and New Hampshire farmers, chefs, bakers, candymakers, winemakers, brewmasters, and restaurateurs who gave us good reason to write this book in the first place. Their heroic response to the devastation wrought in both states by Hurricane Irene in August 2011 was truly inspirational, and we were humbled by their gracious hospitality. We are especially thankful to the cooks and chefs and farmers who shared their recipes for this volume. We offer a memorial salute to the late Laura Strom for conceiving the Food Lovers' series, and thank Amy Lyons for letting us take such an active role in the much expanded series. We also want to thank editor Lynn Zelem for shepherding this manuscript to publication.

Introduction: Vermont & New Hampshire— Four Seasons of Flavor

To get a real taste of Vermont and New Hampshire, you'll have to travel a lot of unpaved roads. A few bumps and ruts aside, there are far worse ways to spend your days than motoring through a rolling countryside of alternating patches of pasture and forest, red barns sheltering dairy herds, twisting furrows of potato fields, and, in late winter, weathered gray cabins with smoke curling from the chimney of a sugar evaporator or a smokehouse.

Many of the specialty products—the cheeses, breads, smoked meats, maple syrup—that you'll find at the end of the road may be available in stores, especially in nearby natural food co-ops. But there's something deeply satisfying about going to the source, seeing where the product is grown or made, and meeting some of the people who grow or make it. A great cheese becomes all the more amazing when you've encountered the grazing cows, sheep, and goats, and then talked with the cheesemaker. Seeing the stony glacial till of the fields gives you a special appreciation for the vegetables a farmer has coaxed from such uncooperative soil. When you gaze across vineyards of espaliered grape vines, you marvel that you are in Vermont or New Hampshire, not Bordeaux or Napa Valley.

At the source, you might also find products not available elsewhere—the experimental wine or beer, the limited production cheese, even the specialty bread that the bakery sells only to its retail customers.

For all their cultural and political differences, Vermont and New Hampshire are two sides of the same northern New England climate—the high landscapes of the Green Mountains and the White Mountains glued together by the Connecticut River Valley. Vermont has the verdant land of the Champlain Valley as its richest farming country, while New Hampshire has the rich soils of the Merrimack Valley and the advantage of a slight but significant marine coast. Both states have grand ski country with their attendant resorts and restaurants. Time of year is always important, as these states have sharply defined seasons. As the tail end of winter transitions slowly into mud season, you will encounter maple sugaring. Over the summer, the harvest seems so bountiful that the landscape almost seems to groan under the weight of great food. By the time the legendary autumn foliage hits its stride, every lawn seems covered with pumpkins and the smell of apples permeates the countryside.

Marketing imagery aside, neither state is entirely rural. In fact, the busy towns and cities are where you will find most of the terrific res- taurants: Burlington with its pedestrian-friendly downtown, Middlebury with its students and professors, Manchester and Nashua with their mill architecture and ethnic influences, Portsmouth with its salty history that looks to the sea.

Long before the boom in culinary education, the New England Culinary Institute in Montpelier began training chefs and other restaurant professionals. There are more than 4,000 alumni of NECI, and a large number of them still work in Vermont and New Hampshire. Even beyond its chef training programs, NECI helped create a culinary awareness that has converged with the worldwide locavore movement. Increasingly, menus describe the pedigree of the ingredients in every dish, using the words "local" and "artisan" even more frequently than we do in these pages. What is astonishing in both states is the level of culinary sophistica- tion. You'll find food with character everywhere from casual bakery cafes to fine-dining restaurants, from historic roadside diners to splendid brick-oven pizza in the back of a rural country store. And the food you find is no more predictable than the place you find it—the fabulous French-Canadian *tourtière* in a rural bakery cafe, Indonesian street food in a former warehouse building on the New Hampshire coast, or *tortilla española* at a tapas bar on the shores of Lake Memphremagog.

The classic flavors of Vermont and New Hampshire persist—apples, maple syrup, and cheddar cheese—but sometimes show up in surprising ways. Maple syrup poured on a stack of pancakes is delicious—but so is a cordial glass of maple liqueur after dinner. We would never want to give up the tart crunch of a good old-fashioned apple, but we also welcome a sip of farmhouse apple brandy. The cheesemaking tradition in Vermont not only gave us wonderful old-fashioned Colby and cheddar cheeses, it's grown into an artisanal revolution. Not only can you find world-class blue cheese, you might even find it enrobed in dark chocolate.

Perhaps the biggest food revolution in both states has been in beverages. Brewpubs and breweries, once ski-country novelties, have matured into world-class craft brewers. Hard cider has made a comeback, and with it, ice cider, a sweet drink modeled on ice wines. Other producers have turned to mead—a fine wine fermented from honey and sometimes flavored with local fruits. The most startling development has been the spread of Vermont and New Hampshire wineries. Some still rely on berries and apples, but many now grow cold-climate wine grapes. It is a nascent industry, but a handful of the best producers are making exceptional wines.

We have always believed that tasting local food is a way to get to know a place and its people. We hope you agree. Please consider this book your introduction.

How to Use This Book

We have divided the two states into 11 regions. Starting in Vermont, the chapters progress from the vibrant restaurant scene of Burlington and the riches of the Champlain Valley across the northern tier of the Green Mountain State to the Stowe-Montpelier axis and then east to the Northeast Kingdom. The guide continues to central and then southern Vermont before jumping over the Connecticut River to New Hampshire. Beginning up north in the White Mountains and the Great North Woods, the chapters work progressively southward in east-west bands, catching the Lakes region, the Sunapee region and Upper Connecticut River Valley, Keene and the Monadnock Region, the Merrimack Valley, and concluding with Portsmouth and New Hampshire's short but sweet seacoast. Each chapter is packed with wonderful places to visit as you're passing through, and other establishments that are destinations in themselves. Alas, space does not permit us to include every worthy spot.

Each chapter includes a map of the region, which can help you plan trips to do your own exploring. While you're on the road, be sure to check chapters for adjacent areas—a terrific surprise might await just a few miles away. Farmstands and farm stores are seasonal by nature, and we've done our best to identify when they're open. Still, it's always a good idea to call ahead. Bring cash in the form of lots of small bills and coins because self-service stands may not have change. Only a few places accept personal checks.

Because we have sliced and diced the regions into manageable portions, we have listed entries in just a few categories:

Foodie Faves

These are principally restaurants and more casual eateries (such as diners and bakery cafes) that represent some of the best dining in the region.

Landmarks

This designation identifies a few places that are iconic, and may have even helped define the regions where they are located.

Specialty Stores, Markets & Producers

This section of each chapter is devoted to places where you can get all the wonderful ingredients to prepare a great meal or a picnic and the shops where you can purchase the kitchen hardware to turn provender into repast. The category also includes pastry shops, bread bakeries, coffee roasters, and breweries and wineries with tasting rooms. We have placed artisanal cheesemakers, confectioners, maple syrup producers, and farms that sell their own butchered meat in this category as well.

Farmstands & Pick Your Own

Farmstands can range from a card table and a hand-lettered sign at the end of a driveway to a year-round store that offers honey, jam, pickles, breads, and maybe even flowers in addition to fresh fruits and vegetables. We could not possibly include every farm selling a few cucumbers from a table by the mailbox, but have tried to include many that are open for longer seasons. Pick-your-own produce and fruit operations are included in this category.

Farm Stays

The ultimate in agricultural tourism is the farm stay—essentially a rural B&B on a working farm. They offer the charm of a retreat in the countryside with additional insight into the day-to-day operations of a farm.

Farmers' Markets

Many Vermont and New Hampshire farms have been in the same families for generations, and farmers' markets are essential venues for meeting the people behind your dinner. Farmers selling at the markets often feel they must offer something special, something you cannot get from the local grocery store. That may be an heirloom fruit or vegetable, an unusual ethnic varietal, or the assurance that the food you buy is free of chemicals. Because the number of farmers' markets continues to proliferate, it's always a good idea to double-check times and locations at either the **New Hampshire Farmer's Market Association** (www.nhfma.org) or the **Vermont Department of Agriculture** (www.vermontagriculture.com).

Food Events

Vermont and New Hampshire love to celebrate, and the calendar is riddled with fairs, festivals, cook-offs, and other culinary events.

Price Code

We've tried to give some guidance on how much it will cost you to eat at the restaurants in this book. The price code is keyed to the cost of a main dish at dinner. Keep in mind that most restaurants are less expensive at lunchtime, and that even expensive restaurants may offer a less-expensive pub or bar menu.

$ Less than $10. This includes most diners and fast food.

$$ Main dishes $10 to $20. These are usually casual dining spots.

$$$ Main dishes $20 to $40. This includes many classy but casual spots as well as many fine-dining restaurants.

$$$$ Main dishes cost more than $40 or restaurant only offers a prix fixe of more than $40. These are usually special-occasion dining options.

Keeping Up with Food News

Edible Green Mountains, www.ediblegreenmountains.com: Quarterly magazine celebrates the local food culture of Vermont with focus on farmers, growers, fishermen, home cooks, and chefs. Magazine available free at many locations. Current issue online.

The Hippo, www.hippopress.com: New Hampshire's weekly tabloid entertainment weekly focuses primarily on Manchester, NH, but also covers dining in the Merrimack Valley. Publishes an annual "Best of" readers' poll that includes many categories of restaurants.

New Hampshire Farm to Restaurant Connection, www .nhfarmtorestaurant.com: This group sponsors Growers' Dinners, which usually take place on a farm from July into September. See the website for schedule and reservation information.

New Hampshire magazine, www.nhmagazine.com: This state-wide lifestyle magazine includes restaurant news and publishes an annual "Best of" issue.

New Hampshire Maple **Producers Association,** www  .nhmapleproducers.com: Publishes an events page and a map to pro-ducers open during sugaring season.

Seacoast Eat Local, www.seacoasteatlocal.com: This organiza-tion sponsors foodie workshops and events, and provides news about food issues on the New Hampshire seacoast.

Seven Days, www.7dvt.com: Burlington-based alternative weekly publishes some food news, with most up-to-date items available on the website Seven Nights (www.7nvt.com).

Vermont Farms Association, www.vtfarms.org: The website posts farm-related events, most having to do with dining.

Tours & Trails

Vermont Grape and Wine Council
www.vermontgrapeandwinecouncil.com
The council publishes an interactive online map of Vermont wineries and vineyards.

Vermont Brewers Association
www.brewersvt.com
The association provides an online brewery tour map.

Vermont Cheese Association
www.vtcheese.com
Membership always seems to be growing. See the latest Vermont Cheese Trail on the website.

New Hampshire Tourism
www.visitnh.gov
New Hampshire's brewery map provides a useful tour: www.visitnh.gov/itineraries/nh-brewery-map.pdf.

New Hampshire Winery Association
www.nhwineryassociation.com
The Association creates and publishes a winery tour map. The link is on the website.

New Hampshire Cheesemaker's Guild
www.nhdairypromo.com
The guild publishes a map and index of its members.

Vermont Fresh Network, www.vermontfresh.net: Vermont Fresh Network encourages farmers, food producers, and chefs to work together. Website posts a number of foodie events, conferences, and confabs.

Vermont Maple Sugar Makers' Association, www.vermontmaple.org: Publishes an events page and a map to producers open during sugaring season.

Vermont Tree Fruit Growers Association, www.vermontapples.org: The association publishes an annual harvest guide in print and online.

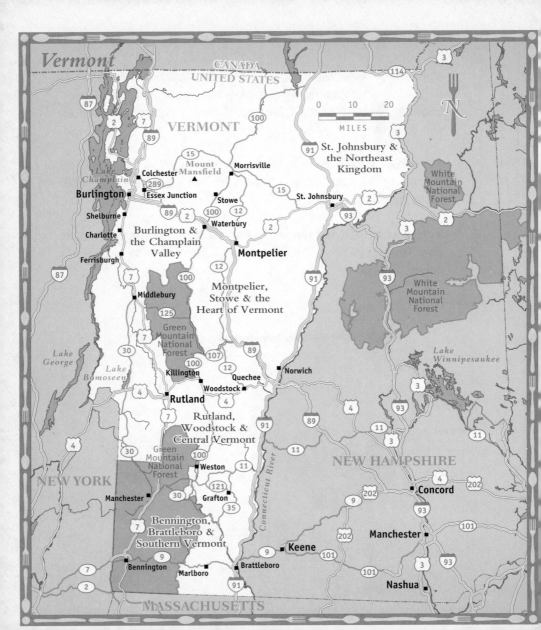

Vermont

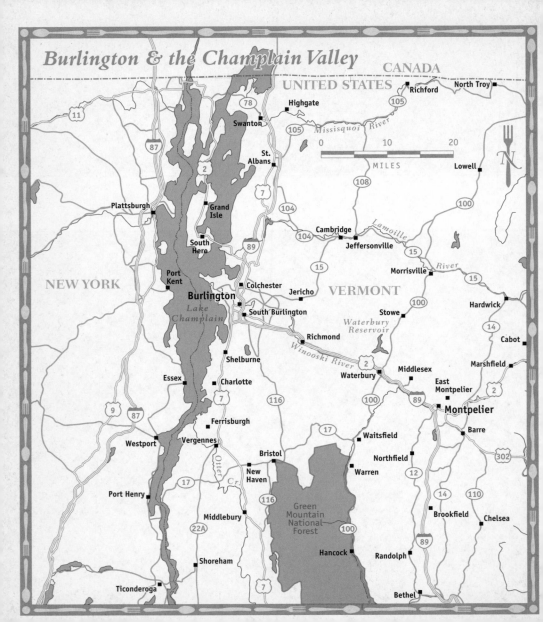

Burlington & the Champlain Valley

CANADA

UNITED STATES

NEW YORK

VERMONT

Lake Champlain

Green Mountain National Forest

Missisquoi River

Lamoille River

Winooski River

Otter Cr.

Waterbury Reservoir

0   10   20

MILES

N

Richford
North Troy
Highgate
Swanton
St. Albans
Lowell
Plattsburgh
Grand Isle
South Hero
Cambridge
Jeffersonville
Morrisville
Hardwick
Cabot
Marshfield
Port Kent
Colchester
Jericho
Stowe
Burlington
South Burlington
Richmond
Waterbury
Middlesex
East Montpelier
Montpelier
Shelburne
Barre
Essex
Charlotte
Waitsfield
Northfield
Warren
Ferrisburgh
Vergennes
Bristol
New Haven
Hancock
Randolph
Brookfield
Chelsea
Bethel
Westport
Port Henry
Middlebury
Shoreham
Ticonderoga

11
78
105
105
87
2
7
108
104
104
100
89
15
15
15
116
116
100
2
100
89
302
9
87
17
17
12
14
110
22A
89
7

Burlington & the Champlain Valley

Vermont's upper left-hand corner draws its complex identity from many different sources, including the outdoorsy environmental consciousness of Middlebury College, the diversity of the land-grant University of Vermont, former hippie enclaves, and hard-core farmers determined to tough it out on the land just as their forebears have over the last two centuries. All these forces combine to make the Champlain Valley a hotbed of farm-to-fork dining. Moreover, while the New England Culinary Institute is based in Montpelier, the restaurants of Burlington and nearby towns are filled with NECI-trained chefs. Restaurants abound in pedestrian-friendly downtown Burlington, making it easily the gourmand capital of Vermont.

It is also hard to overestimate the impact of Lake Champlain on local agriculture. So large that it is sometimes called the "little" Great Lake, Champlain's waters change the local climate by holding heat into the fall and keeping the region cooler during the summer.

As a result, farmers in the valley can grow crops for which most of the rest of the state is too cold. It is no accident, for example, that Vermont's best wineries are concentrated in this chapter. The wineries enjoy the best of two worlds, however. When cold weather does arrive in late November or early December, the conditions are ideal for making ice wine.

Foodie Faves

Al's French Frys, 1251 Williston Rd., South Burlington; (802) 862-9203; www.alsfrenchfrys.com; $. It's not surprising that everyone knows the drill at Al's, since it seems that every customer has at least one family member who has worked at this South Burlington institution since it opened in the late 1940s. The uninitiated should simply join the long line, inch forward to the cashier where you place and pay for your order, then continue shuffling ahead until you can watch the cooks at work in the open kitchen. About the order itself: start with *"frys"* (available in quart, pint or cup servings) and then select your accompaniment, perhaps a chili dog, double cheeseburger, or Philly cheese steak. It really is all about the *"frys"*—which have been freshly cut, quickly blanched, and fried twice before they reach your plate. The surface is crisp and seals in the strong flavor of the potatoes. Al's has expanded over the years, even adding inside booths for dining, but many regulars still prefer to eat in their cars on a nice summer evening. Strip malls have replaced the farmland that once surrounded Al's, but this fast-food stalwart remains undiminished, perhaps explaining why the James Beard Foundation named it as one of America's Classics in 2010.

American Flatbread/Hearth (Middlebury), Marble Works, 137 Maple St., Middlebury; (802) 388-3300; **American Flatbread/ Hearth (Burlington),** 115 St. Paul St., Burlington; (802) 861- 2999; www.americanflatbread.com; $$. The original farm-based **Flatbread Kitchen** in Waitsfield (p. 65) has two in-town siblings. The cavernous hall inside the old Marble Works in Middlebury turns into the pizza equivalent of a beer hall for a few hours in the evening. Pizzaiolas shuffle the signature American Flatbread pizzas in and out of the earthen oven on long peels and the cheerful din of diners fills the room. A similar din with a more urban vibe holds forth at the down- town Burlington location, which also houses **Zero Gravity Craft Brewery,** which has about a dozen of its own beers on tap. At both locations the wine list tends toward affordable, fruity, and fresh, tapping some of the less familiar grapes (Viognier, Grüner Veltliner, and Tempranillo) and less common growing areas (Portugal, the Côtes du Ventoux).

Basin Harbor Club, 4800 Basin Harbor Rd., Vergennes; (802) 475-2311; www.basinharbor.com; $$$. Casual elegance is the theme of the sumptuous Basin Harbor Club resort on the shores of Lake

Champlain. The **main dining** room of the resort offers a modern update of classical fine dining with dishes like roast chicken (from Misty Knoll, of course, see p. 47) glazed with lime and ginger, or pan-roasted duck in an anise-merlot sauce. With its rustic barn decor, the **Red Mill Restaurant** ($$) is a more casual venue, popular for drinks at the bar after a round of golf, and big with locals as well as guests. The menu is part grill (seared tuna with mixed greens, grilled steaks with fries) and part pub fare (braised St. Louis ribs with a bourbon sauce, a half-pound burger).

Belted Cow Bistro, 4 Park St., Essex; (802) 316-3883; www .beltedcowvt.com; $$$. This smart-looking bistro right on the traffic circle in the middle of Essex leads a kind of dual life. Chef John Delpha mainly sticks to wonderfully streamlined American bistro fare like seared scallops with a cauliflower puree or Quebec duck breast and confit leg with carrots, mushrooms, and poached black figs. That kind of cooking is the perfect match to the airy dining room with casual wooden tables and chairs. But Delpha is also the 2009 Grand Champion and twice category champion at the Jack Daniels World Barbecue Championship, so roughly once a week the paper towels and paper napkins come out for a night of barbecue. If you order far enough in advance, he will even do a whole barbecued suckling pig for the table.

Black Sheep Bistro, 253 Main St., Vergennes; (802) 877-9991; www.blacksheepbistrovt.com; $$$. With its dark wooden tables, bentwood chairs covered with multicolored woven seats, and worn wooden floor, Black Sheep looks the part of a Parisian bistro. It also harks back to bistro roots by pricing its food within reach and serving classic homey dishes. Start with chicken liver pâté served with crostini and cornichons, a grape and almond white gazpacho, or nicely garlicky escargots Provençal. That should whet your appetite for a coriander-crusted small steak, a seared tuna Niçoise salad, or ravioli stuffed with Vermont chèvre and served with julienned vegetables. Wines by the bottle start almost as low as we've ever seen in an American restaurant.

Blue Paddle Bistro, 316 Rte. 2, South Hero; (802) 372-4814; www.bluepaddlebistro.com; $$$. Classy comfort food in a historic house makes Blue Paddle worth seeking out. The canoe hanging over the bar suggests the whimsy that keeps co-owners Mandy Hotchkiss and Phoebe Bright sane. Crab cakes are the size of a small fist, and the sea bass (seasoned with a little smoky bacon) is perfect on a bed of local spinach. The owners have tried to take the Gorgonzola-stuffed meatloaf off the menu, but regulars won't have it. Sunday brunch, served spring through fall, has some tasty inventions, including a salmon burger BLT with cucumber and caper mayonnaise. The wine list is eclectic but features **Snow Farm Vineyard** (p. 48).

Bobcat Cafe & Brewery, 5 Main St., Bristol; (802) 453-3311; www.bobcatcafe.com; $$. While the name sounds New England, the Bobcat is a transplanted Alsatian brasserie where brewmaster Mark Magiera crafts beer that he considers more food than drink. His Brickwall double IPA celebrates the hop-growing culture of Vermont, using his own Chinook hops grown on the east wall of the cafe along with hops grown in Lincoln and New Haven. His Unrepentant is a gigantic stout brewed with Indian long pepper and treated with cacao nibs. The result is a peppery chocolate stout with espresso notes on the finish. Of course, he also makes American and German pale ales, which might be better matches for the venison stew, the sage-butter potato gnocchi, or the chèvre and mushroom lasagna. Real hopheads might want to try the stout float for dessert.

Bove's Cafe, 68 Pearl St., Burlington; (802) 864-6651; www.boves.com; $$. Louis and Victoria Bove opened this cafe in 1941 and their grandsons run it today. Not only does Bove's serve a quintessential Italian-American red-sauce menu, it makes and sells the quintessential Italian-American red sauce, or quintessential for Vermont. Bobby Flay did a lasagna *Throwdown* here (and lost), but many diners are partial to the spaghetti and meatballs. (Very *Lady and the Tramp*.) The place has been remodeled a bit over the years, but with the central glowing jukebox and the cozy booths lining the walls, Bove's oozes nostalgia the way its lasagna oozes cheese.

Cafe Shelburne, 5573 Shelburne Rd., Shelburne; (802) 985-3939; www.cafeshelburne.com; $$$. There's nothing faux about the French country food that Chef Patrick Grangien prepares at this tasteful roadside restaurant just across the street from one of the entrances to the Shelburne Museum. Trained in France, Grangien prepares light versions of French classics—pan-roasted veal tenderloin in a white-wine sauce, sautéed duck breast with mushroom risotto, steamed salmon with a lemon-caper sauce. Prices are modest for food that could grace a provincial Michelin one-star restaurant.

Church & Main, 156 B Church St., Burlington; (802) 540-3040; www.churchandmainvt.com; $$$. Bustling and stylish without ever seeming the least bit formal, Church & Main serves simple New American dishes that tend to contrast two strong flavors or two textures or both. The salt-roasted beet salad pairs with a soft cheese soufflé, for example, and the cider-brined pork chop is matched with a duck sausage cassoulet. The kitchen sources most of its meats and produce locally when the season permits, and the farms that supply star ingredients (lamb from Winding Brook Farm, for example) get billing on the menu. The kitchen is particularly adept at preparing meals for diners with gluten or dairy allergies. The outdoor sidewalk tables are extremely popular in the summer, as the restaurant sits on the corner of the pedestrianized section of Church Street.

Daily Planet, 15 Center St., Burlington; (802) 862-9647; www
.dailyplanet15.com; $$. We usually stay away from restaurants
where the menu has a little from this cuisine and a little from that
and some more from another place. That said, even though Daily
Planet samples at least the spice profiles of dishes from around the
world, the kitchen has domesticated them into a cohesive bistro-
lite menu. In the end, the dishes are simple, good food, whether
it's a plate of red beans and rice, or grilled pita bread with
spiced spinach and kale and a farmer's cheese made in the
kitchen. The first plate almost speaks bayou Creole, and
the second is a worthy adaptation of *saag paneer*. Still,
it's even wiser to order closer to home. Big John's Supper,
for example, is a fine plate of barbecued braised pork,
johnny cakes, and apple sauce. It's a nice dish to pair
with Burlington's own Switchback Unfiltered Ale,
a brew that's hard to find since so little is made.

Das Bierhaus, 175 Church St., Burlington; (802) 881-0600; www
.dasbierhausvt.com; $$–$$$. The female servers wear dirndls that
have a bit of a naughty schoolgirl vibe, but we guess that is just
part of the fun at this German restaurant with a rooftop beer garden
and soccer matches playing on a big screen TV. Soft Bavarian-
style pretzels (plain or with cheese) are the nosh of choice with
the German beers on tap. The menu features German, Swiss, and
Austrian specialties, including a range of sausages or *wurst* (with
or without homemade curry sauce), sauerbraten with red cabbage,
and *rouladen* filled with pickles, onion, and bacon. By the way,

cinnamon and chocolate pretzels reappear on the dessert menu along with honey-bourbon and chocolate dipping sauces. Name notwithstanding, if you try speaking German with the staff, you'll probably be met with a look of utter incomprehension.

The Essex, Vermont's Culinary Resort & Spa, 70 Essex Way, Essex; (802) 878-1100; www.vtculinaryresort.com; $$$$. The Essex and the New England Culinary Institute have gone their separate ways, but some of the facilities that worked to train professional chefs are now part of the resort's Cook at the Essex—essentially a series of hands-on classes for amateurs that can run the gamut from a session on preparing Asian noodle dishes to a 3-hour class on cooking a full-on classical French dinner. Take the classes a la carte or bundle them with various options for overnight stays. If you'd rather have someone else do the cooking, you'll find hearty American bistro food at the Tavern (roast local lamb, walnut-crusted trout) and inventive fine dining at Amuse (buffalo sirloin with blueberry verjus, smoked veal breast with polenta). For a true foodie option, reserve spots at the chef's table, which is a marble bar encircling a kitchen right in the main dining room. A dozen guests dine on a tasting menu that the chef prepares literally before their eyes. It's dinner theater and a cooking lesson in one.

Farmhouse Tap & Grill, 160 Bank St., Burlington; (802) 859-0888; www.farmhousetg.com; $$. Great food using a lot of local products makes for terrific eating at Burlington's hottest restaurant. Farmhouse is the joint project of a lot of talented people: Jed Davis worked with Daniel Boulud and Danny Meyer, Chef Phillip Clayton worked at **Hen of the Wood** (p. 66), and Rob Downey and Paul Sayler are the principals behind **American Flatbread** (p. 17). They have the look and the cooking down, but don't take reservations or manage customer flow, creating long lines and embattled receptionists. Diners put up with it because the food is lovingly crafted, tasty, and local almost to a fault (virtually every dish has an ingredient described as "local"). The cheeses, for example, rarely stray more than a few miles beyond the Vermont border. And who doesn't like chicken and biscuits or a burger with grass-fed beef, smokehouse bacon, and Landaff Creamery cheddar? If you want to eat dinner here on a weekend, though, start standing in line before they open at 5 p.m.

Kitchen Door Cafe, Grand Isle Art Works, 259 Rte. 2, Grand Isle; (802) 378-4591; www.grandisleartworks.com; $. The tiny kitchen and dining area are tucked into an old home that has been converted to a showcase and shop featuring the work of Vermont artists and artisans. The breakfast and lunch fare is equally artful—from the sandwich of scrambled or poached eggs on homemade biscuits with homemade sausage to the fish tacos with cabbage slaw, chipotle sour cream, and *pico de gallo* on a homemade flour tortilla. Sunday is usually smoked barbecue brisket day. Closed January.

Kitchen Table Bistro, 1840 W. Main St., Richmond; (802) 434-8686; www.kitchentablebistro.com; $$–$$$. Steve and Lara Atkins met as students at the New England Culinary Institute in 1995, worked together in the Napa Valley of California, and returned to Vermont in 2001 when their son Gabriel was born. They brought some of that California fresh-market sensibility with them, and through the Vermont Fresh Network, they keep their bistro as farm-centric as the places they worked in Napa. Their cooking is heartier than that of typical NECI-trained chefs, with bold dishes like a shepherd's pie made with braised short ribs and a blend of winter veggies under the garlic mash, or roasted **Misty Knoll** (p. 47) chicken breast with bacon and spinach, a pool of cheddar polenta, and a side of apple-roasted brussels sprouts. We want to be part of their family. Last time we stopped during midday prep, Steve was making gnocchi and cheese for Gabriel.

Leonardo's Pizza, 83 Pearl St., Burlington; (802) 862-7700; and 1160 Williston Rd., South Burlington; (802) 951-9000; www .leonardosonline.com; $. This family-run pizza joint has been a Burlington standby for more than 20 years, and no wonder: It's great pizza. As in nearly Naples great. That's assuming you order the traditional crust, of course, though you can get whole-wheat, certified organic wheat, and even gluten-free crusts with a selection of different, often not so traditional sauces (what's with Thai peanut?). Even the white-tiled interior of the Pearl Street location looks Neapolitan. We think of it as the best of both worlds—pretty authentic Neapolitan pizza, or American pies loaded with gooey sauces and lots of toppings.

Leunig's Bistro & Old World Cafe, 115 Church St., Burlington; (802) 863-3759; www.leunigsbistro.com; $$$. Leunig's has been around for what seems like forever, but the Art Nouveau restaurant manages to stay abreast of the way people like to eat. Thus you can order a trio of rabbit, venison, and quail sliders (very au courant) or tuck into a roasted chicken breast stuffed with cranberry and red-currant compote (very old-school European). As ever, it's a warm and cozy place with an old-fashioned sense of hospitality. The wine list, including choices by the glass, is very well chosen—strong on Sauvignon Blanc and real French Chardonnay as well as some excellent California reds.

Libby's Blue Line Diner, 46 Highpoint Center, Colchester; (802) 655-0343; www.libbysbluelinediner.com; $–$$. There are too many choices on the menu, our waitress agreed, as we studied the breakfast (served all day) offerings. For the indecisive, the Number 6 Big Diner Breakfast pretty much covers the options: two eggs any style; a short stack of pancakes (plain, chocolate chip, or blueberry) or french toast; bacon, sausage or ham; home fries; and toast (plain or wheat), an English muffin, or a biscuit. Choices continue with the lunchtime plates such as roast turkey with dressing, meat loaf or eggplant parmigiana, which all come with soup or salad, mash or fries, slaw or vegetable. One of the last 15 Worcester Lunch Car Co. diners ever built, Libby's has held up well. It began life in 1953 in Turner's Falls, Mass., made a stop in Auburn, Mass., and has held down its current hilltop location since 1989. The original interior features 17 stools and six booths. An addition adds three more booths and several tables to better accommodate the Saturday and Sunday morning crowd.

Mary's Restaurant, Inn at Baldwin Creek, 1868 Rte. 116, Bristol; (888) 424-2432; www.innat baldwincreek.com; $$$$. It's reassuring that some things never change. Chef-Owner Doug Mack has been serving his signature cream of garlic soup every night since 1983. The rest of the menu, however, is always in flux, as Mack takes locavore consciousness very seriously. (He was one of the founders of the Vermont Fresh Network.) In July and August he even offers a 50-Mile Dinner series. The New American cooking is more about the flavors of single ingredients than fancy preparations.

Monty's Old Brick Tavern, 7921 Williston Rd., Williston; (802) 316-4262; www.montysoldbricktavern.com; $$. One of the cool things about Burlington is that you can drive for 5 minutes and be out in the country. This tavern is only a short distance east of town, but it feels like a country roadhouse and Chef Shawn Beede's unpretentious menu has all the hallmarks of American bistro food without the rhetorical fuss. His fish-and-chips is broiled haddock over hand-cut fries, his hanger steak comes with garlic mash, and he serves his local veal with a saffron risotto, Milan style. Add eight Vermont craft brews and a good wine list to that confident menu and you have a real winner, especially given that most entrees are less than $20.

North Hero House, 3643 Rte. 2, North Hero; (802) 372-4732; www.northherohouse.com; $$–$$$. Set on one of the Champlain islands practically a stone's throw from the Quebec border, this lakeside compound is one of the North Country's legendary hostelries. But even if you can't stay here, try to book a meal at the restaurant. Much of the produce is grown on-site, the beef is local, the seafood comes from Maine, and the duck is trucked across the border from Quebec. You'll find said duck on the menu either as the confit leg or roasted breast (with roasted peaches, when they're available) almost all year. Since North Hero is on an inland lake and not the ocean (though it certainly looks marine from the front porch), the fish-and-chips features ale-battered walleye. The salmon, honestly, is flown in from the icy waters of the Shetland Islands. The dining room, like the lodging, is open all year, but public dining is limited to weekends in the winter.

On the Rise Bakery, 39 Esplanade, Richmond; (802) 434-7787; www.ontherisebakery.net; $. We were surprised to discover this neo-hippie vegetarian eatery in the midst of Vermont farm country. But On the Rise turns out lovely breads and pastries and hearty meals from their wood-fired oven. The On the Rise breakfast special features toast, scrambled eggs, seitan sausage, mixed vegetables, and cheddar cheese. Their own recipe veggie burger is topped with garlic mayo, lettuce, tomato, cucumber pickles, and red onion (cheddar cheese optional). Dinnertime wraps might be filled with seared tempeh, sprouts, and avocado or with barbecue tofu, red onion, broccoli, and melted cheddar. Check for the evening schedule of live music performances.

Otter Creek Brewing, 793 Exchange St., Middlebury; (802) 388-0727; www.ottercreekbrewing.com; $. Every college town should have its own brewery, don't you think? The tasting room here is only open from 11 a.m. until 6 p.m., so the dining is geared to luncheon foods that go well with beer. The company's Copper Top Ale, for example, forms the backbone of the cheddar ale soup, and the bowl of chili is spiked with Wolaver's IPA. Even the barbecued chicken wrap is slathered with a BBQ sauce featuring Stovepipe Porter. If it's good enough to drink (and all the Otter Creek beers are), it's good enough to cook with.

Penny Cluse, 169 Cherry St., Burlington; (802) 651-8834; www.pennycluse.com; $–$$. If the old sitcom *Friends* (or any of its buddy-show imitations) had been filmed in Burlington, you can bet the characters would have gathered for breakfast or lunch at Penny Cluse. It's that adorable, if just a tad precious with surprisingly good dishes like gingerbread pancakes and secret-recipe granola. Then there's the tofu scramble, but *de gustibus non est disputandum*. It's so popular that it's been on the menu since 1998. Tacos (fish, chorizo and egg, or roasted pepper and egg) are the mainstay at lunch, and you can always count on a perky buzz among the clientele.

A Single Pebble, 133 Bank St., Burlington; (802) 865-5200; www .asinglepebble.com; $$. Chef-Owner Chiuho Duval took over this pioneer Chinese haute cuisine restaurant in 2008. Born in Taiwan and trained at NECI, Duval combines her appreciation of the Chinese culinary legacy with a mastery of contemporary, simpler cooking techniques and a dedication to fresh ingredients from local farms. At the same time, A Single Pebble is extremely vegetarian-friendly. In fact, Duval's version of sesame beef made with crisply fried seitan and vegetables in a sesame garlic sauce is one of her specialties, and her dish of batter-fried walnuts, red peppers, onions, and a bean cake glazed in a sweet and pungent sauce will banish all bad memories of sweet and sour dishes in lesser restaurants. The restaurant also uses a lot of tofu from Vermont Soy, which makes its products from non-GMO soybeans organically grown in Vermont.

The Skinny Pancake, 60 Lake St., Burlington; (802) 540-0188; www.skinnypancake.com; $. Sprung from an itinerant crepes cart, the Skinny Pancake opened in a real brick-and-mortar building on the lakefront in 2007, and it seems like the line to get in hasn't abated yet. You can get savory classics like spinach and fresh feta cheese or apples and brie, or go sweet with the Choco-Monkey (Nutella and ripe banana) or the classic  fresh lemon juice and sugar. In the evenings, Skinny Pancake turns into something of a coffeehouse as indie, folk, and singer-songwriter musicians perform.

Sonoma Station, Bridge St., Richmond; (802) 434-5949; www.sonomastation.com; $$. Chef-Owner Monica Lamay is a native Vermonter who trained at NECI before spending several years cooking in northern California (hence the name of the restaurant). She eventually returned to Burlington to run the kitchen of a well-known restaurant there, but when the Blue Seal Feed store became available in Richmond, she jumped at the chance to branch out on her own. The California sojourn is evident in her extensive use of fresh, often raw vegetables and Asian spicing. But however long she was gone, Lemay is still from Vermont and even uses local tofu, green beans, and sweet potatoes in a Moroccan-spiced plate. Her wine list (no surprise here) is especially well stocked with Sonoma Valley bottles.

Storm Cafe, Frog Hollow, 3 Mill St., Middlebury; (802) 388-1063; www.thestormcafe.com; $$$. It would be hard to ask for a more picturesque setting than riverside in the lower level of Middlebury's old Frog Hollow mill. Chef-Owner John Hughes cooks fresh-market American food that would have had James Beard singing his praises. We can't get enough of his butternut squash and pumpkin ravioli in brown sage butter sauce, and the spiced pear poached in red wine is the perfect accompaniment to charcoal-grilled pork tenderloin. During cool weather, his roasted garlic and potato soup is a perfect appetizer—or a lunch in itself.

Tourterelle, 3629 Ethan Allen Hwy. (Rte. 7), New Haven; (802) 453-6309; www.tourterellevt.com; $$$. The love affair of New York–trained chef Bill Snell and his Brittany-born wife Christine produced a daughter and a series of terrific French restaurants. The first two were in Brooklyn, NY, but since 2009 the couple has re-created the French countryside at their hilltop inn and restaurant outside Middlebury. The house specialties are a litany of French provincial classics, from a bouillabaisse that the chef spices with red curry and saffron aioli to baked salmon in an apple cider glaze. The Snells also offer a separate bistro menu of less-involved but no less tasty classics, including either steak- or moules-frites. The menu displays French technique, French spicing, and French names, but the vegetables, fruits, meats, and even the cheeses mostly hail from Vermont. (*Comment dit-on "locavore" en français?*) There are only three rooms at the inn—just right for wedding parties.

Trattoria Delia, 152 St. Paul St., Burlington; (802) 864-5253; www.trattoriadelia.com; $$$. The standard-bearer for Italian fine dining in Burlington since 1993, Trattoria Delia serves a pan-Italian menu that places a heavy emphasis on the wood grill and the oven. The dining room is romantic with a big wood-burning stone fireplace, dimly lit tables, and a constant low soundtrack of Italian music and opera. Thomas and Lori Delia return frequently to Italy (his family hails from Calabria) to research dishes, and the restaurant prepares some interesting plates uncommon in the US. Even something as simple as pasta with a red sauce becomes *orecchiette con fricone:* little ear-shaped pasta with a fried fresh tomato sauce. The wine list is particularly strong on reds, dividing them between northern, central, and southern Italian zones.

Vermont Pub & Brewery, 144 College St., Burlington; (802) 865-0500; www.vermontbrewery.com; $-$$. The location in the heart of Burlington is terrific, and the prices are good, so the place is always bustling. Moreover, this was Vermont's first craft brewery. Best bets on the extensive menu, though, are the brewpub plates like a ploughman's lunch (bread, cheese, chutney, mustard) or a cock-a-leekie pie (chicken, leek, and vegetable stew with a round of pastry on top).

Shelburne Farms, 1611 Harbor Rd., Shelburne; (802) 985-8686, inn (802) 985-8498; www.shelburnefarms.org; $$$–$$$$. Not every Vermont farm has grounds designed by famed landscape architect Frederick Law Olmsted. But Shelburne Farms is not your average farm. It was created in 1886 by William Seward Webb and his socialite wife Lila Vanderbilt Webb as a model agricultural estate, complete with a huge redbrick mansion perched on the shore of Lake Champlain. The 1,400-acre working farm is now an environmental education center where a herd of 125 Brown Swiss cows graze in the rolling green pastures. Their milk is used for the farm's well-regarded farmhouse cheddar cheese. The farm produces about 130,000 pounds of cheese per year and tours of the estate include the five-story redbrick barn that is now the center of the cheese-making operations. The mansion itself has been converted to a 24-room inn and the Marble Dining Room, which looks out on Lake Champlain. Dinner is truly farm-to-fork, using much of the produce grown on the estate, as well as pork and beef from the resident livestock. The farmstead cheese finds its way into everything from the cheddar flatbread appetizer to the cheddar polenta served with the Shelburne Farms veal scaloppine. The inn and property tours operate from early May through late Oct. A Welcome Center with cheese, maple syrup, and other farm products is open year-round.

Behind the Food

We confess to getting lost more than once while we researched this book. If you'd rather leave the driving and navigating to someone else, the **Vermont Farm Tours** (www.vermontfarmtours.com) guided tours to local farms and food producers are a good alternative. Sampling is, of course, included and full-day tours include a picnic lunch. Founder and guide Chris Howell is a proponent of the Slow Food movement and is committed to giving visitors a personal look at the people who grow and make Vermont's signature foods.

Specialty Stores, Markets & Producers

August First Bakery & Cafe, 149 S. Champlain St., Burlington; (802) 540-0060; www.augustfirst.typepad.com. Old wooden chairs and tables and a chalkboard list of local suppliers lend a homey air to this renovated garage with exposed duct work and concrete floors. That homey feel extends to the hearth-baked breads emerging from the open kitchen, along with scones, brownies, and signature Hungarian sweet rolls filled with a walnut meringue or honey-apricot mixture. Lunchtime salads, soups, and sandwiches include many vegetarian options. Defying predictability, August First is also sometimes used for performances and the space gains an underlying arty vibe from the framed photographs and poetry hanging on the walls.

Boucher Family Farm, 2183 Gore Rd., Highgate Center; (802) 868-4193. We can forgive the punning name of one of the blue cheeses made by Daniel Boucher and Dawn Morin-Boucher. It's called "Gore-Dawn-Zola" and makes a very good Vermont substitute for a mountain-style Gorgonzola from Italy. The Bouchers, in fact, make three blue cheeses in their Green Mountain Blue Cheese label, and they also sell beef, pork, veal, and chickens, both at the farm and at the Burlington Farmers' Market. The Bouchers raise French Normande cattle exclusively. It's a felicitous choice for farmers who only feed their livestock with their own crops (alfalfa, soybeans, corn, and grass) since the breed produces well-marbled meat on a lean diet.

Bristol Bakery & Cafe, 16 Main St., Bristol; (802) 453-3280; www.bristolbakeryandcafe.com. We can always tell that we've stumbled into a real local hangout when the clientele seems equally divided between families with young kids and laptop-toting singles. This big storefront is just such a place and the chalkboard menu surely has something for every taste from a salmon burger sandwich with capers and red onion to a Waldorf salad with chicken or tofu and chopped apple, celery, walnuts, raisins, and grapes. The bakers turn out fresh bagels every day along with muffins, scones, berry and apple pies, cupcakes, and a signature ginger chocolate chip cookie. The cafe has lots of options for vegetarians including a baked potato stuffed with vegetables and melted Vermont cheddar.

Charlotte Village Winery, 3968 Greenbush Rd., Charlotte; (802) 425-4599; www.charlottevillagewinery.com. The folks at Charlotte Village Winery know how to have a good time. The back porch of the winery overlooks the extensive plantings of blueberry shrubs. Customers can pull up a chair at one of the tables, crack open a bottle or two, and drink in the view. In fact, the winery encourages people to bring a picnic and do just that. The winery's three blueberry wines are their best. The dry Midnight Blue has a strong oak component and mates well with food. Other fruit wines are sweeter and fruitier—more novelty sippers than table wines. Charlotte Village also raises some cold-climate grapes, but the vines are too young yet to produce serious wines. In the meantime, the winery buys Chardonnay, Merlot, Riesling, Gamay, and Pinot Grigio grapes from California to vint reasonably priced varietal wines. Open Memorial Day weekend through New Year's Day.

City Market, 82 S. Winooski Ave., Burlington; (802) 861-9700; www.citymarket.coop. Burlington's only downtown grocery store just happens to be its natural foods co-op, better stocked with local products than regional supermarkets. This is the place to get locally roasted coffee, locally raised meats and vegetables, and in the fall, local apples. Since it's a co-op, prices are lower than you might expect, since there is no profit. There is incredible convenience, though, in its long hours—every day from early morning until late in the evening.

Daily Chocolate, 7 Green St., Vergennes; (802) 877-0087; www .dailychocolate.net. Jen Roberts usually makes chocolates four days a week on the two granite tables in her open shop and kitchen. She is known for her delicate lemon lavender white chocolate almond bark. But "I mostly do dark chocolate," she says, noting that the 72 percent dark chocolate that she favors is not too dark or too bitter. "It's a good gateway," she says. "If people were more willing to try dark chocolate they would find out how different it is." Milk-chocolate fans beware: A bite of Roberts' Jamaican black rum caramel with dark chocolate and sea salt or her house-made burnt butter toffee dipped in dark chocolate should be enough to convert even die-hard adherents of chocolate's smoother and sweeter cousin.

Dakin Farm, 5797 Rte. 7, Ferrisburgh; (802) 425-3971; 100 Dorset St., South Burlington; (802) 658-9560; www.dakinfarm.com. The farm shop near Shelburne Museum is popular with individuals and bus groups for its generous samples of cob-smoked and maple-sugar-cured meats, cheddar cheeses, and other farm products. The Cutting family, which has owned the 1792 farm since 1960, cob-smokes 10,000 hams, 5,000 sides of bacon, and 7,000 turkey breasts a year. That's not to mention making maple syrup and cheddar cheeses. The products are for sale individually or in a variety of themed gift packages, such as the Green Mountain Breakfast of cob-smoked bacon, maple syrup, and buttermilk pancake mix or the Tailgate Party with boneless ham and turkey, sharp and smoked cheddars, and spicy honey mustard. The same products are available (without the bus groups) at the South Burlington branch.

Dobra Tea, 80 Church St., Burlington; (802) 951-2424; www .dobratea.com. This restful shop and tea room in downtown Burlington is the first US offshoot of the Dobrà Čajovna tea rooms that opened in Prague after the Velvet Revolution to provide a serene alternative to drinking beer in a crowded bar. According to Nina Beck, co-owner of the Burlington shop, the wide range of green, Japanese, white, yellow, oolong, black, and pu-er teas available in bulk are very traditional. Specialty teas, served only in the tearoom, are more imaginative and include Memories of Prague (black tea mixed with semi-bitter chocolate and served with warm milk and honey) and Taste of Kashmir (green and oolong teas with dried apples, orange peel, and cloves). Most romantic is Casanova, a mix of black tea and rose, served in a double-spouted teapot for two.

Harrington's of Vermont, 5597 Shelburne Rd. (Rte. 7), Shelburne; (802) 985-2000; and Rte. 2, Richmond; (802) 434-7500; www .harringtonham.com. With its headquarters in Richmond and more deli-oriented store in Shelburne, Harrington's was one of the first companies to make corncob-smoked ham a signature Vermont taste.

You can sample that ham in a sandwich from the in-store deli, along with smoked turkey breast sandwiches or a BLT made with Harrington's smokehouse bacon. But we usually opt for a smoked beef sandwich, made Montreal-style with marinated brisket smoked over a hickory fire for about 10 hours. In fact, the smokehouse turns out all kinds of products including baby back ribs and pork chops, duckling and pheasant, and salmon and rainbow trout. And the store also stocks a whole range of products to round out a festive meal, including cheeses, relishes, mustards, sauces, and a range of fancy desserts.

Healthy Living Natural Foods Market, 222 Dorset St., South Burlington; (802) 863-2569; www.healthylivingmarket.com. It speaks volumes about Burlington that one of the biggest chain supermarkets in the suburbs is a natural foods store with an in-store organic cafe. Part of the market's success is its commitment to local suppliers for everything from artisanal cheeses to produce to grass-fed beef. The market also features locally processed foods, such as coffee from Vermont micro-roasters (Capitol Grounds of Montpelier, Vermont Artisan of Waterbury, Vermont Coffee Company of Middlebury, and Uncommon Grounds of Burlington) or tofu from Montepelier's Vermont Soy. The market's Healthy Living Learning Center is on the Dorset Street side of the building and offers a full menu of hands-on cooking classes, cooking demonstrations, and community lectures.

Kiss the Cook, 72 Church St., Burlington; (802) 863-4226; www
.kissthecook.net. The folks who run this cookware store on the
Church Street pedestrian mall clearly believe that good knives are
the cornerstone of a good kitchen. Their extensive displays include
Bunmei, Lamson Sharp, Furitechnics, Global, MAC, Kasumi, Hattori,
Henckel, Victorinox, Wusthof-Trident, and more, along with knife
sharpeners, holders, and drawer organizers. Once you have covered the basics, you can branch out into espresso makers, fondue
pots and raclette grills, crème brûlée sets, and even old-fashioned
stovetop popcorn poppers.

Klinger's Bread Company, 10 Farrell St., South Burlington;
(802) 860-6322; www.klingersbread.com. This bread bakery in a
small office park in the 'burbs is unprepossessing, but nonetheless produces a huge array of artisan breads available on-site as
well as in supermarkets and co-ops all through New Hampshire and
Vermont. The classic sourdough and the Vermont maple walnut are
two of the company's most popular loaves. The bakery also makes
terrific take-out sandwiches that change every day.

**Lake Champlain Chocolates Chocolatier and
Cafe,** 63 Church St., Burlington; (802) 862-5185;
www.lakechamplainchocolates.com. Located on
the Church Street pedestrian mall, this welcoming
shop has a wide range of products for those who
don't want to visit the factory store (p. 44) or simply
crave a caramel apple or cup of mint-flavored hot chocolate.

COLD-CLIMATE GRAPES

Vermont and New Hampshire vineyards have sprung up optimistically since the 1990s. Some pioneer growers thought that they might be able to raise European wine grapes, but most of the best-known European grapes can't survive the northern New England winters. While a few growers have succeeded with Gamay and Riesling—grapes that hail from the northernmost growing regions in Europe—the most successful grapes are those bred for cold climates. A few were created years ago in France, but most result from Minnesota, Wisconsin, and Quebec breeding programs. Here are some of the most important:

Frontenac Noir: Created at the University of Minnesota, this grape is becoming a standard for New England red wines despite a slightly ashen aftertaste. Carefully vinted, it produces a wine akin to Beaujolais, though some producers make good port-style sweet wines with it.

Frontenac Blanc: The white grape version of Frontenac is a sturdy white with a good acid profile. It is often blended with other grapes.

Frontenac Gris: A relatively recent grape that appeared spontaneously in a number of vineyards, it promises to make the best of Frontenac white wines. Properly vinted, Frontenac Gris resembles the white wines of the Loire Valley—tart and aggressive.

La Crescent: This super-hardy grape (vines survive temperatures as low as -34°F) produces extremely aromatic wines with hints of peach, apricot, and citrus. It has a strong acid profile that allows winemakers to produce German-style table wines as well as concentrated late-harvest dessert wines.

Louise Swenson: Probably the best of the cold climate grapes bred by Wisconsin viticulturalist Elmer Swenson, it is named for his wife.

Very hardy, it can be stressed by drought, producing wines that are bright and peppery-tart—an almost perfect complement to cheddar cheese.

Marquette: A grandchild of Pinot Noir through crosses with Frontenac and other French-American hybrid grapes, this grape was only released by the University of Minnesota in 2006. It is already proving to be a reliable early-ripening red wine grape that produces wines with notes of cherry, blackberry, and black pepper in both the nose and the mouth.

St. Croix: Originally bred in Wisconsin, this red grape does well in the north, where the long days of summer allow it to attain higher sugar concentrations. It is used mostly in blends, since the wine is fruity and lacks tannins.

Seyval Blanc: Developed in northern France between the world wars, Seyval is both the tenderest of the French-American hybrids and the most "French" in its flavor. It can resemble Sauvignon Blanc and is noted for making excellent sparkling wines.

Vidal Blanc: Originally bred for cognac production in France, this cross of Ugni Blanc (a Rhône Valley grape) with a hybrid grown in the Loire Valley is a winter-hardy vine that holds its grape clusters well after frost hits. With flavors akin to Muscat and Riesling, it is most often used for sweet late-harvest wines and for ice wines.

Vignoles: This French-American hybrid is an American-bred grape with similar flavors to Vidal Blanc but even thicker skin, making it ideal for late-harvest and ice wines.

Lake Champlain Chocolates Factory Store, 750 Pine St., Burlington; (802) 864-1807; www.lakechamplainchocolates.com. More than 25 years ago Jim Lampman began giving handmade truffles to diners at his Burlington restaurant. That generous gesture has grown into Vermont's largest and best-known chocolate company. Today the truffles, caramels, clusters, barks, bars, and novelty items are all made in a 24,000-square-foot building on the outskirts of town. Visitors can check out the full line of products and order a hot chocolate or ice cream from the cafe. A few tables overlook the workroom with its equipment for tempering, enrobing, and molding chocolate. Factory tours are also offered on weekdays and one corner of the shop is devoted to factory seconds at discount prices.

Lincoln Peak Vineyard, 142 River Rd., New Haven; (802) 388-7368; www.lincolnpeakvineyard.com. One of the two best wineries in northern New England, Lincoln Peak is also the biggest grape grower in Vermont and one of the few wineries in this book producing 100 percent estate-grown and -bottled wines. Lincoln

Peak grows many of the same cold-climate hybrid grapes as other wineries, but concentrates on Marquette for its signature dry red and Frontenac Gris for its dry white. The Marquette makes a nice, fleshy wine with black currant and cherry notes and a finish with a bit of black pepper. The Frontenac Gris is vinted in the style of a Loire Valley white, with a hint of green apple and very little of Frontenac's characteristic back-of-the-throat bite. (At this writing the Frontenac Gris production is limited and only available at the winery.) The hilltop location outside Middlebury gives both the ventilation (to keep down fungal infections) and radiational cooling to reliably produce ice wines with late November or early December pickings. Lincoln Peak wines are featured on the wine lists of many of Vermont's better restaurants. Open Memorial Day to New Year's Day.

Magic Hat Brewery, 5 Bartlett Bay Rd., South Burlington; (802) 658-2379; www.magichat.net. Whimsical beer has been the hallmark of Magic Hat since 1994, and the shop at the "Artifactory" reflects that with its T-shirts, glassware, and beer tchotchkes. Best of all, both the tours and the tastings are free. In fact, the Growler Bar (which, of course, refills growlers) is pouring glasses pretty much nonstop as a fair number of Magic Hat fans show up here for afternoon samples that include all the small-batch seasonal ales as well as the year-round standards.

Middlebury Chocolates, 52 Main St., Middlebury; www.middlebury chocolates.com. Husband and wife team Stephanie and Andy

Jackson have raised the bar, so to speak, for chocolate. "We make all our chocolates straight from the bean," says Andy. "We crack, winnow, and grind." Andy calls their Red Bar "a throwback to the earliest known recipes," and describes its mix of sour, mellow, toasted, and sweet notes as a "flavor journey." It's not for everyone, he admits, but customers have no such ambivalence toward the couple's truffles (which have a notably strong chocolate flavor because no dairy products are added) or their sipping chocolates (seasoned with vanilla bean; cinnamon, allspice, and nutmeg; or with aji peppers). Their shop is down a flight of enclosed stairs from Middlebury's Main Street, but is well worth seeking out.

Middlebury Natural Foods Co-op, 1 Washington St., Middlebury; (802) 388-7276; www.middleburycoop.com. Founded in the 1970s to provide wholesome food at a fair price, this cooperative has embraced the growth in local small-scale food production and stocks a great range of local products. In addition to maple products, produce, wines, and ciders, the store also stocks harder to find local white and whole-wheat flours in bulk. The cheese case mixes international and Vermont options, including award-winning Tarentaise (an Alpine-style cheese from Spring Brook Farm) and Manchester (an aged goat's milk *tomme* from Consider Bardwell Farm, see p. 165).

Mirabelle's Cafe & Bakery, 198 Main St., Burlington; (802) 658-3074; www.mirabellescafe.com. If we lived in Burlington we'd probably pop into Mirabelle's every morning for a delicious apple cinnamon scone. Hearty breakfast eaters might opt instead for a biscuit with egg and cheese or a popover with herb-scrambled eggs and hash browns. There are equally satisfying lunch choices for every appetite— from a turkey and pepper jelly sandwich with cheddar cheese, avocado, and sprouts to a red-wine braised beef panini with grilled red onions and peppers, and mozzarella. Cookies run the gamut from homey peanut butter sandwiches to elegant macaroons in a rainbow of colors. Need a dessert for a dinner party? Pick up a pear-caramel charlotte or a triple chocolate-mocha mousse cake.

Misty Knoll Farms, 1685 Main St., New Haven; (802) 453-4748; www.mistyknollfarms.com. You'll find Misty Knoll chickens (and sometimes turkeys) on the menus of many of the best restaurants in Vermont, New Hampshire, and parts of eastern New York. Not only does Misty Knoll raise all its poultry, it also processes and markets them. Turkeys are true free-range, given access to pastured fields. The chickens are uncaged but spend most of their lives wandering around in giant barns. As it works out, that's the most humane way to raise great-tasting chicken, and the proof is in the poultry. Anyone who wants to see the operation is welcome, but it's best to call in advance. (The immaculate processing plant is clean and wet, but not for the squeamish.) Chickens and turkeys (in season) are available at the farm.

Otter Creek Bakery, 14 College St., Middlebury; (802) 388-3371; www.ottercreekbakery.com. The bakers love to turn out sculpted breads for holidays and special events, including bats, bunnies, bears, and even Old Man Winter. But you don't need a special occasion to stop in for a honey oatmeal scone or cinnamon twist in the morning, bowl of soup or roasted vegetable salad for lunch, or a maple oatmeal raisin cookie or brownie in the afternoon. A selection of breads along with house-made pâtés (venison, rabbit, duck, or a country pâté of pork, chicken, and vegetables) are perfect for a party appetizer. Finish the meal with a linzer torte or chocolate mousse cake.

Shelburne Vineyard, 6308 Shelburne Rd., Shelburne; (802) 985-8222; www.shelburnevineyard.com. One of Vermont's oldest vineyards, Shelburne nonetheless makes the bulk of its wines with grapes grown in other regions (especially New York's Finger Lakes). The busy tasting room right on Route 7 pulls in the curious, and many tasters bring a picnic to enjoy on the premises. Best among the Vermont-grown wines are Louise Swenson, a tangy white with a pleasant green-apple sharpness that goes well with cheese, and the various sweet late-harvest wines, made with a mixture of grapes mostly from Shelburne's own vineyards.

Snow Farm Vineyard, 190 W. Shore Rd., South Hero; (802) 372-9463; www.snowfarm.com. Dating from 1996, this Champlain Islands vineyard may produce the best line of wines in northern

New England. All wines are estate grown and bottled, and wine-maker Patrick Barrelet shows a particular ability to coax balanced wines with varietal characteristics from the vineyard grapes. In practice, this means that some of the wines are sweeter than most people imagine they like, but in the signature Snow White blend of Cayuga and Seyval, the residual sugar disguises the foxy character of Cayuga, and the Seyval gives the wine sufficient back-bone to stand up to rather rich foods. The late-harvest Vignoles is an extraordinary sweet dessert wine, full of apricot notes and very lush. It is surpassed (among the dessert wines) only by Snow Farm's Vidal ice wine, which ranks with some of the best made in Canada's Niagara Peninsula. The surprise, however, is Snow Farm's Pinot Noir. A distinctly cold-climate pinot, it is velvety with bright cherry notes. Alas, the Pinot Noir, the Vignobles, and the American Riesling are produced in such small quantities that they can only be purchased at the vineyard. Tasting room open May through Dec.

Snowflake Chocolates, 81A Rte. 15, Jericho; (802) 899-3373; and 150 Dorset St., South Burlington; (802) 863-8306; www.snowflake chocolate.com. Snowflake Chocolates is named in honor of local farmer Wilson "Snowflake" Bentley (1865–1931) who was the first person to photograph a single snow crystal and, in all, photo-graphed about 5,000 unique snowflakes. Along with a variety of hand-dipped creams and caramels, one of Snowflake's signature treats is a molded white chocolate replica of one of Bentley's pho-tographic images. But the shop is known for other specialties as well, including pumpkin fudge and Candy Cane Delight. "It comes out on November 1," says store manager Shelly Dionne, of the concoction of crushed candy canes mixed with white chocolate and then enrobed in dark chocolate. "People wait for it all year." The shop is also known for its handmade candy canes. "We make them every Saturday in November," says Dionne. A big window looks into the workroom, so visitors might glimpse the candymakers at work pulling the sugar mixture. And they will certainly catch a whiff of peppermint or wintergreen. If you can't make it to Jericho, there's an outlet in South Burlington.

Vergennes Laundry, 247 Main St., Vergennes; (802) 870-7157; www.vergenneslaundry.com. Talk about dedication. Didier Murat and Julianne Jones have to stoke the wood-fired Swedish oven in their laundromat turned bakery and espresso bar at 3:30 a.m. But eager eaters assure them that it is well worth the effort—and the loss of a few hours' sleep. The couple's commitment to local products combines with Murat's French background to create apple tarts with heirloom apples, *gougère* cheese puffs with Grafton cheese, or Provençal-style tomatoes baked in little glass mason jars. One of their specialties is *tarte flambée,* the Alsatian answer to Italy's pizza. Murat and Jones might top theirs with cauliflower, or with new potatoes, fresh herbs, and crème fraiche. Try a *canelé* pastry, with a rich custard interior and caramelized crust, with a shot of espresso.

Champlain Orchards, 3597 Rte. 74 West, Shoreham; (802) 897-2777; www.champlainorchards.com. The warming effects of Lake Champlain give the orchards a climatological boost with less risk of frost during the spring bloom and warmer days and nights to extend the fall harvest. With this leg up from Mother Nature, Champlain Orchards grows plums, cherries, peaches, raspberries, and some organic vegetables, but it's really all about the 40 varieties of apples. Visitors can pick their own or sample them in a wealth of products including apple butter and applesauce, apple cider and apple cider doughnuts, and apple pies and turnovers. The apples also find their way into Pruner's Pride Hard Cider and Honey Crisp Ice Cider, made in conjunction with Eden Ice Cider Company.

Douglas Orchards and Cider Mill, 1050 Rte. 74 West, Shoreham; (802) 897-5043. We didn't realize that you could freeze apple cider until Bob Douglas clued us in. Pour a little bit out of the plastic bottle first to allow for expansion during freezing, he told us, and shake the cider well after it has thawed and before drinking. Like many orchardists, Douglas has his own preferred mix of apples for cider and a number of varieties are also available for picking on the fourth-generation farm. Picking season starts in mid-June with strawberries, followed by raspberries a month later. Open mid-June through Thanksgiving.

Hackett's Orchard, 86 South St., South Hero; (802) 372-4848; www.hackettsorchard.com. Ron and Celia Hackett are the third owners and dedicated stewards of this island orchard first established in 1900. They grow about 45 varieties of apples, press about 4,000 gallons of cider each season, and turn out countless pans of apple crisp. "We think that we make the best apple cider doughnuts in the world," says Ron, and a lot of folks must agree. The doughnut machine churns out 250 dozen doughnuts a day during PYO weekends. Kids will get a real treat out of watching the apple-packing line in action. Thirteen-bushel bins of apples are lowered into a tank of water; after the apples float to the surface they run over soft brushes to clean and shine them, and then pass over a 2.5-inch hole. Any small apples that fall through the hole are set aside for cider. The remaining apples make their way to a revolving table where a person (often the Hacketts' grandson) inspects them and removes any blemished fruit. We can't explain it, but somehow the apples taste better when you see the care that goes into their selection. There aren't many sugar maple trees on the Champlain Islands, but the Hacketts purchase bulk syrup from other Vermont producers and sell it to their customers. Open Apr through Dec.

Happy Valley Orchard and Farmstand, 217 Quarry Rd., Middlebury; (802) 388-2411; www.happyvalleyorchard.com. Pull into the parking lot at this farmstand and PYO orchard and you will be greeted by a row of trees with brilliant red Northern Spy apples hanging from every branch. Good for baking, eating, and storing over the winter, they are only one of a number of traditional and heirloom apples, mostly growing on dwarf stock for easy picking. The farm also raises pumpkins, squashes, and potatoes, along with Concord grapes. Open late Aug through late Nov.

Hudak Farm, 599 Saint Albans Rd., Swanton; (802) 527-1147. Hudak's farmstand, with its weathered barn and hand-carved folk-art designs, is a true work of art. Inside the tall-ceilinged space heads of garlic hang on log rails and a season-long harvest of vegetables raised following organic practices fills the bins. In the fall, Hudak is a favorite with families who come to pick out a pumpkin and grab a bottle of apple cider. Open May through Thanksgiving.

Jericho Settlers Farm, 22 Barber Farm Rd., Jericho; (802) 899-4000; www.jerichosettlersfarm.com. Founded in 2002, the farm encompasses two of the earliest settled homesteads of Jericho (hence the name). The main focus is on pasture-raised pork and chicken as well as 100 percent grass-fed beef and lamb, and the meats are available at the farmstand all year, along with fresh eggs. Farm vegetables are available in season. The farm also attends the Burlington winter and summer farmers' markets.

Sam Mazza's Farm Market, Bakery & Greenhouses, 277 Lavigne Rd., Colchester; (802) 655-3440; www.sammazzafarms.com. Events at this large farm store celebrate the seasons from a June strawberry festival to a July blueberry breakfast to an October giant pumpkin weigh-in. Mazza's own produce is available, along with other local products and a more unusual line of Amish pickled vegetables, including beets, mushrooms, and watermelon rind. The big bakery case is filled with quiches made with Cabot cheddar, fresh breads, and two styles of apple or raspberry turnovers—enclosed in pie crust or puff pastry.

Shelburne Orchards, 216 Orchard Rd., Shelburne; (802) 985-2753; www.shelburneorchards.com. There's no more inspirational spot to pick apples (or sour cherries or peaches) than this beautiful hilltop orchard with stunning views of Lake Champlain. But the staff doesn't take it all too seriously, cajoling pickers to take a whirl on the rope swing hanging from a big old tree. Visitors are also welcome to stick their heads into the vinegar house for a whiff of cider vinegar, or to check out the outdoor wood-fired brick oven where big pans of apple brown betty are often baked. Shelburne also offers the farmstand staples of apple cider, cider doughnuts, and apple pies, but we like their more unusual products. Ginger Jack is a mixture of apple cider and ginger that is cooked all day and bottled at night. "It's our nonalcoholic whiskey," says an orchard employee, "with all of the burn and none of the buzz." A smoother apple drink is also in the works. Shelburne Orchards opened a distillery a couple of years ago with the aim of making an apple brandy in the style of the Calvados of northern France. It's aged in oak barrels for seven years and some of the first vintages are ready for release. Open mid-August through October.

Farmers' Markets

Bristol Farmers' Market, Village Green, Bristol. Sat from 11 a.m. to 2 p.m., June through September.

Burlington Farmers' Market, City Hall Park, Burlington. Sat from 8:30 a.m. to 2 p.m., May through October.

Burlington New North End Farmers' Market, 925 North Ave., Burlington. Thurs from 3 to 6:30 p.m., June through September.

Burlington Old North End Farmers' Market, 6 Archibald St., Burlington. Tues from 3 to 6:30 p.m., June through October.

Burlington Winter Farmers' Market, Memorial Auditorium, corner of Main and South Union Streets, Burlington. Every other Sat from 10 a.m. to 2 p.m., November through April.

Champlain Islands Grand Isle Farmers' Market, St. Joseph's Church, Rte. 2, Grand Isle. Sat from 10 a.m. to 2 p.m., late May through late September.

Champlain Islands South Hero Farmers' Market, Saint Rose of Lima Church, Rte. 2, South Hero. Wed from 4 to 7 p.m., June to late September.

Enosburg Falls Farmers' Market, Lincoln Park, Main St., Enosburg Falls. Wed from 3 to 6 p.m. and Sat from 9 a.m. to 1 p.m., May through October.

Five Corners Farmers' Market, Lincoln Place off Railroad Ave., Essex Junction. Fri from 3:30 to 7:30 p.m., June to early October.

Hinesburg Lions Farmers' Market, Route 116, Hinesburg. Thurs from 3:30 to 6:30 p.m., June through August.

Jericho Mills Riverside Farmers' Market, Mills Riverside Park, Rte. 15, Jericho Mills. Thurs from 3 to 7 p.m., June through September.

Middlebury Farmers' Market, Marbleworks, Maple St., Middlebury. Sat from 9 a.m. to 12:30 p.m., early May to late October, and Wed from 9 a.m. to 12:30 p.m., mid-June to mid-October. Winter market every Sat 9:30 a.m. to 1 p.m. in November and December, and the second and fourth Sat, January to April.

Milton Grange Farmers' Market, Grange Hall, Rte. 7, Milton. Sat from 9:30 a.m. to 1:30 p.m., June through October.

Richford Farmers' Market, 21 Main St., Richford. Sat from 9 a.m. to 1 p.m., mid-June through September.

Richmond Farmers' Market, Volunteers Green, Richmond. Fri from 3 to 6:30 p.m., June to mid-October.

St. Albans Northwest Farmers' Market, Taylor Park, St. Albans. Sat from 9 a.m. to 2 p.m., late May through October.

Shelburne Farmers' Market, Rte. 7 and Church St., Shelburne. Sat from 9 a.m. to 1 p.m., late May to early October.

South Burlington Farmers' Market, 222 Dorset St., South Burlington. Every other Sun from 10 a.m. to 2 p.m.

Westford Farmers' Market, Town Common, Rte. 128, Westford. Fri from 3:30 to 6:30 p.m., mid-June to mid-October.

Williston Farmers' Market, Village Green, Rte. 2, Williston. Sat from 10 a.m. to 2 p.m., June to mid-October.

Winooski Farmers' Market, Champlain Mill Green, Winooski Falls. Sun from 10 a.m. to 2 p.m., mid-June to early October.

Addison County Fair & Field Days, www.addisoncountyfielddays
.com. Vermont's largest agricultural fair is held in New Haven in
mid-August and includes competitions in apple baked goods, honey
and honey baked goods, dairy foods, canning, and baked beans.

Burlington Wine and Food Festival, www.burlingtonwineand
foodfestival.com. Waterfront Park is the setting for this mid-June
event which features tastings of Vermont artisan breads and
cheeses, wines from Vermont and around the world, along with
seminars by chefs and winemakers.

Champlain Islands Open Farm and Studio Tour, www.open
farmandstudio.com. For one weekend in mid-July, artists, crafts-
people, and farmers welcome visitors to explore the culture and
cuisine of the Champlain Islands.

Champlain Valley Fair, www.cvexpo.org. This Essex Junction
extravaganza stretches from late August to early September and
features midway rides and a packed schedule of entertainment
along with a celebration of agricultural traditions.

Festival of the Islands, www.champlainislands.com. The
Champlain Islands celebrate summer in this late July event that
includes visits to farmstands and wine and ice cream tastings, along
with concerts, flea markets, and art shows.

Franklin County Field Days, www.franklincountyfielddays.org. Food and maple are among the products in the judging competitions at this annual event that takes place in late July or early August in Highgate. Look also for a food auction and chicken barbecue.

Shelburne Farms Harvest Festival, www.shelburnefarms.org. Hayrides, crafts demonstrations, live music, and plenty of food highlight this mid-September celebration of Vermont's agricultural heritage.

Tour de Farms, www.vtbikeped.org. This one-day September bike ride in Addison County is a fundraiser to help keep Vermont's agritourism alive and to celebrate farm and cycling culture. It's a joint project of the Vermont Bicycle & Pedestrian Coalition, Rural Vermont, and the Addison County Re-Localization Network (ACoRN). Waves of cyclists depart at staggered start times for the 30-mile route, then the 22-mile route, and finally the family-friendly 10-mile route. At each stop, they're treated to harvest samples, from tomatoes to apples to maple candy.

Vermont Brewers Festival, www.vermont brewers.com. This mid-July event in Burlington is a good opportunity to sample and compare Vermont brews with others from New England, Quebec, and sometimes as far away as California.

Vermont Cheesemakers' Festival, www.vtcheesefest.com. Vermont claims the most artisanal cheesemakers per capita of any state and about forty of them gather for this late July event at Shelburne Farms. Visitors can sample more than 100 cheeses, along with products from local wineries, breweries, and other food producers. Cooking and cheesemaking demonstrations and a dinner at the Shelburne Farms restaurant round out a busy day of activities.

Vermont Dairy Festival, www.vermontdairyfestival.com. Enosburg Falls lays claim to the title of "dairy center of the world." This early June event helps make that case with food booths, dairy-baking competitions, a pancake breakfast, and tours of dairy farms.

Vermont Maple Festival, www.vtmaplefestival.org. This late April event in St. Albans features sugarhouse tours, a pancake breakfast, a maple-themed buffet dinner, cooking contests, and more. Be sure to try the maple cotton candy.

Montpelier, Stowe & the Heart of Vermont

Sandwiched between the rich growing area of the Champlain Valley on the west and the wooded uplands of the Northeast Kingdom on the east, the heart of northern Vermont lies along the Lamoille and Mad Rivers. This is the region that encompasses the capital of the Green Mountain State, Montpelier, and several of the state's major ski areas—Stowe Mountain Resort, Sugarbush, Smugglers' Notch, and the retro hardcore skier–owned Mad River Glen. It is a region of beautiful alpine villages like Stowe and Jeffersonville and quaint riverside hamlets like Warren and Waitsfield.

Waterbury is located almost in the dead center of the region, and is home of two of the biggest agri-businesses in the state: Green Mountain Coffee and Ben & Jerry's Ice Cream. Even the Cabot Creamery cooperative has a major presence here with the Cabot

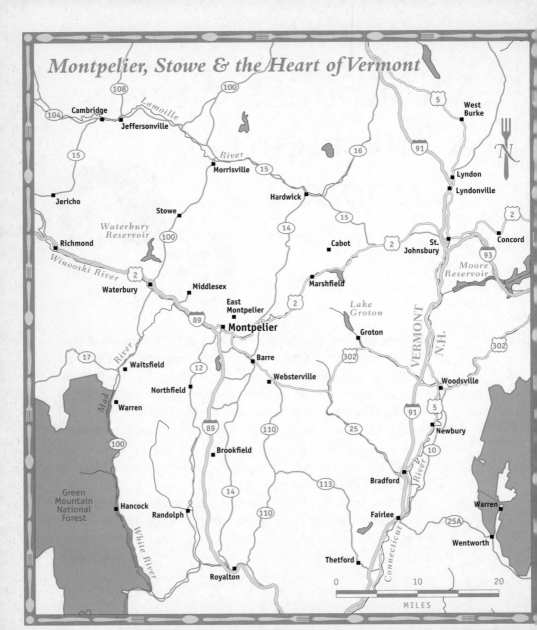

Annex, completing the triumvirate of Vermont food giants. Yet the area is also dotted with micro-roasters of coffee, tiny brewers of beer, small cheesemakers, maple syrup producers, and even a few wineries.

Perhaps even more significantly, Montpelier is home to the New England Culinary Institute (NECI). It sometimes seems every chef in Vermont over the age of 45 has taught at NECI, and every chef under 35 has studied there. The culinary school has been instrumental in fostering the locavore sensibility in Vermont, and is one of the gold-level sponsors of the Vermont Fresh Network, which was founded to advance relationships among farmers, chefs, and consumers with the aim of expanding markets for locally grown food.

Foodie Faves

The Bee's Knees, 82 Lower Main St., Morrisville; (802) 888-7889; www.thebeesknees-vt.com; $$. Suppose you had a good friend who was a terrific cook and invited you over for dinner every night? That's a little what it feels like at The Bee's Knees, which bills itself as producing "home-cooked meals emphasizing locally grown and organic ingredients." Indeed, the cheesemaker who created the cheddar in the mac and cheese and the stockman who herded the grass-fed beef used in the burgers are so local that they probably eat here. It's hard to imagine a small place with such a varied menu that sources its food quite this close to home. The veggies come from **Pete's Greens** (p. 109), and the tofu in the vegan and vegetarian entrees comes from Vermont Soy in Hardwick. The Bee's Knees is an all-day eatery (organic local eggs at breakfast, naturally) and there's usually live music in the evenings.

Burger Barn, 4968 Rte. 15, Cambridge; (802) 730-3441; $. It is almost impossible to resist the bright green homemade-food trailer with a black-and-white Holstein roof sitting on the side of Route 15 between Cambridge and Jeffersonville. Jud Gravel and Kierstin Colacecci use only grass-fed local beef for their burgers and have come up with 31 combinations of toppings, including their own maple and honey mustards. One of the more popular combos is the "Nutty Goat," with chèvre, maple-crusted walnuts, caramelized onions, and a touch of mayonnaise. But the biggest seller is the classic, with lettuce, tomato, and a slice of red onion. In both cases, the star is the burger itself—amazingly rich and beefy and surprisingly tender for such a lean patty. Alas, the Burger Barn is only open May through Oct.

Cliff House, Mount Mansfield, Stowe; (802) 253-3000; www.stowe .com; $$. Located at the top of the Stowe gondola at an altitude of 3,625 feet, this chalet-style room has panoramic views from picture windows. Meals tend to be simple fare, ranging from crepes to venison chili to lamb stew. A good winter warmer is the cheese fondue for two. After lunch, you can hike or ski back down, depending on the season. Special locavore and wine-themed dinners are available on select Saturday nights during ski season. The Cliff House is open whenever the gondola is operating.

Dutch Pancake House, Grey Fox Inn, 990 Mountain Rd., Stowe; (802) 253-8921; www.greyfoxinn.com; $–$$. With all that maple syrup just itching to be poured, the pancake house has become a staple of North Country dining. The Dutch Pancake House raises the humble breakfast food to a new level. Their 12-inch pancakes are cooked in a traditional Dutch skillet and are thinner—and more crepe-like—than their American cousins. Diners can choose from about 50 different toppings that range from simple (cinnamon apple slices and raisins) to elaborate (apple, shredded potato, pineapple, raisins, ham, cheddar, and curry).

Flatbread Kitchen, 46 Lareau Rd., Waitsfield; (802) 496-8856; www.americanflatbread.com; $$. Established in 1986, American Flatbread makes gourmet pizza with organically grown wheat and imaginative toppings. This is the original location and since the bakers are producing gourmet frozen pizza for groceries and natural foods stores during the first half of the week, the restaurant is only open Thursday through Sunday. Seating is first-come, first served, though you can put your name on a "wait list" to be seated at an approximate time if you show up in person at 4 p.m. Pizza choices are every bit as locavore as you might expect from a place that touts "all-natural pizza baked in a primitive wood-fired oven." The New Vermont Sausage, for example, features naturally raised Waitsfield pork in homemade maple-fennel sausage, combined with sun-dried tomatoes, caramelized onions, mushrooms, mixed cheeses, and herbs. Other branches of Flatbread are located in Middlebury (p. 17) and Burlington (p. 17).

Hen of the Wood, 92 Stowe St., Waterbury; (802) 244-7300; www .henofthewood.com; $$$. Few chefs are so finely attuned to the foodscape around them as Eric Warnstedt, who has been cooking up a storm at Hen of the Wood since 2005. Given half a chance, he waxes eloquent about sustainable agriculture and promoting the viability of the local farm economy. That focus makes it hard to predict a given night's menu, since Warnstedt rolls with whatever is being harvested or foraged. He works closely with about 20 different farms, buying the lion's share of his produce from **Pete's Greens** (p. 109). The local provender feeds his imagination, producing such terrific dishes as goat's milk gnocchi with king trumpet mushrooms, celery root, and pine nuts, or a local cornmeal polenta and duck sausage served with a sunny-side-up duck egg from Gopher Broke Farm in nearby Wolcott. The setting in an old grist mill is truly romantic, and there are a few tables on the porch overlooking the waterfall during warm weather. For dessert, you can't beat the selection of at least 15 artisan cheeses. Warnstedt admits to being hooked by the *affineurs* at **Jasper Hill** (p. 107).

La Brioche Bakery & Cafe, 89 Main St., Montpelier; (802) 229-0443; www.neci.edu; $. Students at the New England Culinary Institute begin preparing the day's breads and pastries at 4 a.m., but big windows might give you a glimpse of them still at work in the kitchen when you stop in at a more civilized hour for a croissant, muffin, or scone for breakfast. The breads emerge from the oven around 11 a.m. and form the basis for lunchtime sandwiches and a daily panini choice such as roast turkey, cranberry relish, and cheddar cheese on rosemary focaccia. You might want to pick up some big chocolate chip or molasses cookies, a chocolate éclair or a fruit tart for later, since La Brioche is not open in the evening.

Michael's on the Hill, 4182 Waterbury-Stowe Rd., Waterbury Center; (802) 244-7476; www.michaelsonthehill.com; $$$–$$$$. Locavore pioneers, even among Vermont restaurateurs, Laura and Michael Kloeti serve what they call European-influenced farm-to-table cuisine and what we call New American at its most local and best. That might include appetizers such as slow-roasted lamb ribs with a fall vegetable slaw or a Maine crab cake with an heirloom tomato salad. The entree could be skillet-roasted chicken with a succotash of sweet corn and fava beans, or a smoked pork loin with apple, braised greens, and cheddar-sausage bread pudding. Chef Michael also offers cooking classes for groups up to six. Laura runs the front of the house, and the pair were named Vermont restaurateurs of the year in 2011.

NECI on Main, 118 Main St., Montpelier; (802) 223-3188; www.neci.edu; $$$. The farm-to-table classroom of the New England Culinary Institute, NECI on Main is staffed by students at all levels—from the dishwashers to the serving staff. The menus change often, reflecting the changing harvest, but most dishes have the light NECI touch—a style of contemporary American cooking that aims to highlight the flavors of the key ingredients while showing a certain flair for classical technique. A perfect NECI appetizer might be the tartlet of smoked duck breast with peas, pickled beets, and chopped roasted hazelnuts. There's almost always some version of pan-seared scallop on the menu, since such dishes are an essential part of every chef's training. In summer, the scallops might be paired with a pea puree, crispy polenta, and a little Vermont smoked bacon.

Norma's, Topnotch Resort and Spa, 4000 Mountain Rd., Stowe; (802) 253-8585; www.topnotchresort.com; $$$. Half the folks who flock to Topnotch come for the comfortable lodging between trips up (and down) Stowe's ski hills. And the other half come to be rubbed the right way in the spa and maybe go home a few pounds lighter and sporting a healthy glow. As the main restaurant at the resort (it's open to nonguests as well), Norma's walks a fine line between the two clienteles. Skiers might opt for the roasted Berkshire pork with braised greens, spaetzle sausage hash, and a rosemary reduction, while the spa folk order the perch with roasted fennel, crispy eggplant, and braised tomato butter. (Butter on the side, please.) Live a little and order the Notch Burger topped with chorizo chili, maple onions, a slice of melted cheddar, and a fried egg. It comes with fries.

Perfect Pear Cafe & Vermont Beer Company, Main St., Bradford; (802) 222-5912; www.theperfectpearcafe.com; $$. The picturesque location just above the Wait River Falls is hard to beat, and casual American bistro food like cod cakes or a rosemary ale and lamb stew are the perfect foil for chef-turned-brewer Adam Coulter's beers, which are available only on the premises. The 10-gallon brewing system means frequent changes, but he usually has an IPA and either a red ale or a porter in the two house taps, reserving the other two for other craft brews.

Salt Cafe, 207 Barre St., Montpelier; (802) 229-6678; www.saltcafe vt.com; $$$. Fresh-market cooking means the menu changes every 3 weeks at this intimate New American dining room. The young staff bubbles with enthusiasm for using Vermont materials with classical techniques, resulting in full-bodied dishes like chicken roulade stuffed with a Dijon mustard and rosemary-spiced filling and served with caramelized onions, a side of sautéed carrots and celery root, and a toasted farro pilaf. On the other hand, the pastry chef is happy to play around with New England classics, too, serving a maple whoopie pie filled with sweet cream cheese and quince jam. Salt also offers occasional cooking and food-writing classes.

The Skinny Pancake, 89 Main St., Montpelier; (802) 262-CAKE (2253); www.skinnypancake.com; $. Known to fans as the "mini Skinny," this scaled-down version of the Burlington crepe house (p. 30) serves the same mix of savory and sweet crepes minus Burlington's concert series.

Solstice, Stowe Mountain Lodge, 7412 Mountain Rd., Stowe; (802) 253-3560; www.stowemountainlodge.com; $$$. Ski-country dining is often a haze of heavy alpine dishes (emphasis on the cheese), but Solstice offers refined New American food in relaxed surroundings. The artisan cheese plate couldn't be more local: 11 of the 12 cheeses are from Vermont, the other one is from a few miles over the border in New Hampshire. Chef Cody Vasek keeps the menu pretty simple and straight-forward—six or seven starters, eight or nine main dishes. The pairings are inspired—roast lamb loin with local blueberries and watercress puree, duck breast with baby turnips and a rhu-barb puree, cauliflower risotto with lobster. The best bargain is the nightly 5-course tasting menu with or without the optional wine pairing.

Timbers Restaurant, Sugarbush Resort, Sugarbush Access Rd., Warren; (800) 53-SUGAR (78427); www.sugarbush.com; $$$. Few dining locations are quite as dramatic as this slopeside restau-rant at the Lincoln Peak complex. The post-and-beam architecture resembles a round barn but boasts 45-foot vaulted ceilings and huge windows to take in the view. The New American menu emphasizes local ingredients without being doctrinaire about it. Chef Tim Chalifoux and executive chef Gerry Nooney have created some terrific versions of well-known dishes. Their "shepherd's pie," for example, combines bison short ribs braised in porter with caramelized cipollini onions and mashed root vegetables. Ask about special Fungi Fest dinners that combine an afternoon of foraging with the resort's resident mycologist with a mushroom-centric dinner. Timbers also offers Locavore Community Table Dinners between June and September. Each ski season, Nooney prepares several special country dinners focused on Vermont foods at Allyn's Lodge—a facility at the top of Gadd Peak at the end of the Super Bravo lift. Diners ascend on a Cabin Cat (a snow groomer) and feast on fondue, salad, a main dish, and then ski down or return on the Cat for dessert and brandy by the fireplace at Timbers. Reservations for the Allyn's Lodge dinner are made at (802) 583-6590, and fill up weeks if not months in advance. Allyn's Lodge also serves hot drinks, sandwiches, chili, and soups during the day whenever the lifts are operating. See Chef Nooney's recipe for **Vermont Farmhouse Potato Chowder** on p. 351.

Trapp Family Lodge, 700 Trapp Hill Rd., Stowe; (802) 253-8511; (800) 826-7000; www.trappfamily.com; $$$. After fleeing Austria in 1938, the von Trapp family selected Vermont as their new home and began creating a little bit of Austria in the Green Mountain State. That heritage is certainly alive and well in the resort's kitchens—from the elegant pastries in the bakery to the Austrian-style lager in the brewery. The pub in the main lodge has the most pronounced Austrian flavor with its simple, hearty dishes (bratwurst with sauerkraut and red potatoes or wiener schnitzel with spaetzle and lingonberries), while the main dining room offers a more continental menu with entrees such as duck breast with duck-filled dumplings. Count on apple strudel and linzer torte on the dessert menu.

275 Main, Pitcher Inn, 275 Main St., Warren; (802) 496-6350; www.pitcherinn.com; $$$. Executive chef Sue Schickler faces a tall order—to cook meals that befit the Magical Realism rooms of the over-the-top inn. So she pickles her own baby turnips for an antipasto plate, toasts the brioche that goes with the bacon-topped sautéed soft-shell crab, and makes a carrot fritter to accompany her pan-roasted quail. The flavor combinations are inspired, and the kitchen makes some of the most complex dishes appear effortless. The grilled veal rib chop meets its perfect counterpoint in asparagus risotto and a lemon-herb sauce. Whatever Schickler dreams up, sommelier Ari Sadri can pair with just the right bottle from the extensive cellar. No wonder 275 Main is one of Vermont's best restaurants for wine lovers. The menu for the inn's tavern, Tracks, recapitulates the small plates of 275 Main in a more casual environment.

Specialty Stores, Markets & Producers

Alchemist Cannery, 35 Crossroad, Waterbury; (802) 244-7744; www.alchemistbeer.com. The much-beloved Alchemist Pub in downtown Waterbury was a casualty of the 2011 flooding caused by Hurricane Irene. But John and Jennifer Kimmich continue to produce beer at the Cannery, concentrating on a Double IPA. The tasting room, retail shop, and self-guided tour are open to the public.

Ben & Jerry's Factory Tour, Rte. 100, Waterbury; (802) 882-1240 ext. 2300; www.benjerry.com. There are probably very few people who don't know the story of how childhood friends Ben Cohen and Jerry Greenfield took a $5 correspondence course in ice cream making and opened a little shop in a reno-vated gas station in Burlington in 1978. But the tour of their mega-factory still begins with a video history and an appreciation of the local farmers and their cows who pro-vide the milk and cream for Karamel Sutra, Cherry Garcia, and dozens of other flavors. Visitors get a birds-eye view of the production line, which generally operates Monday through Friday, and end their tour with a tasting—sometimes of a new flavor under consideration—in the Flavoroom. Visitors can also pay their respects to their favorite discontinued ice cream (Tennessee Mud, perhaps, or Ethan Almond) at the tongue-in-cheek Flavor Graveyard behind the factory.

Black Cap Coffee, 144 Main St., Stowe; (802) 253-2123; www
.blackcapcoffee.com. Located inside the old IGA store on the
north end of Stowe's village, Black Cap is run by the
Townsends: Chris the roaster and Heidi the baker. The
select coffees are roasted off-premises in micro-lots
with shades of subtlety best appreciated by true bean-
heads. Chris tends to treat each shipment of green
beans a little differently, adjusting time and temperature to bring out the *terroir*. The sweets are perfect
for coffee drinkers—raspberry shortbread bars, chocolate
chip cookies, macaroons . . .

Boyden Valley Winery, 64 Rte. 104, Cambridge; (802) 644-8151;
www.boydenvalley.com. Located in a restored 1878 carriage barn at
a bend in the Lamoille River, Boyden Valley Winery shares the farm
with the Boyden Valley Farm beef operation. The tasting room is
open year-round, and it's the best place to get a good overview of
the operation. Boyden Valley grows a wide variety of cold-climate
hybrid grapes, producing red and rosé blends and a few white varietals. The Seyval Blanc is dry and crisp, while "Cow Tipper," made
from Le Crescent, is a fruity and soft pale blush. The most unusual
wines are made from frozen fruit. "Vermont Ice," made from Le
Crescent grapes, has a pleasing acidity and apricot undertones that
balance the sugars. "Vermont Ice Red" is made from Frontenac
grapes and shows strong jammy flavors with an overtone of oak
from the barrel aging. The final frozen nectar is a luscious and
sweet Vermont ice cider.

Bragg Farm Sugarhouse & Gift Shop, 1005 Rte. 14 North, East Montpelier; (802) 223-5757; www.braggfarm.com. "It's traditional to sell your maple syrup off your front porch," says Barbara Bragg, remembering the humble origins of her family's year-round gift shop with attached sugarhouse. Her husband Doug is an eighth generation sugarmaker, who still collects all his sap in buckets, rather than using less labor-intensive tubing. "We do 2,200 buckets," says Barbara. "That's the way Doug learned as a kid and he honors his ancestors." The shop is busiest during the late February to early April sugar season, but a short film in the sugarhouse gives visitors an overview of the process at any time of year. In addition to their own maple products, the Braggs stock other local foodstuffs including maple mustard, maple barbecue sauce, maple tea, and maple cream cookies. The warm-weather favorite is a maple "creemee" (soft-serve ice cream mixed with Grade B syrup) topped with Maple Apple Drizzle Sauce, which Barbara describes as "apple pie in a jar."

Brown & Jenkins Gourmet Coffee, 286 Old Rte. 15; Cambridge; (802) 862-2395; www.brownjenkins.com. Principally a mail-order coffee roaster with access to top beans from regions around the world, Brown & Jenkins keeps the door open for anyone who happens to be driving past (it's a few hundred yards from Boyden Valley Winery, see p. 74). You can sip a cup of freshly brewed coffee or buy some bags of whatever has just cooled down.

Cabot Annex Store, 2657 Waterbury-Stowe Rd. (Rte. 100), Waterbury; (802) 244-6334; www.cabotcheese.coop. This complex along Route 100 captures a lot more passing traffic than the rural location of the factory in Cabot (p. 103), so it offers great visibility for the cooperative. Sample almost all the Cabot cheeses except for the ultra-premium Clothbound Cheddar, and shop for Vermont-y tastes like pancake mix, Woodstock Granola, maple syrup and local honey. You can also buy other artisan Vermont cheeses, including products of **Vermont Butter & Cheese Creamery** (p. 85), **Jasper Hill Farm** (p. 107), **Neighborly Farms** (p. 83), and others. The shop has a broad wine selection as well as a small tasting area for **Snow Farm Vineyard** (p. 48).

Capital Kitchen, 18 State St., Montpelier; (802) 229-2305; www .capitalkitchenvt.com. Shop owner Jessica Turner believes that everyday tools can be both beautiful and functional and likes to test the items for her store in her home kitchen. You might not find the broadest choice of spatulas or French press coffee makers, but you will find the ones that Turner likes best. And she realizes that the small details matter—like the perfect balance of a stainless steel whisk or chef's knife or the pour spout and nonskid bottom on a deep mixing bowl.

Capitol Grounds, 27 State St., Montpelier; (802) 223-7800; www.capitolgrounds.com. This coffee shop and art gallery features the Fair Trade coffees roasted by Capitol Grounds at a facility in East Montpelier. The cafe serves breakfast and lunch sandwiches and a wide variety of desserts and snacks—presumably so you'll have something to wash down with the coffee. Many of the coffees go beyond being shade-grown, organic, and Fair Trade. They are also certified as "bird friendly" because the farms plant shade trees critical as nesting habitats.

Cold Hollow Cider Mill, 3600 Waterbury-Stowe Rd., Waterbury Center; (802) 244-8771; www.coldhollow.com. It takes about 12 pounds of apples to make one gallon of cider and Cold Hollow presses those apples year-round using a traditional rack and cloth press from the 1920s. But not all apples end up as cider, as they also figure prominently in many of the other treats in this large operation that is popular with tour groups. The bakery, for example, features apple turnovers, apple crumb pie, and, of course, apple cider doughnuts. Cold Hollow encourages visitors to sample its products, including maple mustard dipping sauce, cider chipotle barbecue sauce, spiced apple butter, and apple cider jelly, once a staple of every New England kitchen.

Eaton's Sugarhouse, 5894 Rte. 14 (junction Rte. 107), South Royalton; (802) 763-8809; www.eatonssugarhouse.com. In the time-honored tradition of rural New England serial architecture, this structure began as a cider mill around 1865. A sugarhouse was

Making the Grade

It might seem counterintuitive, but whatever the color, all grades of Vermont maple syrup consist of pure maple sap from which enough water has been removed that it has a density of 66.9 percent sugar. The Vermont Maple Producers Association recognizes four grades of table syrup based on color. They range from the lightest, produced at the beginning of the season, to the darkest, produced at the end. There is no single "best" grade—taste is up to the consumer. The grades are the same in New Hampshire except that Fancy is labeled Grade A Light Amber.

Fancy
Displaying a light amber color with a delicate maple bouquet, this is the mildest-flavored maple syrup. It is especially good on pancakes, waffles, and ice cream.

Grade A Medium Amber
This syrup is darker, with a medium amber color and a pronounced maple aroma. It is perhaps the most popular syrup for all-around use.

Grade A Dark Amber
Darker yet, this syrup has a strong maple aroma and a hearty maple flavor. It is produced toward the end of the 4- to 6-week sugaring season and is also a popular table syrup.

Grade B
Strong and dark, this syrup is produced at the tail end of the season. The maple flavor is very strong, making it good for cooking, but some people dislike its green, sappy overtones. It is an excellent syrup for making cake icings, marinating meats, or for use in other recipes.

added in the 1950s and the space was renovated to accommodate a restaurant about a decade later. In the spring, visitors can watch maple sap being converted to syrup. Any time of year, they can see that syrup being made into maple cream, maple fudge, and maple-sugar candy—or try some of it on a big stack of pancakes, waffles, or french toast. Lunch fare tends toward soup and sandwiches and most folks make a point of saving room for a slice of maple pecan pie. Eaton's syrup and other local products are also available at the country store in the complex.

Grand View Winery Tasting Room, Rte. 100, Waterbury Center; (802) 456-7012; www.grandviewwinery.com. Although the winery is located up in the **Northeast Kingdom** (p. 105), this location is far more convenient for sampling the wares. Grand View produces fruit wines as well as a few grape wines (Riesling and two French-American hybrids: the white Seyval and the red De Chaunac). The light, dry Mac Jack Hard Cider has won a number of awards.

Green Mountain Coffee Factory Store, 40 Foundry St., Waterbury; 802-882-2134. **Green Mountain Visitor Center & Cafe,** 1 Rotarian Place, Waterbury; (877) TRY-BEAN (879-2326); www.waterburystation.com. Despite the flurry of micro-roasters that has sprung up in recent years, Green Mountain Coffee dominates the Vermont java trade. The Factory Store has cups of brewed coffee and sells a wide variety of sometimes discounted coffee paraphernalia, including several versions of the Keurig

System. Green Mountain bought the patent rights to K-cups, and sells its own coffees and some by other producers at the outlet store. The Visitor Center, located in the old train station, was severely damaged by Hurricane Irene in 2011 but has been restored to its Victorian charm. Exhibits highlight the history of Green Mountain Coffee and snacks and coffee are for sale.

Harvest Market, 1031 Mountain Rd., Stowe; (802) 253-3800; www.harvestatstowe.com. About halfway between Stowe village and the ski slopes, this bustling gourmet shop stocks everything you would need to prepare quick meals in your vacation condo. The selection is especially strong on pastas and sauces. They pair well with the breads (Parmesan grissini, rosemary and sea-salt focaccia) that come hot out of the ovens at the back of the store. Other fresh baked goods include muffins and scones, crumble-top fruit pies, brownies, and lemon bars. The deli has a good selection of cheeses, olives, and cured meats, along with salads, samosas, and a few entrees such as pomegranate chicken or pork and rice stir-fry. To save you a trip to another store, there's also a small wine and beer selection.

J.K. Adams—The Kitchen Store, Cabot Annex, 2657 Waterbury-Stowe Rd. (Rte. 100), Waterbury Center; (802) 560-4116; www .thekitchenstoreonline.com. This retail shop carries many of the beautiful wood products of the J.K. Adams factory in Dorset (p. 169), as well as a wide range of bakeware, small electric appliances, cookware, glassware, linens, and fun little gadgets. Many of the wood products can be monogrammed.

The Kitchen at The Store, 5275 Main St. (Rte. 100), Waitsfield; (802) 496-4465; www.kitchenatthestore.com. Woks and tajines and cast-iron skillets all seem right at home in this 1834 former Methodist Meeting House that has been restored and converted into a warm haven for cooks. In addition to cookware, baking supplies, cookbooks, and all sorts of gadgets (that the staff call "fun toys"), the shop has a wonderful selection of tableware from painted Tunisian ceramics to rich, jewel-colored earthenware from Germany. In-house chef John Lumbra offers cooking classes year-round in a beautifully designed and stocked kitchen at the rear of the store. See Chef Lumbra's recipe for **Pork Loin Stuffed with Blue Cheese and Caramelized Apples** on p. 358.

Lake Champlain Chocolates Chocolatier and Cafe, Cabot Annex, 2657 Waterbury-Stowe Rd. (Rte. 100), Waterbury Center; (802) 241-4150; www.lakechamplainchocolates.com. This pocket shop in the Cabot Annex complex has a good selection of Lake Champlain chocolates, although it has a smaller selection of factory seconds than the factory store in Burlington (p. 44).

Laughing Moon Chocolates, 78 S. Main St., Stowe; (802) 253-9591; www.laughingmoonchocolates.com. At first we thought that the chocolatiers might be taking the "locavore" food trend a little too far by making truffles with natural ingredients that are either local or locally sourced. But one taste of the basil and black pepper truffle proved us wrong. And the chamomile and lavender truffle with goat cheese was even better. Since the truffles contain no preservatives, locally distilled vodka is used to extend their shelf life. Young chocolate lovers—or those with simpler tastes—can select Laughing Moon's fudge, chocolate-covered caramel apples, or chocolate turtles (with or without granola). The shop features an open kitchen so that visitors can see the chocolatiers mixing up the centers in old fashioned copper pots and hand-dipping each treat in smooth, rich chocolate. Every afternoon at 2 p.m., there's a mini demonstration of chocolate-making techniques.

Morse Farm, 1168 County Rd., Montpelier; (800) 242-2740; www.morsefarm.com. Morse Farm claims to be home to the original maple "creemee" of soft-serve ice cream mixed with maple syrup. We can't vouch for the claim, but we can say that Morse's creemee has an intense maple flavor. The Morse family traces its Vermont roots and its sugaring heritage back to 1782 and seems to have a passion for all things maple—from their own syrup, cream, and candy to maple-cured bacon and maple kettle corn. Guests are welcome to hike the nature trails on the property (they become a ski touring center in winter). In the spring, the sugarhouse gets a workout, boiling down about 40 gallons of maple sap for each gallon of syrup.

Mountain Cheese & Wine, 1799 Mountain Rd., Stowe; (802) 253-8606; www.mtncheesewine.com. The name tells most of what you need to know. This shop on the road between Stowe village and the ski slopes sells a huge array of cheeses (including most of the Vermont and New Hampshire artisanal cheeses) and an even huger array of wines. The wines tend to favor Italy and California, but some of the better Vermont vineyards are also represented.

Neighborly Farms of Vermont, 1362 Curtis Rd., Randolph Center; (802) 728-4700; www.neighborlyfarms.com. Visitors can stop into the farm store from Monday through Friday to purchase some of Neighborly Farms' organic cheese. But time your visit to a Monday or Thursday and you will probably see Linda Dimmick and her assistants making cheese in the production area behind the shop and next to the barn. Linda and her husband Robert milk 60 cows and make 65,000 pounds of cheese a year. "We transitioned to organic in the late 1990s," says Linda. "We love it and our animals are so much healthier." Neighborly Farms makes 10 different cheeses, including Colby, feta, Monterey Jack, and a number of flavored cheddars. But the best sellers are the plain sharp and mild raw-milk cheddars. "We stagger the calving," explains Linda, "so that we have a fresh supply of milk for cheese year-round."

Red Hen Baking Co., 961B Rte. 2, Middlesex; (802) 223-5200; www.redhenbaking.com. This roadside eatery could not be more homey, with its well-worn couches and rocking chair and the smell of fresh-baked bread in the air. Red Hen's artisanal loaves include olive, potato, ciabatta, and the Vermont *miche,* a round loaf with a caramelized crust and chewy interior that's made with wheat and rye grown in Vermont. The breads are used for lunchtime grilled sandwiches that often sell out quickly. Red Hen is also a Wi-Fi hot spot and many patrons simply grab a cup of coffee and a maple-glazed sticky bun and settle in with their computers at one of the round cafe tables.

Rock Art Brewery, 632 Laporte Rd. (Rte. 100), Morrisville; (802) 888-9400; www.rockartbrewery.com. It is amazing how each Vermont brewery manages to make beers unlike its compatriots. Rock Art (which uses Anasazi petroglyphs of Kokopelli as its signature design) makes large, bold brews. Its smooth and malty Vermonster, for example, is 10 percent alcohol, and its Ridgerunner qualifies as a barley wine. The Double IPA, however, might be the most characteristic of the heavily hopped brews. It pours with a frothy head and is the perfect match to venison chili or an extra-sharp aged Vermont cheddar. Tastings are available at the brewery with the purchase of a souvenir glass. (It's so distinctive, you might end up buying a set.)

Snow Farm Vineyard Tasting Room, Cabot Annex, 2657 Waterbury-Stowe Rd. (Rte. 100), Waterbury; (802) 244-7118; www.snowfarm.com. Vermont's oldest commercial vineyard and grape winery was established in 1996 in South Hero, one of the Champlain islands. The microclimate permits them to make several outstanding estate wines from both hybrid and vinifera grapes. The Vidal Ice

Wine is a consistent award winner, while we like the estate Riesling. Tasting at the winery (p. 48) is much more atmospheric, but this corner of the Cabot Annex pours the same wines—and sells them as well.

Stowe Kitchen Bath & Linens, 1813 Mountain Rd., Stowe; (802) 253-8050; www.stowekitchen.net. This well-stocked shop seems to have the special tool for every cooking need—from asparagus steamers to spaetzle makers, copper bowls to individual sandwich-size cast-iron griddles. If you're looking for an elegant way to serve your Vermont maple syrup, check out the array of syrup dispensers and simple glass pitchers in graduated sizes. Beautiful wooden salad bowls and serving utensils make great gifts.

Vermont Artisan Coffee & Tea Co., 80 Commercial Dr., Waterbury; (802) 244-8338; www.vt artisan.com. Technically a wholesale business, Vermont Artisan Coffee has a window where they sell brewed coffee (and tea) to folks who stop by. Try the robust signature Mané's Blend of Central and South American coffees with just a little East African. The aroma is intense and the rounded, nutty flavor lingers on the palate.

Vermont Butter & Cheese Creamery, 40 Pitman Rd., Websterville; (800) 884-6287; www.vermontcreamery.com. Founded

Now We're Cooking

Allison Hooper, cofounder of Vermont Butter & Cheese, published a wonderful cookbook in 2009 that celebrated the 25th anniversary of the creamery. Many celebrity chefs, including Eric Ripert of Le Bernardin in New York, use the creamery's products and contributed recipes from their menus. Recipes range from a fabulous goat cheese parfait salad to crème fraîche scones. Moreover, Hooper goes into detail about how each of the cheeses (and other dairy products) differ and how they work best in the kitchen. As a result, *In a Cheesemaker's Kitchen* (Countryman Press, 2009) is an invaluable resource for cooking with cultured dairy products. The dishes also taste really good . . .

in 1984, Vermont Butter & Cheese was in the vanguard of artisanal cheesemaking in the US, importing French techniques (and recipes) to use with Vermont goat's and cow's milk to produce wonderful soft-ripened cheeses, fresh cheeses, and even that miracle ingredient of French cookery, crème fraîche. Founders Allison Hooper and Bob Reese have continued to elaborate, and their creamery supports the production of 20 family farms. The cow's milk goes primarily to cultured butter, fromage blanc, marscapone, crème fraîche, and quark.

The goat's milk cheeses are split between fresh cheeses (chèvre, feta, a fresh *crottin*) and magnificent aged cheeses. The supreme jewel of the aged cheeses is the ash-covered Bonne Bouche, named best aged goat cheese in the US. Given the importance of Vermont Butter & Cheese to artisanal cookery in Vermont, we were surprised to find the creamery is located in a small industrial park, rather than a quintessential Vermont farmyard. Nonetheless, visitors can peer through small windows at the cheesemakers at work and peruse the full line of products.

Vermont Liberty Tea, 1 Derby Lane #4, Waterbury; (802) 244-6102; www.vermontlibertytea.com. Waterbury may be better known as the home of **Green Mountain Coffee** (p. 79), but this plucky purveyor is also putting tea on the map—and into people's cups. The name makes reference to the teas made from local herbs that Revolutionary War patriots drank to protest the British tax on tea. And, in fact, Vermont Liberty began by offering herbal teas, but now blends and packages green and black teas as well. A sample of brewed tea is usually available in the shop, which also features a good selection of teapots and other accessories.

Vermont Maple Outlet, 3929 Rte. 15, Jeffersonville; (802) 644-5482; www.vermontmapleoutlet.com. Seven generations of the Marsh family have made maple syrup for more than 100 years. You can find it for sale, along with the Marshes' maple candy and maple cream in this gift shop/sugarhouse. As in most such places, the Marshes also stock a number of other Vermont products including cob-smoked ham and bacon, cheeses, honey, jams, and pancake mixes. They also make a very good maple "creemee."

Warren Store, 284 Main St. (Rte. 100), Warren; (802) 496-3864; www.warrenstore.com. Housed in a venerable old building in Warren's tiny downtown, this emporium is like a country store for the 21st century. The upper level sells stylish clothing, offbeat toys, and original jewelry. The main floor concentrates on food, with scones, muffins, cookies, and pies from the bakery, lunchtime sandwiches, soups, and salads from the deli, and a selection of wine to go with the takeaway dinner entrees.

Farmstands & Pick Your Own

Cedar Circle Farm & Education Center, 225 Pavillion Rd., East Thetford; (802) 785-4737; www.cedarcirclefarm.org. The farm's beautiful organic vegetables serve as inspiration for some of the more unusual pickles and preserves that we've encountered, including Ginger Carrots, Fennel Cukes, and Tomato Chili Jam. If you want to add to your own cooking repertoire, the education center offers some intriguing cooking classes such as how to ferment sauerkraut and kimchee or how to make no-knead breads to accompany fall soups. The kitchen classroom is right on the property, as is a cute little cafe with coffee, cookies, and a few other small nibbles. Open May through Oct.

Four Corners Farm, 306 Doe Hill Rd., South Newbury; (802) 866-3342; www.4cornersfarm.com. If Hollywood scouts were looking for a picture-perfect farmstand, we'd send them to Four Corners family farm. The big barn up a small hill has stunning views across a green valley. Bob and Kim Gray grow all the produce that they sell and many of the fruits and vegetables actually look as if they were arranged by a stylist: red, yellow, and orange peppers spilling out of baskets; giant red and white onions next to tall buckets of sunflowers; piles of cucumbers for pickling beside big bunches of dill with bright yellow flowers. It's all too pretty not to eat. Open May through Thanksgiving.

Liberty Orchard, 2622 Rte. 65, Brookfield; (802) 276-3161; www.libertyorchardvt.com. The Liberty apple is a hybrid type developed by the New York State Agricultural Experiment Station to be especially disease resistant and require no pesticides. It was released to the public in 1974 and has slowly been catching on across the Northeast. This orchard specializes in pick-your-own Liberty apples and five other newer disease-resistant varieties. They are all planted on dwarf stock for easy picking. Open Sept through late Oct.

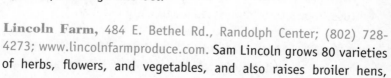

Lincoln Farm, 484 E. Bethel Rd., Randolph Center; (802) 728-4273; www.lincolnfarmproduce.com. Sam Lincoln grows 80 varieties of herbs, flowers, and vegetables, and also raises broiler hens, pigs, and Thanksgiving turkeys. He takes the definition of "local" seriously, and his small farmstand also stocks finished beef from a nearby farm and cheese and yogurt made only 5 miles away. It's a bit of a drive along a tree-lined dirt road to reach Lincoln Farm, but the views of old farms and rolling pastureland make it well worth going out of the way. Lincoln Farm hosts a number of events in the summer and fall, such as cooking demonstrations, a chicken barbecue or a pumpkin festival.

Farmers' Markets

Barre Granite Center Farmers' Market, City Central Park, Barre. Wed from 3 to 6:30 p.m., mid-May to mid-October.

Chelsea Farmers' Market, North Common, Chelsea. Fri from 3 to 6:30 p.m., late May to mid-October.

Eden Farmers' Market, On the Green, Eden. Sun from 11 a.m. to 3 p.m, early July to late September.

Johnson Farmers' Market, United Church, Rte. 15, Johnson. Tues from 3 to 6 p.m., late May to early October.

Lamoille Valley Farmers' Artisan Market, Pleasant St., Morrisville. Wed from 3 to 6:30 p.m., early May to late September.

Montpelier Capital City Farmers' Market, corner State and Elm streets, Montpelier. Sat from 9 a.m. to 1 p.m., May through October.

Northfield Farmers' Market, Village Common, Northfield. Tues from 3 to 6 p.m., late May to mid-October.

Plainfield Farmers' Market, Mill Street Park, Plainfield. Fri from 4 to 7 p.m., June to early October.

Randolph Farmers' Market, Rte. 66, Randolph. Sat from 9 a.m. to 1 p.m., mid-May to mid-October.

Stowe Farmers' Market, Rte. 108, 2 miles from intersection of Rtes. 100 and 108, Stowe. Sun from 10:30 a.m. to 3 p.m., mid-May to mid-October.

Stowe Mountain Resort Farmers' Market, Spruce Peak Plaza, Stowe. Fri from 11 a.m. to 3 p.m., July through September.

Waitsfield Farmers' Market, Mad River Green, Rte. 100, Waitsfield. Sat from 9 a.m. to 1 p.m., late May to mid-October.

Waterbury Farmers' Market, Rusty Parker Park, Rte. 2, Waterbury. Thurs from 3 to 7 p.m., mid-May to mid-October.

Food Events

Bradford Wild Game Supper, www.bradforducc.org. For more than 50 years the Bradford United Church of Christ has held the Super Bowl of game suppers, usually the weekend before Thanksgiving. Reservations must be made up to 4 weeks ahead by using a form available on the church website. Proceeds support maintenance of the church.

Lamoille County Field Days, www.lamoillefielddays.com. Begun in 1961, this family-oriented agricultural fair is held in Johnson in late July and includes food, crafts, and agricultural exhibitions.

Solstice Brew-Grass Festival, www.sugarbush.com. Vermonters celebrate the beginning of summer in late June at Sugarbush in Warren with a day of listening to bluegrass bands while enjoying such small-scale local craft brews as Switchback, Rock Art, and Dogfish Head.

Stowe Oktoberfest, www.stoweoktoberfest.com. Freshly brewed Vermont beer pairs well with such traditional German dishes as bratwurst and knockwurst with sauerkraut and potato salad. This late September event in Stowe also features a grand parade and lively entertainment.

Tunbridge World's Fair, www.tunbridgefair.com. Only the 1918 flu epidemic and World War II have interrupted this agricultural fair that was first held in 1867. The event takes place in mid-September in Tunbridge.

Washington County Fair & Field Days, www.vtfairs.org. This low-key fair is held in early August in Waitsfield and includes 4-H displays and a pie-eating contest.

Wine & Food Classic, www.stowewine.com. Stowe is the setting for this late June event that features wine tastings and seminars, cooking demonstrations, and a gala dinner.

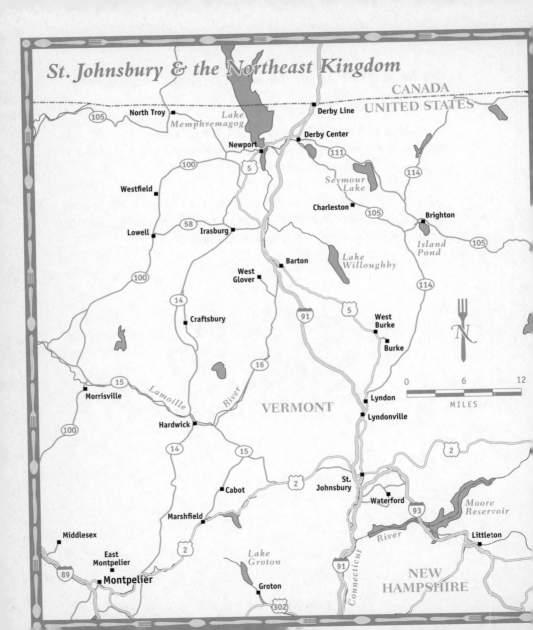

St. Johnsbury & the Northeast Kingdom

CANADA

UNITED STATES

105 North Troy

Lake Memphremagog

Derby Line

Derby Center

Newport

100

5

111

114

Westfield

Seymour Lake

Charleston

105

Brighton

Island Pond

105

Lowell

58

Irasburg

West Glover

Barton

Lake Willoughby

100

14

91

5

114

Craftsbury

West Burke

Burke

16

15

Morrisville

Lamoille River

0   6   12

MILES

N

VERMONT

Lyndon

100

Hardwick

Lyndonville

14

15

2

Cabot

2

St. Johnsbury

Marshfield

Waterford

93

Moore Reservoir

Middlesex

River

Littleton

East Montpelier

89

Montpelier

Lake Groton

91

Connecticut

NEW HAMPSHIRE

Groton

302

St. Johnsbury & the Northeast Kingdom

In a 1949 speech, the late Senator George D. Aiken first called the northeast quadrant of Vermont the "Northeast Kingdom," a moniker that perfectly captured the mythical qualities of a corner of Vermont otherwise known for fall foliage, winter skiing, and maple syrup. The Kingdom (as residents sometimes call it) is so rural that its largest town, the Caledonia County shire town of St. Johnsbury, has only 7,500 people and the only city, Newport, has just 5,000. The other 50-plus spots on the map are even smaller.

Roughly 80 percent of the Northeast Kingdom is covered in forest, which might explain why it sometimes seems that every rural mailbox has a sign next to it advertising maple syrup for sale. The presence of Cabot, New England's largest dairy cooperative, demonstrates that a paucity of open land doesn't keep the Kingdom from being dairy country. While the Kingdom is perhaps the toughest place in Vermont and New Hampshire to actually raise food, it has some of New England's fiercest local food advocates. In practice, this means that anyone looking for local produce, bread, honey, beer, mead, fruit, cheese, or meat can find it in most markets and on the menus of most restaurants.

Foodie Faves

Claire's Restaurant & Bar, 41 S. Main St., Hardwick; (802) 472-7053; www.clairesvt.com; $$. "Farm to table" is more than a slogan at Claire's. Proclaiming as his motto "local ingredients open to the world," Chef-Proprietor Steven Obranovich puts his money where his mouth is. He makes 90 percent of the restaurant's food purchases in the immediate region, most within a 15-mile radius, even buying Vermont sunflower oil and wine for cooking. The "open to the world" part means that his essentially New American cooking can speak with a Middle Eastern accent in one dish (Jacob's Cattle bean falafel), Mexican-Irish in another (pork rib braised in stout with tomatillos) and Heartland American in yet another (a burger with fries, lettuce, and tomato). The restaurant opens for coffee, bar service, and pastry in the mid-afternoon as well as for dinner and Sunday brunch. Obranovich differentiates only between small plates and main courses, with the former outnumbering the latter three to one. In practice, this means groups generally order a table full of tastes.

Elements Food and Spirit, 98 Mill St., No. 1, St. Johnsbury; (802) 748-8400; www.elementsfood.com; $$. Chef Eric Kadle believes that good food doesn't have to be fancy—it just has to have character and integrity. That spirit is even summed up by the setting for Elements: an 1853 mill building with exposed brick, an outdoor terrace on the river, zinc bar, and copper-clad tables. A huge brick oven does double duty as decor and cooking appliance. Pasta and fish change daily, and the menu is unadorned and straightforward New American bistro fare. Steak and fries are prominent. Depending on the season, you might find an eggplant roulade (rolled and stuffed with ricotta) as the centerpiece of a vegetarian plate, or a lobster BLT for diners with light appetites. The daily prix-fixe menu includes soup or salad, three entree choices (meat, vegetarian, poultry/fish), and a few dessert choices of classics like apple strudel a la mode or flourless chocolate torte. Given that the prices are as honest as the fare, it's no wonder that Elements is a top choice by North Country foodies for a fun night out.

Juniper's at the Wildflower Inn, 2059 Darling Hill Rd., Lyndonville; (802) 626-8310; www.junipersrestaurant.com; $$. The extensive menu at Juniper's ranges from burgers that feature beef from a neighboring farm to a seitan stir-fry for vegans to a grilled meatloaf entree or a roasted chicken breast. As much as possible, the ingredients come from around the Northeast Kingdom, and the Vermont beer list is one of the best in the state. Juniper's also has an extensive gluten-free menu and special empathy for diners with dietary restrictions. It is a cheery place to dine, as the big windows of the dining room overlook an idyllic farmlike setting.

Lago Trattoria & Catering, 95 Main St., Newport; (802) 334-8222; www.lagotrattoria.com; $$$. Sharing the same fine views of Lake Memphremagog as **Le Belvedere** (below), Lago is Newport's veteran fine-dining venue. Chef-Owner Frank Richardi specializes in Italian dishes that emphasize the quality of ingredients, many of which he sources locally from northern Vermont and the Eastern Townships of Quebec. A perfect starter might be his beef carpaccio seasoned with black pepper and served on a salad of arugula and Parmigiano Reggiano cheese. The ever-popular maple-glazed quail often comes with a confit duck leg and Richardi's own ravioli filled with sweet potato.

Le Belvedere, 100 Main St., Newport; (802) 487-9147; $$. Eating out should be fun, or at least that's the premise behind Le Belvedere, the year-round tapas restaurant in the state office building on Newport's waterfront. Local boy Jason Marcoux (who was away long enough to get a degree from the New England Culinary Institute, another certificate from the CIA, and serve as chef de cuisine in one of Alaska's hottest restaurants) runs the kitchen. Although it took a while for small-plate dining to catch on in Newport, Le Belvedere won customers over with the most eclectic and social dining experience in town. The dishes are smart, too. For example, Marcoux serves spanakopita filled with chèvre and duck confit. One night a week, he features sushi and sashimi. For dessert, try his brie baked in a crust and served with blueberry compote.

Parker Pie Co., 161 County Rd., West Glover; (802) 525-3366; www.parkerpie.com; $. From the front porch, the Lake Parker Country Store looks like any number of small-town establishments that offer basic staples and a sense of community in equal measure. But step inside and the smell of garlic and tomatoes will lead you past the bulk grains and video displays to the rear of the store. That's where Parker Pie Co. has set up a wooden counter and a few tables to serve customers eager for one of their pizzas. The best way to appreciate the tender but chewy crust (nearly on a par with those we tasted in Naples, Italy) is to order a simple Margherita with plum tomatoes, mozzarella, Parmesan, garlic, and fresh basil. But since this is Vermont, after all, it's a shame not to try the Green Mountain Special, replete with cheddar cheese, baby spinach, red onion, smoked bacon, apples, and fresh garlic—all drizzled with maple syrup.

Rabbit Hill Inn, 48 Lower Waterford Rd., Lower Waterford; (802) 748-5168; www.rabbithillinn.com; $$$$. As befits this elegant B&B, the dining room at the Rabbit Hill Inn has just 14 candlelit tables and the farm-to-fork menu is prix-fixe. It is also in constant flux. When the pig from a neighboring farm is ready, there's suddenly a lot of pork. Cabbage and apples and root vegetables are prominent in cool weather, while summer explodes with the bounty of tomatoes and corn. The New American preparations are unfussy—a grilled rib eye steak served with a potato–Cabot cheddar puree, for example,

Let It Grow

From a backyard enterprise growing 28 varieties in 1996, **High Mowing Organic Seeds** has expanded dramatically to become one of New England's largest suppliers of organic vegetable, fruit, herb, and flower seeds. The company still grows much of the seed on its own 40-acre farm, providing 450 varieties. Most are open-pollinated heirlooms, but some (like the sweet corn and a few tomatoes) are first-generation hybrids. Founder Tom Stearns is something of a missionary about rebuilding food systems that respect the land and restore the environment. Good, healthy food, he believes, begins with good, healthy seeds. The company's 2-acre trial and showcase garden is open for self-guided tours from about the middle of May through Columbus Day. Seeds are available at the company headquarters, at food and garden stores throughout the region, or through the website.

High Mowing Organic Seeds, 76 Quarry Rd., Wolcott; (802) 472-6174; www.highmowingseeds.com

or venison medallions with roasted root vegetables and a side of spaetzle. The inn also has a separate small but full-service bar.

Trout River Brewing Co., 58 Rte. 5, Lyndonville; (802) 626-9396; www.troutriverbrewing.com; $. Dan and Laura Gates love their beer, and they are among the few brewmasters in northern New England who refuse to filter their ales and lagers. In practice, that means that the beers can be a tad cloudy, especially at the end of a keg, but that they also pack a lot of flavor. The Rainbow Red Ale, an American-style red ale, is the flagship. It's soft and fruity. The Scotch Ale is a richly malty brew, while Hoppin' Mad Trout is brighter and lighter but carries a snappy bite of hops. The brewery opens its pub for just a few hours on Friday and Saturday evening, serving a selection of pizzas to go with the beers. One pizza choice, in particular, parallels the beer: smoked trout, red onions, plum tomatoes, capers, and fresh scallions. It's called the Smokin' Hot Trout.

Specialty Stores, Markets & Producers

Artesano Meadery, 1334 Scott Hwy. (Rte. 302), Groton; (802) 584-9000; www.artesanomead.com. During a stint in the Peace Corps, Mark Simakaski and Nichole Wolfgang taught beekeeping in Paraguay. So when the couple returned to the States and wanted to start a business, they focused on mead. "We are taking an ancient beverage and applying modern technology," says Simakaski, as he points at the five fermentation tanks in the back of the old general store that also serves as Artesano's showroom. "We go for subtle and balanced. I want to make something light and crisp." Working in a small winery with state-of-the-art equipment, they produce about 1,000 cases a year of traditional meads (both semisweet and dry), and seasonal fruit meads, which include a particularly elegant mead infused with raspberries. The distinctive half-liter bottle makes Artesano stand out on the shelf. The couple also makes fantastic ice cream. "We took the same ice cream course as **Ben & Jerry** (p. 73)," says Wolfgang. "We started making it on a whim to help pay the rent while we got the meadery up and running." One of the most popular flavors is *dulce de leche,* a reminder of the years the couple spent in Buenos Aires. Simakaski finds it perfectly logical to focus on two different, but all natural products. "There is a synergy," he says. "People can develop their palates if they think about what they are tasting. If they think about what they are smelling." Open Memorial Day through Columbus Day.

Bentley's Bakery & Cafe, 20 Hill St., Danville; (802) 684-3385; www.bentleysbakeryvt.com. Portions are generous at Bentley's, where the kitchen turns out plump muffins and platter-sized cookies. "One of the services we offer is to help you eat it," Nancy Frampton jokes as she serves customers lined up at the counter. She and husband Jeff are originally from Montreal. "We want our shop to have a Montreal feel," says Jeff. Sure enough, the Framptons offer a range of plain and filled croissants and lovely éclairs and tarts. Quiche is one of the most popular light lunches at this breakfast and lunch only community gathering place. But the Framptons have also embraced their adopted home and bake what might be the cutest cookie in Vermont. Called "Kingdom Cow," the bovine-shaped sugar cookie is slathered with vanilla icing and dappled with chocolate spots.

Buffalo Mountain Food Coop and Cafe, 39 Main St., Hardwick; (802) 472-6020; www.buffalomountaincoop.org. Hardwick likes to proclaim itself the town saved by local food, and Buffalo Mountain is, in some ways, the heart of the town. The store's motto of "food for people, not for profit" translates into an abundance of local products (cheese, maple syrup, baked goods, fruits, vegetables, meat, milk . . .) presented with just a touch of smug self-righteousness. All in all, it's a wholesome place full of food that is good for you. Much the same can be said of the integrated cafe, which serves breakfast and lunch. The dietary inclusiveness is perhaps summed up in the TLT/BLT sandwich, which offers a choice of Vermont smoked bacon or smoked tempeh, lettuce, and a choice of tomato or avocado. (Would you like sprouts with that?)

Cabot Visitors Center, 2878 Main St., Cabot; (800) 837-4261; www.cabotcheese.coop. Cabot is the largest of the 40-plus members of the Vermont Cheese Council and its plant tends to dominate its namesake town. In fact, it's one of the Cabot Cooperative's three cheese plants and the only one open to the public. The factory tour begins with a short video that recounts the origins of the cooperative in 1919 when 94 farmers each chipped in a cord of wood and $5 per cow to buy out the Cabot village creamery. The operation has certainly grown since then and the tour leads visitors through the modern facility where they can view the cheesemaking equipment through large windows. If you want to be sure to see the facility up and running, call ahead for the cheesemaking schedule. When operating at full production, the plant can make 43 tons of cheddar a day. Like all good factory tours, Cabot's ends in the gift shop/ tasting room where visitors can sample and purchase the cooperative's cheddar cheeses, flavored cheddars, and assorted dips.

Caledonia Spirits & Winery, 46 Buffalo Mountain Commons Dr., Hardwick; (802) 472-8000; www.caledoniaspirits.com. Rooted in beekeeping, this unusual beverage maker crafts a limited number of honey-fruit wines (or mead). They also make some striking distilled products, including honey vodka, honey–juniper berry gin, and elderberry cordial with honey and apple. The distillery store sells all these products as well as raw honey and some herbal medicines.

Goodrich's Maple Farm, 2427 Rte. 2, Cabot; (800) 639-1854; www.goodrichmaplefarm.com. The Goodrich family has been making maple syrup for seven generations and share their knowledge and enthusiasm in casual tours throughout the year. But the best time to visit is during sugaring season in March and April when the evaporator—one of the largest and fastest in the world and roughly the size of a Sherman tank—is up and running to boil down the sap from about 40,000 trees. Of course, the family also offers a full range of maple products.

Grand View Winery, 2113 Max Gray Road, East Calais; (802) 456-7012; www.grandviewwinery.com. Grand View produces fruit wines as well as a few grape wines (Riesling and two French-American hybrids: the white Seyval and the red De Chaunac). The light, dry Mac Jack Hard Cider has won a number of awards. The location has, as advertised in the name, grand views, and opens for tastings May through November. It is also a popular spot for country weddings. The retail outlet and tasting room at **Cold Hollow Cider Mill** in Waterbury (p. 77) is a more convenient location for trying the wines.

Maple Grove Farms of Vermont, 1052 Portland St., St. Johnsbury; (802) 748-5141; www.maplegrove.com. Launched in a farmhouse kitchen in 1915, Maple Grove now claims to be the largest packer of maple syrup in the United States and the largest manufacturer of maple candies in the world. After watching a video on the sugaring process, you can sample four grades of syrup or the sweet little candies or purchase a soft-serve maple "creemee." Maple Grove makes its candies in the traditional maple-leaf mold, but also nods to the seasons with other shapes such as mini pilgrims or Santas. The shop features an array of other products

including dressings, jellies, fruit syrups, pancake and waffle mixes, and maple cream cookies. Be sure to check the discount shelves for savings of up to 50 percent on some items.

Rainbow Sweets, 1689 Rte. 2, Marshfield; (802) 426-3531. Ask William Tecosky how he came to make such delicious sweet and savory pastries in this tiny Vermont town and he'll turn coy and tell you to wait for the book about his life. But we don't really mind because his food speaks for itself. For lunch, diners can grab a seat at one of the few small tables and watch Tecosky pull treats from the giant oven as they savor an Argentine-style empanada (ground beef, onions, olives, raisins, and cumin in pie pastry) or a Moroccan B'stilla (shredded chicken, almonds, cinnamon, and saffron in phyllo dough) with a small salad. Tecosky is particularly proud of his sweets, including a chocolate whipped cream torte, a vanilla buttercream poppy seed cake, and linzer tortes. "You'd have to know someone in Austria to get one this good," he says half in jest. Tecosky encourages diners to split a dessert, unless they order the St. Honoré. He calls this creation of whipped cream, puffed pastry, and profiteroles filled with cream and dipped in hot caramel the "Johnny Depp of desserts" and insists that it's too good to share.

The Cheese Underground

When brothers Mateo and Andy Kehler founded **Jasper Hill Farm** in Greensboro in 2003, they decided that they would make cheese—and they would make a difference. Dairy farms were going out of business all around them as they assembled their small herd of Ayrshire cattle. But they were determined to show, in their own words, that it "is still possible to prosper on a rocky hillside farm [and] create a vehicle for the renewal of our local dairy economy in the form of a business model that can be replicated on other dairy farms."

Making cheese was almost the easy part. Most cheeses only develop their character as they mature. So the Kehlers had the Cellars at Jasper Hill constructed to serve as "a bridge between small-scale production and large scale markets." The cellars consist of seven underground vaults, each with a different ambient temperature and humidity to age cheeses to perfection.

They handle their own highly decorated cheeses—bark-wrapped bloomy-rind Harbison, buttery bloomy-rind Moses Sleeper, Bailey Hazen Blue, washed-rind Winnimere, and the tangy lactic-set bloomy-rind Constant Bliss—and the production of a handful of other cheesemakers. Cabot Creamery's Clothbound Cheddar, for example, is aged here, as is Landaff Creamery's Caerphilly-style tomme. The Kehlers also handle the marketing and sales of the cheeses that they mature, and the cheeses are available in many shops and on the menus of fine restaurants.

Jasper Hill Farm does not permit visitors, but you can purchase cheese directly through the website: www.cellarsat jasperhill.com, (802) 533-7772.

Berry Creek Farm, 1342 Rte. 100, Westfield; (802) 744-2406; www.berrycreekfarmvt.com. "My husband is from France, so food has always been a focus," says Rosemary Croizet, who operates this 158-acre organic farm with her husband Gerard. Stopping at the farm to pick some of the Croizets' luscious strawberries is almost a rite of early summer in this part of the Northeast Kingdom and the farmstand keeps the treats coming all season with everything from artichokes to eggplant, celeriac to Swiss chard. The Croizets also grow more than 30 different herbs and Rosemary makes her own honey and jams, including strawberry maple and strawberry honey for those who missed the picking season. The farmstand stocks a small selection of other local products including goat cheese from Lazy Lady Farm, yogurt and cream from Butterworks Farm, and Maple Mudd (a rich peanut butter and maple spread) from Jed's Maple Products. Open May through Oct. See Rosemary's recipe for **Chocolate Strawberry Tarte** on p. 365.

Burtt's Apple Orchard, 283 Cabot Plains Rd., Cabot; (802) 917-2614; www.burttsappleorchard.com. Burtt's grows about 35 varieties of apples on a 6-acre plot. The relatively new orchards were planted with pick-your-own customers in mind, meaning that tree branches are low and different apple varieties are grouped close together. Burtt's also presses its own cider and tailors some of its batches for hard-cider aficionados who can fill a carboy with juice and let it work its natural magic over the winter. Open mid-September through October.

Pete's Greens at Craftsbury Village Farm, 266 S. Craftsbury Rd., Craftsbury; (802) 586-2882; www.petesgreens.com. Pete's is familiar to shoppers at natural foods stores all around New England because the farm produces both consumer packs and restaurant bulk packs of organic greenhouse greens all year long. But there's more to Pete's than mesclun. The farm grows about 75 varieties of vegetables and operates a four-season CSA. Retail customers can check the farmstand for overflow.

Farm Stays

Couture's Maple Shop Bed & Breakfast, 560 Rte. 100, Westfield; (802) 744-2733; www.maplesyrupvermont.com. Guests are welcome at the 4-room bed-and-breakfast in the 1892 farmhouse any time of year and can watch Jacques Couture feed and milk his herd of about 125 cattle. But the most interesting time to stay might be during maple season when the Coutures are collecting sap from 7,500 taps and the sugarhouse is in full operation. Breakfast, of course, features maple syrup, which can also be purchased at the Coutures' maple shop. The wide variety of products available includes Maple Fire Hot Sauce, maple cotton candy, and maple almonds.

Emergo Farm Bed & Breakfast, 261 Webster Hill, Danville; (802) 684-2215; www.emergofarm.com. Emergo is what most people imagine when they picture a Vermont farm: a white farmhouse with big front porch on a hill overlooking a field of black and white Holstein cows. The farm has been in Bebo Webster's family since 1858 and he and wife Lori offer guests the chance to stay in 4 guest rooms on the second floor of the 1890 farm house. Guests are also welcome to lounge in the parlor or on the front porch or watch Bebo and his son Justin at work in the barns. Early risers might even catch the morning milking, though Bebo finds that most guests favor afternoon. Emergo Farm is a member of the Cabot Cooperative, so Lori uses Cabot products along with local eggs and organic produce in her farm-style breakfasts.

Hollister Hill Farm, 2193 Hollister Hill Rd., Marshfield; (802) 454-7725; www.hollisterhillfarm.com. Bob and Lee Light chose to "go back to the land" in 1972 and don't seem to have ever looked back. After a career as full-blown dairy farmers, they've stepped back to milk a few Jerseys and raise some chickens and pigs and run a B&B where guests can get a taste of Vermont farm life. The barn is open during the day so guests can visit—or even help with some chores like watering or bedding the animals. Kids are allowed—even encouraged—to play in the hay mow. Even if you're not staying in one of the 2 double rooms or the 2-room suite, you might want to stop at the farmstore for Hollister Hill Farm's own Beefalo beef, pork, chickens, turkeys, eggs, and maple syrup as well as organic vegetables and berries in season. You can also purchase raw milk from the four Jerseys.

Farmers' Markets

Craftsbury Common Farmers' Market, On the Common, Craftsbury. Sat from 10 a.m. to 1 p.m., late May through mid-October.

Danville Farmers' Market, Rte. 2 between West Danville and Danville Village. Wed from 9 a.m. to 1 p.m., early June to early October.

Derby Farmers' Market, Rte. 5, Derby. Sat and Tues from 9:30 a.m. to 2:30 p.m., late May to early October.

Greensboro Farmers' Market, Town Hall Green, Greensboro. Thurs from 3 to 6 p.m., June to early September.

Groton Growers' Market, Veterans Memorial Park, Groton. Sat from 10 a.m. to 1 p.m., June to late September.

Hardwick Farmers' Market, Granite St., Hardwick. Fri from 3 to 6 p.m., May through October.

Lunenberg Farmers' Market, Town Common, Rte. 2, Lunenberg. Wed from 2 to 6 p.m., June to mid October.

Lyndonville Farmers' Market, Bandstand Park, Lyndonville. Fri from 3 to 7 p.m., mid-May to mid-October.

Newport Northeast Kingdom Farmers' Market, 246 The Causeway, Newport. Sat from 9 a.m. to 2 p.m. mid-May to mid-October and Wed from 9 a.m. to 2 p.m., mid-June to mid-October.

Peacham Farmers' Market, Green Space, Village Center, Peacham. Thurs from 3 to 6 p.m., late May through September.

St. Johnsbury Farmers' Market, Pearl St., St. Johnsbury. Sat from 9 a.m. to 1 p.m., May through October.

Willoughby Lake Farmers' & Artisans' Market, Rte. 5A and Long Pond Rd., Westmore. Thurs from 3 to 7 p.m., early June to mid-September.

Food Events

Apple Pie Festival, www.cabothistory.com. The Cabot Historical Society sponsors this community event on the Saturday after Columbus Day. Children and adults enter their best pies in the apple pie contest. Visitors can purchase a pie to take home, grab a snack at the lunch bar, and shop among the crafts booths.

Caledonia County Fair, www.vtfair.com. A lively midway and daredevil demolition derby tend to get a lot of attention, but this late-August fair in Lyndonville also features 4-H exhibits, a maple display area, and farm-fresh foods.

New England Pie Breakfast, www.travelthekingdom.com. The folks in Woodbury celebrate the old Yankee tradition of eating pie for breakfast at this mid-March event that features more than 100 pies and quiches along with live entertainment and a silent auction.

Orleans County Fair, www.orleanscountyfair.net. Held in the village of Barton in mid-August, this fair is more than 140 years old and still celebrates such agricultural traditions as horse, pony, and ox pulling, along with 4-H livestock competitions. More unusual displays include an interactive milking parlor and a cheese-processing unit.

St. Johnsbury Maple Fest, www.worldmaplefestival.org. We're not really certain that St. Johnsbury is the "Maple Center of the World," as the organizers of this mid-April event have proclaimed. But the city does throw a good party, complete with a parade, craft exhibits, and food vendors. Syrup producers compete for awards for best syrups in four grades (Fancy, Medium Amber, Dark Amber, and Grade B), as well as for Best of Festival.

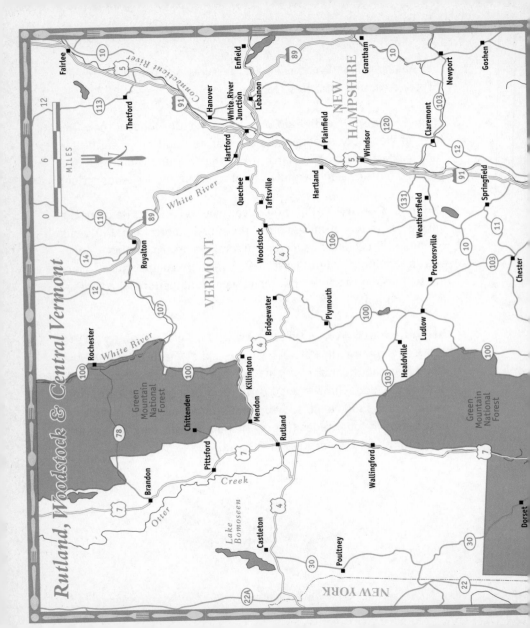

Rutland, Woodstock & Central Vermont

While the topography of the Green Mountains makes it tempting to think of Vermont as a series of north-south vertical stripes—mountain ridges and the valleys between them—the east-west corridor a few miles on each side of Vermont Route 4 represents a fascinating cross-section of the state. The highway strings together lowland burgs and highland villages like a strand of pearls running across the middle of the state.

Farming on the east end of the corridor was profoundly influenced in the 19th century by the scientific farming movement exemplified by Woodstock's own gentleman farmer, Frederick Billings. The middle sector stands high in the mountains, where alpine dairy traditions thrive, while the western end of the corridor was planted early on in apples and retains an identity as orchard country. This entire slice of Vermont has proved irresistible to urbanites whose summer farm retreats and winter ski chalets provide support for a vibrant restaurant scene.

Foodie Faves

Birdseye Diner, 590 Main St., Castleton; (802) 468-5817; www .birdseyediner.com; $. In its current location since 1952, the Birdseye is a central Vermont institution. The Silk City diner from the 1940s was "updated" in the 1950s to replace wooden parts of the interior with chrome, then retrofitted in the 1990s to restore the original design. The food is timeless diner fare, including an excellent burger piled with fresh veggies, a solid meatloaf, roast pork, and a traditional Italian-American lasagna. All the breakfast specials come with home fries—except the pancakes and French toast, which are accompanied by real Vermont maple syrup. In classic diner fashion, the coffee is bottomless.

Cafe Provence, 11 Center St., Brandon; (802) 247-9997; www .cafeprovencevt.com; $$. How lucky can one town get? Chefs Robert and Line Barral changed the food landscape of Brandon when they settled here and opened Cafe Provence. The restaurant is primarily Robert's purview, while Line produces the great breads and pastries of **Gourmet Provence Bakery and Wine Shop** (see p. 130). The former executive chef of the New England Culinary Institute,

Robert brings his mastery of French technique to local meats, cheeses, fruits, and vegetables. The result is unmistakably New American cuisine done with French finesse. He makes his own cherry tomato chutney, for example, to top the baked haddock, and uses beef from the Spotted Dog Family Farm in Brandon to craft his "Local Grass-Fed Beef Burger." (Ask for it with Vermont cheddar.) Since the cafe is equipped with a hearth oven, he also produces exquisite pizzas—a dish that happens to be native to his home region of Provence. Barral also offers an extensive gluten-free menu. The restaurant is very family friendly: Children dine free from the children's menu on Sunday. On most Monday afternoons except in the summer, Barral also offers inexpensive cooking classes in classical French technique so students can replicate restaurant menu entrees and desserts at home.

Countryman's Pleasure, 3 Town Line Rd., Mendon; (802) 773-7141; www.countrymanspleasure.com; $$$. For authentic tastes of Mitteleuropa, don't miss Hans and Kathleen Entinger's white farmhouse restaurant just off Route 4. A native of Austria, Hans originally trained in Munich and cooked in Switzerland, England, France, and Canada before settling here in 1978. Many of his specialties feature veal, including wiener schnitzel and veal á la Holstein (with pan-fried eggs), and veal Entinger (his own version with king crab, artichokes, and Hollandaise sauce).

Farmers Diner, 5573 Woodstock Rd., Quechee; (802) 295-4600; $. The souvenir T-shirt pretty much says what you need to know about this oddball diner located off to the side of the parking lot at Quechee Gorge Village: "Think Locally. Eat Neighborly." The diner sources as much of its food as close to home as possible, and while the coffee, tea, and cocoa aren't from Vermont or adjacent New Hampshire, the beef, chicken, eggs, bacon, and salad vegetables are. Farmers Diner is proof that locavore dining doesn't have to be precious. They serve real diner food in a 1947 Worcester Lunch Car Co. diner. As Mark Twain once wrote, "The report of my death is an exaggeration." Ditto reports of the death of Farmers Diner. It did change hands in 2011 and the menu was simplified to include more comfort food (chicken and biscuits, meat loaf and mashed potatoes), but the cooking remains up to snuff and the foodstuffs remain as local as possible.

Harpoon Brewery, 336 Ruth Carney Dr., Windsor; (802) 674-5491; www.harpoonbrewery.com; $. Harpoon bought out Vermont's own Catamount Brewery back in 2000, giving Boston-based Harpoon a foothold in western New England. The Harpoon Riverbend Taps and Beer Garden shares the brewery building, and true to its name, it is right on a bend in the Connecticut River just a short distance above the flood-control dam. Alas, there's no view from the tap-room, but the full line of Harpoon beers is available on draft, and you can take a tour of the brewery on weekends. The 100-barrel limited edition beers change constantly. If you're lucky, you might even find a Catamount revival on tap. Food at the Taps and Beer

Garden consists of beer-friendly fare like burgers, wraps, panini, salads, and good old-fashioned fries.

Inn at Long Trail, 709 Rte. 4, Sherburne Pass, Killington; (800) 325-2540; www.innatlongtrail.com; $$. First-time diners are always surprised to find that the dining room has been built around a giant boulder. Less surprising is that innkeepers Murray and Patty McGrath feature hearty Irish dishes on the menu. Beef stew simmered in Guinness stout or an Irish Reuben (rye bread topped with corned beef, cabbage, and melted swiss cheese) are equally satisfying to skiers, long-distance hikers, or car-driving leaf peepers. Amazingly, many diners still find room for double chocolate Irish soda bread pudding with Irish whiskey cream sauce. The adjacent McGrath's Irish Pub has live music (Irish, need we say it?) on weekends.

Inn at Weathersfield, 1342 Rte. 106, Perkinsville; (802) 263-9217; www.weathersfieldinn.com; $$$. On the border between central and southern Vermont, the 1792 country inn maintains its rustic charm, though modern renovations have given private baths to all 12 guest rooms. Chef Jason Totrup has made the inn a locavore dining destination, not just a convenient base for Okemo skiers. The inn even offers its guests a customized GPS tour of its farm partners. Restaurant Verterra offers a menu that Totrup calls "A Taste of Place." For example, the "Whole Hog Heaven" dish changes nightly but always features Springmore Farms pork. The more casual Lucy's Tavern serves lusty bistro fare, including "Chicken Under a Brick," often plated with a cider glaze.

Long Trail Brewing Co., 5520 Rte. 4, Bridgewater Corners; (802) 672-5011; www.longtrail.com; $. This craft brewer has been a fixture in northern New England since 1989, when they began brewing Long Trail Ale in the basement of the former Bridgewater Woolen Mill. Hikers, skiers, and the general public gave the brew a thumbs-up, and the company built this eco-brewery up the road in a former hayfield. (The thermal savings of the design alone make it a model "green" brewery.) Doing good isn't enough—you have to "make good" too, and the beers are wonderfully crafted. The flagship Long Trail is in the style of a German *Altbier,* but the brewery also produces an American Pale Ale, a Traditional IPA, Double Bag strong ale, and Blackberry Wheat all year. Seasonal ales include the high-alcohol Brewmaster Series and a few lighter ales. The food is definitely a cut above that at most brewery pubs, and includes a cheddar ale soup, a steak and cheese sandwich (with Cabot cheddar, of course), and Long Trail Bratwurst from Green Mountain Smokehouse. The brat is served with cooked onions and maple mustard and does its job of giving you a powerful thirst.

Mangowood Restaurant, Lincoln Inn at the Covered Bridge, 2709 Woodstock Rd., Woodstock; (802) 457-3312; www.lincolninn .com; $$. The Asian accents at this otherwise New American dining room shouldn't be a surprise. Chef Teresa Tan originally hails from Singapore, so the aged ginger vinegar reduction she uses to dress a grass-fed sirloin steak comes naturally. Ditto the creamy coconut she incorporates into her risotto cakes, and the crispy duck she pairs with mango in a quesadilla. Located west of town along the river, Mangowood is a fresh change of pace. Tan offers a bargain 4-course prix-fixe deal as well as serving everything a la carte.

Mountain Creamery Restaurant, 33 Central St., Woodstock; (802) 457-1715; www.mountaincreameryvt.com; $$$. Talk about farm to table. Proprietors Boris and Sheila Pilsmaker also own Hinterland Farm in Killington so their breakfast and lunch menus make ample use of local products, including their own beef for hamburgers, roast beef, and barbecue brisket. But the Creamery is perhaps best known for its mile-high apple pies, each made with three pounds of local apples. You can purchase a whole pie or opt for a slice topped with Vermont cheddar cheese or a scoop of the Creamery's homemade ice cream. Purists opt for vanilla; the more adventurous favor maple walnut.

Mountain Top Inn & Resort, 195 Mountain Top Rd., Chittenden; (802) 483-2311; www.mountaintopinn.com; $$$. Mountain Top has always been a no-fuss resort, offering elegant stays at the inn without tony posing. The same holds true of the Highlands Dining Room and Highlands Tavern alike. The inn is an active member of the Vermont Fresh Network, so local products show up throughout the menus, whether it's a salad of local beets and goat cheese or a local chicken roasted with lemon thyme from the kitchen garden. The wine list, including the sparkling wines, is almost exclusively New World. For a special occasion, ask to reserve the romantic table with two wing chairs in front of the dining room fireplace.

Norwich Inn, 325 Main St., Norwich; (802) 649-1143; www .norwichinn.com; $$$. This venerable hostelry dates from 1797. It offers the same menu throughout the property, whether in the formal dining room, the warm and atmospheric pub, or outdoors on the patio, weather permitting. Casual fare leans toward smoked brisket, burgers (including a vegetarian black bean burger), and an excellent plate of charcuterie—all the better to go with the four Jasper Murdock ales brewed on premises and only sold at the inn. Brewmaster Jeremy Hebert uses English malts exclusively to make a red ale, a stout, a porter, and an IPA. Some of the hops come from the inn's own hop vines, which twine around the outdoor patio. The inn serves all meals, including Sunday brunch.

Osteria Pane e Salute, 61 Central St., Woodstock; (802) 457-4882; www.osteriapaneesalute.com; $$$. Owners Deirdre Heekin and Caleb Barber take great pains to point out that they are members of both the Vermont Fresh Network and Slow Food. They try to grow a lot of their own vegetables and work with local farmers to grow heirloom Italian varieties of lettuce, vegetables, and herbs. The restaurant name means "tavern of bread and health," and the couple aspires to replicate the experience of eating at a rural tavern in the Italian countryside. So their antipasto menu might include foraged dandelion greens with pancetta, or crostini with fresh local ricotta, wild mushrooms, and fresh thyme. They grow leeks, onions, and chives in their rose garden and feature all three in a spring pasta dish. On a chilly night, you might prefer to order

ORIGIN OF A PALATE

While her husband Caleb Barber crafts the food at **Osteria Pane e Salute** (often from wonderful old recipes the pair collected in Italy), Deirdre Heekin has managed the wine cellar and dabbled in the alchemy of distilled spirits. Her collection of interlinked personal essays, *Libation: A Bitter Alchemy* (Chelsea Green Publishing, White River Junction, 2009), meditates on the development of her nose and palate and her interests in the often arcane world of liqueurs. It chronicles that journey through taste and smell and *terroir* to its inescapable conclusion: her struggle to grow wine grapes and make her own quality wines in the unlikely locale of central Vermont. Simultaneously evocative and informative, *Libation* mixes the magic of memory with the pleasures of the table.

the roasted (local) chicken leg with rosemary sprigs and lemon confit. The wine list is predominantly Italian and organic or bio-dynamic to boot. They do, however, serve some of the wines from Vermont's own **Lincoln Peak** (p. 44) and the couple has planted their own vineyard where they intend to make wine.

Red Rooster, Woodstock Inn & Resort, 14 the Green, Woodstock; (800) 448-7900; www.woodstockinn.com; $$$. Opened in 2011, this bright and airy restaurant overlooks the expansive back lawns of the

Woodstock Inn & Resort, and the menu nicely complements the view. By focusing on local products, the Red Rooster has replaced the inn's traditional American fare with a New American paean to Vermont agriculture. Entrees lean toward hearty fare—cider-brined pork chop with toasted-vegetable pearl barley, for example, or duck confit with chanterelle mushrooms and brussels sprouts. But even if the oysters aren't from Vermont, don't miss a chance to start the meal with oysters Rockefeller. Laurence Rockfeller, who built the inn, would surely approve.

Simon Pearce Restaurant, The Mill, 1760 Quechee Main St., Quechee; (802) 295-1470; www.simonpearce.com; $$$. Long an outpost of the contemporary Irish style, this gorgeous riverside dining room has expanded its world view to also incorporate Mediterranean and Asian accents under Chef Joshua Duda. The plates remain light and flavorful, like the perennial favorite sesame-seared chicken with an apricot dipping sauce, noodle salad, and pickled ginger. Duda is just as likely to offer penne pasta with chunks of roasted pumpkin, or roasted trout with butternut squash hash. If you're taken with the table- and glassware, you can buy them at the attached Simon Pearce showroom and even watch the glassblowers and potters at work.

Sugar & Spice, Rte. 4, Mendon; (802) 773-7832; www.vtsugar andspice.com; $. This breakfast and lunch institution is housed in a sugarhouse and diners can catch the action during sugar season. But any time of year, they can chow down on pumpkin pancakes with maple syrup or maple walnut waffles with whipped cream. The signature sugar and spice pancakes are seasoned with cinnamon and maple sugar in the batter. Lunch offerings lean toward sandwiches, including one that combines grilled turkey, smoked ham, and Vermont cheddar. Sugar and Spice also makes its own ice cream—which can be served atop waffles or in maple crunch or maple syrup and walnut sundaes.

Table 24, 24 Wales St., Rutland; (802) 775-2424; www.table24. net; $$. The wood-fired grill and rotisserie seem to inspire Chef-Owner Stephen Sawyer. He prepares whole chickens and prime rib by slow-roasting with the rotisserie, and tosses baby back ribs, rib eye and filet mignon steaks, and maple-cured pork tenderloin on the grill. The clean lighting and colorful layout of Table 24 make it the perfect date-night destination, and Sawyer doesn't extract a pound of flesh for you to eat here, either. His five-cheese macaroni and cheese, chicken potpie, and mushroom meat loaf offer full comfort for modest prices, and he happily serves sandwiches and burgers at dinnertime. The same handheld fare and tasty salads are also available at lunch.

Specialty Stores, Markets & Producers

Aubergine, 1 Elm St., Woodstock; (802) 457-1340; www.purple-egg plant.com. This small shop bills itself as "inspiration in the kitchen" and stocks a carefully selected line of products including Revol French porcelain casseroles, onion soup crocks, and crème brûlée ramekins with handles. Among the Swiss Diamond nonstick cookware is a specially designed pan for ball-shaped Danish *aebleskiver* pancakes, which are sometimes cooked with apples but more often served with jam. Elegant hand-turned rolling pins made from maple, cherry, or walnut are available in tapered French and classic Shaker styles.

The Baker's Store, 135 Rte. 5 South, Norwich; (802) 649-3361; www.kingarthurflour.com. Founded in Boston in 1790 (and relocated to Vermont in 1984), King Arthur claims to be the country's oldest flour company. We certainly can't think of any other institution that has done more to keep America baking. The complex, with its education center, cafe, and retail store, is a bit like walking into an animated version of the famous King Arthur Flour catalog. It's a great opportunity to check out the mechanisms on the hand-cranked grain mills and nut grinders, determine the heft of a cast-iron skillet, examine the details on scone pans and cinnamon bun bakers, and pick up a dough whisk, tablespoon cookie scoop, or baker's peel. Shoppers can select from a full range of King Arthur flours, baking mixes (including gluten-free), chocolate (chips, wafers, bars, chunks, cocoa, and powders), and other flavorings. There's almost always something going on in the demonstration kitchen along with a full schedule of hands-on classes in the Baking Education Center. We usually get all the inspiration we need from perusing the scones and croissants, chiffon cakes and specialty cupcakes, berry pies, and streusel coffee cakes for sale in the cafe. They're the perfect sweet treat after a sandwich on King Arthur's whole wheat or honey wheat bread.

Cabot Quechee Store, 5573 Woodstock Rd., Quechee; (802) 295-1180; www.quecheegorge.com. We often dismiss this shop at the Quechee Village complex as a tourist trap. But it's worth a stop because it is so big that it has shelf space for a lot of unusual local products that we don't see often, such as flavored maple syrups (cranberry, apple, habañero, apricot, and orange), High Meadow yellow cornmeal, Vermont Harvest conserves (blueberry bourbon or apple rum walnut), and even Rabbi's Root Horseradish. Visitors can sample from the extensive **Cabot** cheese line (p. 76) and purchase Cabot and other local cheeses. **Snow Farm Vineyard** (p. 48) and **Putney Mountain Winery** (p. 172) both offer tastings. Be sure to look for Madhouse Munchies Sea Salted Kettle Cooked potato chips. Made in South Burlington, they are a favorite snack of New Hampshire native and Olympic gold-medal skier Bode Miller.

Castleton Village Store, 583 Main St., Castleton; (802) 468-2213; www.castletonvillagestore.com. Lurking behind the facade of this 100-year-old country store is one of Vermont's best wine selections (local, domestic, and imported) along with a nice range of local craft beers, maple products, cider jelly, cheeses, and fresh eggs, meats, and produce from local farms. It's also the place to pick up bags of wheat, rye, maple, pumpkin or rosemary Castleton Crackers. Handmade in Castleton, they've been praised in the *New York Times* for their versatile texture, equally suited to nibbling or dipping.

Cobb Hill Cheese, 5 Linden Rd., Hartland; (802) 436-4360; www.cobbhill.org/cheese. Members of the Cobb Hill co-housing community began making cheese in late 2000 and they quickly became adept, winning national and international plaudits for their Ascutney Mountain alpine-style cheese (developed from a Swiss recipe for Appenzeller). They have since added an excellent Caerphilly-style cheese, Four Corners. Both are produced from raw whole milk from the farm's small herd of Jersey cows that graze on chemical-free pastures. (The cows get organic grain over the winter.) The cheeses are available at the Norwich Farmers' Market (Rte. 5, Norwich; Sat from 9 a.m. to 1 p.m., May through Oct), many stores, cheesemongers, and restaurants—and at the farm.

Crowley Cheese, 14 Crowley Lane, Healdville; (802) 259-2340; www.crowleycheese.com. Crowley Cheese claims to be the oldest cheese factory in Vermont and the weathered brown clapboard structure certainly looks the part. Winfield Crowley built the factory in 1882 to expand on his family's farmhouse cheesemaking operation that used milk from their dairy herd. In the world of cheeseheads, Crowley is an "American Original," a cheese with a North American pedigree that owes nothing to the old country. The company has eschewed mechanization, but still turns out an impressive range of aged and flavored cheeses. According to cheesemaker Ken Hart, the whole process takes about 6.5 hours. It begins when he pumps 5,000 pounds of whole raw milk into a stainless-steel tub to be heated and concludes when the curds are packed into molds. Call ahead to find out which days are scheduled for cheesemaking. Even on non-production days you can still sample and purchase. Cheese aficionados prefer Crowley's cloth-bound, waxed wheels to the cut bars. Wheels of the aged cheeses (mild, medium sharp, sharp, extra sharp) are available in 2.5- and 5-pound sizes. The 23-pound wheel is available by special order. See Crowley's recipe for **Crowley and Bacon Scones** on p. 346.

F. H. Gillingham & Sons General Store, 16 Elm St., Woodstock; (802) 457-2100; www.gillinghams.com. This fixture in Woodstock's quaint downtown has been expanded several times since it was founded in 1886, but F. H. Gillingham's descendants appreciate the country store basics of worn wooden floors, merchandise piled in barrels or on long wooden shelves, and store cats to greet customers and angle for handouts. Gillingham stocks a large selection of local products, but Woodstock has become a sophisticated little town and residents and visitors will also find several shelves of olive oils, balsamic vinegars, local and imported cheeses, and a great wine selection. If a product was made in Vermont—or featured in *Bon Appétit*—there's a good chance you can find it at Gillingham. The store also has its own baked goods and its own brand of coffee, including a Vermont maple French roast. Gift items include picnic backpacks and cheese knives and salt and pepper mills made from Vermont marble.

Gourmet Provence Bakery and Wine Shop, 37 Center St., Brandon; (802) 247-3002; www.cafeprovencevt.com. "Please do not lean on the glass," implores a sign on a glass display case in this scrumptious shop. It should probably say "Please do not drool." The casual sibling of **Cafe Provence** (p. 116) offers an almost mind-boggling array of breads and baked goods. Regulars (and there are many) all seem to have a personal favorite, from sticky buns and almond croissants to éclairs and triple-chocolate terrines. For lunch, it's a toss-up between slices of quiche lorraine or a Provençal panini with hard-boiled egg, salami, lettuce, tomato, and mayonnaise on a baguette. Don't let the pastry cases distract you from checking out the adjoining rooms, where Robert and Line Barral stock a serious selection of wine, along with a few gourmet products such as sea salt and olive oil from Spain and mustards, cornichons, vinegars, and jams from France.

Green Mountain Smokehouse, 341 Rte. 5 South, Windsor; (802) 674-6653. "We control everything," says Koreen Henne of the business she and husband Jake started in 1990. The Hennes smoke all their meats on the premises and sell to individuals only at their factory. In fact, much of their output goes directly to major hotel chains, restaurants, or other local purveyors. The Hennes smoke cheese for **Plymouth Artisan Cheese** (see p. 133) and a beer bratwurst for **Harpoon Brewery** (p. 118). Koreen describes their maple smoke as "light and gentle" and their Vermont maple breakfast sausages are extremely popular all year, while the maple-sugar-cured boneless hams are a Christmas favorite. But the maple-sugar-cured, hickory-smoked bacon is the most popular. "A lot of chefs buy the bacon ends," says Koreen, "to use for chowders or stews, or to mix with eggs or sprinkle onto salad." At home, she dices and cooks the bacon ends then sprinkles them with salt and white vinegar. "They keep in the refrigerator and are great for seasoning," she says.

Neshobe River Winery, 79 Stone Mill Dam Rd., Brandon; (802) 247-8002; and **Tastes of the Valley,** 6-8 Park Street, Brandon;

(802) 247-9463; neshoberiverwinery.com. The picturesque vine-yards are on the grounds of the Old Mill Inn B&B outside of town. The winery supplements the production by purchasing grapes grown in Vermont, California, and the Finger Lakes. Wines are whimsically named—except for the cassis, a straightforward wine made from black currants. Purple Haze, a high-alcohol blend, epitomizes their style. As the label says, "40 years ago, 32 of the best-known musicians of the day appeared during the sometimes rainy weekend in front of nearly half a million concertgoers in Woodstock, New York. This bold wine is a blend of our best red grapes, and we hope you enjoy the experience." Tastings are available at both the winery and the in-town shop, which carries other local agricultural products.

New England Maple Museum, 4578 Rte. 7, Pittsford; (802) 483-9414; www.maplemuseum.com. There's a small admission charge to the museum which traces the history of maple sugaring with an extensive collection of artifacts and more than 100 feet of murals painted by artist Grace Brigham. Or you can simply pick up some maple syrup or other more unusual products such as maple tea, maple syrup baked beans or rubber molds to make your own maple sugar candy. Though we haven't tried it ourselves, we've been told that it's a fairly simple process of heating syrup to the proper temperature and then pouring it into the molds where it will harden quickly.

Otter Valley Winery, 1246 Franklin St. (Rte. 7), Brandon; (802) 247-6644; www.ottervalleywinery.com. One of Vermont's newest

wineries, Otter Valley focuses on winter-hardy grapes: Marquette, Frontenac, Frontenac Gris, St. Croix, La Crescent and Frontenac Blanc. The 6-acre vineyard was planted 2007–2008 on the site of an old miniature golf course and produced its first small harvest in 2010. The initial bottling of estate wines included a semisweet white blend and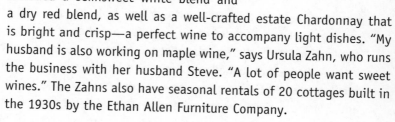
a dry red blend, as well as a well-crafted estate Chardonnay that is bright and crisp—a perfect wine to accompany light dishes. "My husband is also working on maple wine," says Ursula Zahn, who runs the business with her husband Steve. "A lot of people want sweet wines." The Zahns also have seasonal rentals of 20 cottages built in the 1930s by the Ethan Allen Furniture Company.

Plymouth Artisan Cheese, 106 Messer Hill Rd., Plymouth Notch; (802) 672-3650; www.plymouthartisancheese.com. Plymouth is a cheese with a presidential pedigree. The original company was founded in 1890 by five farmers including Colonel John Coolidge, the father of our 30th president, Calvin. In fact, John (who was also a notary public) administered the oath of office to his son in 1923 when news of the death of President Warren Harding reached Plymouth Notch. The area, including the president's boyhood home, a schoolhouse, church, and the cheese factory, is now a state historic site. The upper level of the cheese factory displays original wooden cheese-making vats lined with tin, along with old cheese molds and presses, and period photos. On the first floor, visitors can peek into the modern production room where the raw milk cheeses are usually made on Friday and Saturday (Saturday and Sunday, some weeks). The Original Plymouth is a nicely dry and tangy cheddar. The company also produces a robust Hunter and a buttery young cheddar called East Meadow.

Singleton's General Store, 356 Main St., Proctorsville; (802) 226-7666; www.singletonsvt.com. Since 1977 this family-run store has been a resource for classic woolens and shoes and boots fit for farm or field. But the real specialties are the store's own cold-smoked meats, including slab bacon, hams, bone-in pork chops, salmon, pepperoni, Canadian bacon, and ham hocks. The Singleton family makes a full line of sausages, from breakfast links to kielbasa and a Mexican-style chorizo. The store also carries a number of artisanal cheeses, and farm-raised game (elk, venison, ostrich, bison) in both cuts and as ground meat. Pheasant and boneless quail are also available.

Sugarbush Farm, 591 Sugarbush Farm Rd., Woodstock; (802) 457-1757; www.sugarbushfarm.com. This farm, established in 1945, is not very far from the village of Woodstock. But once you have navigated the 3-plus-mile winding dirt road, you will be convinced that this hilltop spot is in another, simpler, world. The working farm is especially welcoming. Visitors are encouraged to peek into the sugarhouse and follow a walking trail through the maple grove. In addition to syrup, Sugarbush makes 14 varieties of cheese, and staff members pause from work in the packaging room to slice samples of the aged, smoked, and flavored cheddars for visitors to taste. Generous samples of other products, including the farm's maple syrup are also available. The cheeses are packaged in wax, and the small 4-ounce pieces are perfect for putting together a sampler of flavors or a gift package.

Taftsville Country Store, 404 Woodstock Rd., Taftsville; (802) 457-1135; www.taftsville.com. Very few country stores still double as the village post office, and fewer still have Taftsville's terrific selection of Vermont artisanal cheeses and craft beers. This red-brick, circa 1840 landmark also sells deluxe cigars.

Trap Door Bakehouse & Cafe, 176 Waterman Hill Rd., Quechee; (802) 698-8075. Theodora Damaskos trained in classical French pastry before she opened her bakery and cafe. Her skills shine in her beautiful baguettes, croissants (including a hazelnut chocolate version), quiches, cookies, and brown-butter tarts with pears, apples or plums. "The tarts are one of my specialties," she says, "but I let seasonal products determine my savory dishes." As a departure from the precision of baking, Damaskos uses her taste and intuition in her daily soup and salads, such as curried roasted cauliflower or roasted vegetables and basmati rice. Paninis, such as provolone and twice-roasted pork, are a lunchtime favorite to eat on the small outdoor terrace with a magnificent view of the Ottauquechee River far below. See Trap Door's recipe for **Pumpkin Bread** on p. 348.

Upper Valley Food Coop, 193 N. Main St., White River Junction; (802) 295-5804; www.coopfoodstore.coop. In 2010, the Upper Valley Food Co-op of Vermont joined the **Co-op Food Stores of New Hampshire** (p. 243) as one big happy family with tremendous buying clout for their members and other customers. In addition to getting good deals and healthy food for their members, the stores also show a dedication to local agriculture and business, preferentially stocking local cheeses, cider, maple syrup, and even flour.

Village Butcher, 18 Elm St. #1, Woodstock; (802) 457-2756. George Racicot is one of a dwindling breed: a real butcher who knows how to properly age his meat and how to cut like a surgeon. The dry-aged beef and other local meats are so lovingly displayed that they could almost make a vegetarian hungry. The shop also sells pastries, sandwiches, and soups, as well as Vermont wines.

Farmstands & Pick Your Own

Killdeer Farm Stand, 55 Butternut Rd. (off Rte. 5), Norwich; (802) 649-2852; www.killdeerfarm.com. This organic farm sells CSA shares redeemable at its farm store, but you don't have to subscribe to shop here. Killdeer Farm grows most of the vegetables and fruits available at the stand, and their other products—organic milk, meat, artisanal cheese, flour, and baked goods—come from neighboring farms. Open May through early Dec.

Mendon Mountain Orchards and Country Farm Store, 16 Rte. 4, Mendon; (802) 775-5477; www.mendonorchards.com. The orchards were first planted in the 1920s and include a number of heirloom apple varieties on trees that have been carefully pruned to make it possible to pick without ladders. Most of the harvest is pick-your-own, though the family that operates the facility does sell apples at its roadside store. The country store also carries pies, apple turnovers, jams, preserves, honey, apple butter, and maple syrup from a big barrel with a spigot. Flowers and bedding plants are available in the spring.

Sunshine Valley Berry Farm, 129 Ranger Rd., Rochester; (802) 767-3989; www.vermontberries.com. The picking season begins in early July with raspberries and continues unabated until the first hard frost (late September or early October). Blueberries and sour cherries are available between the early July and late August raspberry crops, and blackberries follow around mid-September. All the fruit at Sunshine Valley is certified organic. Pick your own or buy pre-picked at the farmstand, which also offers jam, maple syrup, hot coffee, and books. Open July 4 through Columbus Day.

Wellwood Orchards, 529 Wellwood Orchards Rd., Springfield; (802) 263-5200; www.wellwoodorchards.net. This family-owned farm starts the pick-your-own season in June with strawberries and segues seamlessly into raspberries and blueberries before its prime season, the apple harvest, begins in late August. Free wagon rides to the orchards are available on weekends in September and October. The country store, open through October, sells Wellwood's apples and pumpkins as well as fresh apple pies, honey, and Grafton cheese.

Farm Stay

Liberty Hill Farm Inn, 511 Liberty Hill, Rochester; (802) 767-3926; www.libertyhillfarm.com. After you've taken the **Cabot** factory tour (p. 103) or even just sampled the extensive line of cheeses, there is no better way to get a sense of the farmers who are the backbone of the cooperative than to book a stay at this working dairy farm. Bob and Beth Kennett purchased the farm in 1979. "When we arrived, there were 40 dairy farms operating in our little stretch of the White River Valley," says Beth. "Now we're the only one left." While Bob and grown sons Tom and David have nurtured the family's own pedigree line of Holsteins, Beth has become known as a great country cook. Visitors who stay overnight in one of the 7 guest rooms with quilt-covered beds are treated to hearty

Passion of a Scientific Farmer

Frederick Billings had his hand in a lot of pies. The lawyer, conservationist, and railroad builder established his farm in 1871 as a model of scientific farming practices. In less than two decades the farm had nurtured a top herd of soulful Brown Jersey cows, known for their rich, high-butterfat milk. Today the property is part of a museum dedicated to preserving Vermont's rural way of life called the **Billings Farm & Museum.** About 75 Jersey cows and a small herd of Southdown sheep still graze in the green pastures and the museum hosts a number of special events that celebrate farm life, including wagon and sleigh rides. During the popular mid-October Harvest Weekend visitors can roll up their sleeves and help to dig potatoes, thresh grain, press cider, and make butter and ice cream.

Billings Farm & Museum, Rte. 12 and River Rd., Woodstock; (802) 457-2355; www.billingsfarm.org. Open May through Oct and winter weekends.

farm breakfasts and dinners served family style around the family's dining table. Beth often cooks from updated versions of her grandmother's recipes and is always generous in her use of Cabot milk and butter and Vermont maple syrup. See recipe for **Beth's Baked Oatmeal** on p. 345.

Farmers' Markets

Brandon Farmers' Market, Central Park, Brandon. Fri from 9 a.m. to 3 p.m., late May to early October.

Castleton Farmers' Market, Main St., Castleton. Thurs from 3:30 to 6 p.m., mid-June to early October.

Chester Farmers' Market, Rtes. 11 and 103, Chester. Sun from 11 a.m. to 2 p.m., June to early October.

Fair Haven Farmers' Market, Village Green, Fair Haven. Fri from 3 to 7 p.m., mid-June to mid-October.

Hartland Farmers' Market, Town library, Hartland. Fri from 4 to 7 p.m., June through September.

Ludlow Farmers' Market, 53 Main St., Ludlow. Fri from 4 to 7 p.m., June through early October.

Mount Holly Farmers' Market, Village Green, Belmont. Sat from 10 a.m. to 1 p.m., June through September.

Mount Tom Farmers' Market, Rte. 12 north of Woodstock. Sat from 9:30 a.m. to 12:30 p.m., late May to mid-October.

Norwich Farmers' Market, Rte. 5, Norwich. Sat from 9 a.m. to 1 p.m., May through October.

Poultney Farmers' Market, Main St., Poultney. Thurs from 9 a.m. to 2 p.m., late June to early October.

Quechee Farmers' Market, Rte. 4, Quechee Gorge Village. Sun from 10 a.m. to 2 p.m., late May to mid-September.

South Royalton Farmers' Market, Town Green, South Royalton. Thurs from 3 to 6:30 p.m., late May to early October.

Springfield Community Market, 6 Main St., Springfield. Sat from 10 a.m. to 1 p.m., late May to early October.

Vermont Farmers' Market, Depot Park, Rutland. Sat from 9 a.m. to 2 p.m., early May to late October. Tues from 3 to 6 p.m., mid-May to mid-October.

Windsor Farmers' Market, Town Green, Windsor. Sun from 1 to 4 p.m., late May through October.

Woodstock Market on the Green, Town Green, Woodstock Village. Wed from 3 to 6 p.m., early June to early October.

Famous Roast Beef Suppers, www.hartlandbrickchurch.org. In a great show of community spirit, Hartland's Congregational Church has been offering roast beef dinners—complete with homemade rolls, pies, and side dishes—for more than 35 years. They are held on nine consecutive Saturdays beginning in late January.

Killington Wine Festival, www.killingtonchamber.com. More than 400 wines from around the world are available for tasting at this late July event that features a Champagne brunch, complimentary hors d'oeuvres, and gondola rides to the top of Killington Peak.

Plymouth Cheese & Harvest Festival, www.historicvermont .org. With its graceful old buildings set on a rolling hillside, the President Calvin Coolidge State Historic Site in Plymouth is especially idyllic in the fall. This one-day festival makes a good excuse to visit in mid-September for tours of the Plymouth Artisan Cheese factory, a cheese recipe contest, barbecue, and other activities.

Quechee Scottish Festival and Celtic Fair, www.quecheescot tishfestival.com. Pipe band competitions, sheepdog championship trials, athletic contests, Scottish and American food, and lots of music highlight this late August event at the Quechee Polo Field.

Taste of Woodstock, www.woodstockvermont.com. Food vendors are a big part of the street party that takes over downtown Woodstock for one Saturday in mid-August.

Vermont State Fair, www.vermontstatefair.net. Begun in 1846, the Vermont State Fair is held in Rutland from late August through early September and features an extensive schedule of free entertainment, along with 4-H exhibits and judging in a variety of categories, including culinary arts, maple products, and giant pumpkins.

Vermont State Zucchini Festival, www.yourplaceinvermont .com. Zucchini fries, cookies, breads, and cakes are among the culinary treats at this mid-August event in Ludlow. Besides eating, attractions include giant zucchini and crafts displays, zucchini carving, and the quirky but popular zukapult to launch the honored vegetable through the air.

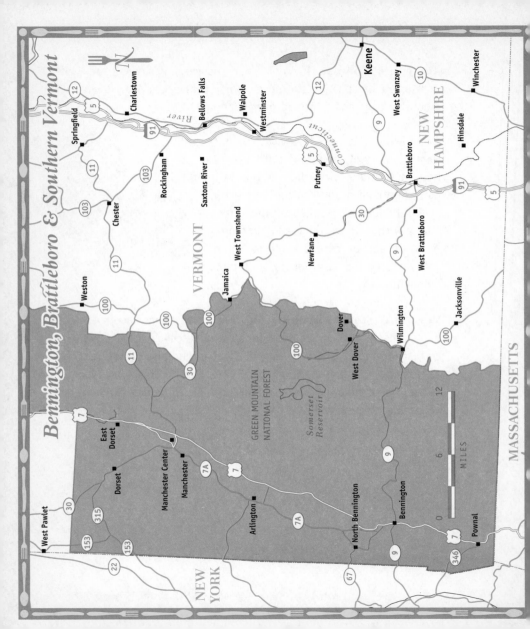

Bennington, Brattleboro & Southern Vermont

Bennington on the west and Brattleboro on the east anchor southern Vermont. Between them lie the southerly portion of the Green Mountains with their historic small-mountain ski resorts (Mt. Snow, Stratton, Bromley) and a clutch of beautiful little hilltop and river-valley towns. It is an area historically rich in apple orchards and sugar bush, but just as devoted to dairy farming as the broader-pastured areas farther north. Cheesemakers abound, as do microbreweries, artisanal coffee roasters, and small fruit and grape wineries.

Southern Vermont is also blessed with some spectacular restaurants, which are found as often in the countryside as in the more urban enclaves of Manchester, Bennington, and Brattleboro. Tourism at this end of Vermont is heavily slanted toward Manhattan—the ski resorts are close enough to New York to drive up Friday after work. This orientation has encouraged a number of high-end country inns with dining rooms to match. Yet some of the funkiest New Age throwback coffeehouses, bakeries, and eateries also thrive in southern Vermont. It is a landscape of contradictions—tasty on both sides.

Foodie Faves

Allegro, 520 Main St., Bennington; (802) 442-0990; www.allegro ristorante.com; $$$. Allegro might just be the perfect college-town restaurant. At this very good contemporary Italian restaurant, visiting parents can get real meals, students on a date can bat eyes over the pasta, and the college faculty can pretend they're back in Europe. There's definitely an Italian-American influence in the handling of fried calamari (beer batter) and the heavy cream in many non-tomato sauces, but you have to admire a place that keeps grilled swordfish piccata and braised wild boar on the menu.

Asta's Swiss Restaurant, 3894 Rte. 30, Jamaica; (802) 874-8000; www.astasswissinn.com; $$$. Jamaica is just down the road from the ski mountains of Stratton and Bromley, so maybe it should not be a surprise that chef Michel de Preux specializes in the hearty cooking of his Swiss homeland. He and wife Bonnie opened the restaurant and adjoining B&B in 2002. During the winter, he has raclette and a choice of meat or cheese fondues on the menu. If you're eager to escape cheese for a while, he's also known for his spicy sauerbraten with spaeztle and for serving rösti (a Swiss potato cake) with a grilled filet mignon.

Bistro Henry, 1942 Depot St., Manchester; 802-362-4982; www .bistrohenry.com; $$$. If there's a fault with Vermont bistros, it's that most of them have interchangeable menus, as if they had been issued with a diploma from the New England Culinary Institute. Not Bistro Henry. Chef Henry Bronson has a distinct point of view and tastes that ignore gastronomic borders. Most of the menu reflects the traditions of southern France (grilled harpoon-caught swordfish with an orange-basil beurre blanc) and northern Italy (wild-mushroom risotto with locally foraged hen-of-the-woods). But Henry's recent passion for slow-roasted barbecue has spilled over to become "Slosmoke Sundays." It's a smart-looking place, with posters of the French Riviera the only distraction from the plates. It's also a family operation. Pâtissière and spouse Dina Bronson does the desserts (she also runs the catering business called Dina's Vermont Baking Company). The wine list nicely balances European and American bottles that complement the food.

Bob's Diner, 2279 Depot St., Manchester; (802) 362-4681; $. This massive stainless steel Silk City diner well out of town features a dozen stools, eight leatherette-upholstered booths, a long black Formica counter with worn wooden rail, and a handful of tables and chairs. In proper diner form, breakfast is available all day, and we enjoy watching the cook at the exposed grill work those magic wrists to turn the eggs truly over easy. The burgers are extremely popular and the house has three specialty patties: the smoked Gouda burger (beef burger and melted smoked Gouda cheese with roasted red-pepper mayo), the turkey burger (ground turkey with melted Swiss cheese and sautéed mushrooms), and the "veggie delight" (a veggie burger topped with Vermont cheddar, sliced avocado, and pesto mayonnaise).

Chantecleer, 8 Read Farm Lane, East Dorset; (802) 362-1616; www.chantecleerrestaurant.com; $$$. Swiss chef Michel Baumann and his wife Melanie have been dishing up the classics of French (and sometimes German) cuisine here since 1981. "We still offer frogs' legs with garlic and capers and we make the Caesar salad at the table with all the traditional flourishes," Melanie notes. It took much of those three decades to collect the wonderful folk-art roosters that perch in the windows and even on the beams of this barn converted to a gemütlich country inn dining room. The Baumanns' tastes may be European, but a lot of the supplies are local, including the **Misty Knoll** chicken (p. 47), Vermont cheddar, and **Jasper Hill**'s heavenly blue cheese (p. 107). Be sure to start with the chef's own pâtés. One of his specialties combines venison, duck, apricot, and hazelnuts.

Chelsea Royal Diner, 487 Marlboro Rd., West Brattleboro; (802) 254-8399; www.chelsearoyaldiner.com; $. A diminutive 1938 Worcester Lunch diner in cream with green trim, the Royal Diner reprises both the home cooking of ages past (Swiss steak, turkey croquettes, baked ziti) and some more recent dishes straight from the pages of the supermarket checkout line food magazines (Jamaican jerk pork chops with chutney, teriyaki chicken breast). Breakfast is available all day; we suggest eggs and the corned-beef hash made on premises. Best of all, the diner makes its own ice cream from scratch on the premises and usually has three dozen or more flavors available.

Curtis' All American BBQ, 7 Putney Landing Rd., Putney; (802) 387-5474; www.curtisbbqvt.com; $$. To paraphrase a certain chicken company, it takes a Tuff man to make tender barbecue. Curtis Tuff, to be exact. Since 1964, he has been out in all weather from spring through fall slow-roasting and smoking meat in his pair of blue schoolbuses. Far from gruff, he is a kind-hearted man who just loves it when people swoon over his barbecue. He keeps it simple: ribs and chicken, half or whole (slab or bird), and just a few sides. (Go for the corn on the cob in season.) His postal address is 40 Old Depot Rd., but if you're using GPS, plug in the Putney Landing address. Open Apr through Oct.

Dorset Inn on the Green, 8 Church Street, Dorset; (802) 867-5500; www.dorsetinn.com; $$$. When Steve and Lauren Bryant, owners of **Mountain Top Inn & Resort** (p. 121), purchased the Dorset Inn from legendary chef/owner Sissy Hicks, they knew they had to keep up Hicks's high culinary standards. As it has been since opening in 1796, the dining room remains a top gastronomic destination in southern Vermont. The inn serves all three meals (the Bryants got the sign painter to finally squeeze "breakfast" onto the hanger out front), but dinner remains the principal attraction. All the plates demonstrate commitment to local products, with starters like a roasted beet salad with local chèvre, an entree of roasted chicken with a maple glaze, and Hicks's famous sautéed calf's liver with cob-smoked bacon. Vegan options—sesame-crusted cakes of quinoa, cracked wheat, and grilled vegetables over a tomato-lentil stew, for example—are interesting enough to intrigue even hardcore carnivores. The relaxed atmosphere makes the Dorset Inn a good place to introduce children to fine dining.

Equinox Resort and Spa, 3567 Main St. (Rte 7), Manchester Village; (802) 362-7823; www.equinoxresort.com; $$$. Try to avoid the entrance to the spa when you dine at the Equinox. It is guarded by a massive antique scale that Golden Age visitors used to make sure they had gained weight during their stays. (Those were the days when girth was considered to be directly correlated with health and well-being.) The meals today in the formal Chop House and more relaxed Marsh Tavern are designed to appeal to taste rather than pack on the avoirdupois. Chop House specialties are grilled steaks or rack of lamb. The Marsh Tavern menu is simple Vermont bistro—seared duck breast, maple-glazed salmon roasted on a plank, a plate of local charcuterie.

Fireworks Restaurant, 69-73 Main St., Brattleboro; (802) 254-2073; www.fireworksrestaurant.net; $$. Chef-Owner Matthew Blau has created a foodie magnet where the dark wood, twinkling lights, and open kitchen are brought to life by the steady buzz of excited diners. The brick oven is the heart of the operation, marrying Vermont and Campania with pizzas like butternut squash, sage pesto, chicken and Gorgonzola, or local veggies with goat cheese. The pastas are rustic and simple—such as a hearty plate of spaghetti tossed with mussels, clams, pancetta, sausage, garlic, and hot peppers.

Four Columns Inn, 21 West St., Newfane; (802) 365-7713; www.fourcolumnsinn.com; $$$. "In the summer you'd think we only had the tables by the windows, and in the winter you'd think there were just the three by the fireplace," says owner-innkeeper Debbie Pfander. But given the popularity of this contemporary New American restaurant with Colonial Revival decor, not everyone gets the choice table. By the time the food begins to arrive it hardly matters—who's looking at the view when there's a plate of panko-crusted scallops with a sour cream, mustard, honey, and red curry sauce to dispatch? Local rabbit (usually braised in vegetable broth) is often available, and pheasant breast with a tart cherry, ginger, and currant sauce is a favorite. Count on two or even three daily soup specials that are also a little out of the ordinary, like a bisque of grilled eggplant and roasted garlic.

Front Porch Cafe, 133 Main St., Putney; (802) 387-2200; $$. This breakfast and lunch establishment is located in the historic Putney Tavern building and sets out a few tables on the long front porch. Even during chilly weather, some regulars eschew the warm indoor dining room in favor of the porch so that they can enjoy their morning corned-beef hash or sausage and bacon frittata while watching the comings and goings on Main Street. The cafe also offers a variety of bagels, croissants, and muffins for breakfast, along with salads and sandwiches for lunch. Many options are vegetarian-friendly, including breakfast's vegetable hash or the Middle-Eastern luncheon plate of hummus, stuffed grape leaves, and spanakopita. A string band performs during the Sunday buffet brunch.

The Hermitage, 25 Handle Rd., West Dover; (877) 464-3511; www.hermitageinn.com; $$$. Head Chef Paul Eschbach came to The Hermitage after 7 years in Jean-Georges Vongerichten's New York kitchens and fell in love with the countryside and the farmers. Bringing an intense farm-to-fork sensibility to the menu, Eschbach makes it seem almost effortless—until you read the list of farms, creameries, bakeries, and other suppliers who made it all possible. There's no attempt to mystify here. When it's corn season, you really must have the corn chowder with local corn, local bacon, and pieces of local tomato. And even when the central part of the dish comes from a distance (like West Coast fresh wild salmon), he's likely to pair it with local apples, celery, and herbs. Lighter plates available in the tavern have just as much local accent: a burger of Sleeping Dog Farm beef with caramelized onions and Vermont smoked cheddar, for example, or a duck *poutine* with cheddar curds from nearby Bennington.

Inn at Weston, 630 Main St., Weston; (802) 824-6789; www .innweston.com; $$$. The candlelit restaurant at this cozy inn is so romantic that dinners are often punctuated by whoops of joy from a well-planned proposal. Chef Michael Kennedy stays close to home for many of his dishes, ranging from a Vermont cheese plate with local honey to local venison, duck, and pork charcuterie, to pan-seared *foie gras* with ricotta gnocchi. Fish, by necessity, have to be trucked in, but the meats are from New York and Vermont, and the wild mushrooms are often foraged in the nearby hills. The principally New World wine list is especially good on Oregon Pinot Noirs.

Little Rooster Cafe, 4645 Main St. (Rte. 7A), Manchester Center; (802) 362-3496; $$. Not surprisingly, when Rachael Ray stopped here for an episode of *Rachael Ray's Tasty Travels,* she featured the recipe for the corned-beef hash. She could as easily have featured the "cock-a-doodle-doo": two poached eggs on sourdough toast with smoked salmon, caper-dill-mustard sauce, and a side of the hash brown potatoes with Vermont cheddar. Breakfast is a big deal here, but since Little Rooster stays open into the afternoon, it also serves some tasty sandwiches. We like the portobello mushroom and grilled eggplant sandwich heaped with roasted peppers, fresh basil, and mozzarella—all on a piece of focaccia. What a break from the outlet mall shopping!

Madison Brewing Co., 428 Main St., Bennington; (802) 442-7397; www.madisonbrewingco.com; $$. Opened in 1994, Madison was southern Vermont's first successful brewpub, and it's easy to see why. It's a friendly and relaxed place where the beer is fresh and the food is simple. The six standard brews include a fruity English-style ale (Old 76 Strong Ale), a Pacific Northwest dry-hopped pale ale (Crowtown), a couple of wheat beers (an American honey wheat and a Belgian-style white beer), a light German beer (Sucker Pond Blonde), and a classic malty red Scottish ale. One of the most popular appetizers is a plate of Irish Lounge Fries—ale-battered fried potatoes topped with melted Cabot cheddar, diced onions and tomatoes, and crispy bacon. Each day there's a special ravioli, steak, and catch of the day.

McNeill's Pub and Brewery, 90 Eliott St., Brattleboro; (802) 254-2553; www.mcneillsbrewery.com; $$. Sometimes brewpubs are restaurants that happen to have a brew kettle. McNeill's is a brewery that has beer-hall tables, and it's a local institution among serious students of craft brews. That makes it a "character" bar, and some real Brattleboro characters (from drag queens to lumberjacks) walk through the doors. Food is so much an afterthought that locals often bring take-out pizza to sop up their suds. Brewmaster Ray McNeill has been at it in this location since 1982, and usually has nine beers on tap. They run the gamut of English and American styles, but many fans swear by his Dark Angel stout.

Pangea Fine Dining, 1 and 3 Prospect St., North Bennington; (802) 442-7171; http://vermontfinedining.com; $$$. The pair of buildings sitting above the mill falls in proletarian North Bennington house no fewer than five different rooms where you can eat—but fortunately only one kitchen. Chef-Owner Bill Scully was a pioneer of farm-to-fork dining here more than a decade ago, and he works his own kind of gastronomic magic that ignores trends. His boar and brie baked in a pastry crust would have won plaudits in the 1970s—and still does today. His pan-roasted Long Island duck breast on saffron risotto and his crispy fried-oyster Cobb salad, on the other hand, are completely of the moment. Bennington-area residents often save Pangea for special-occasion dining, enjoying the rich wine list and ending with a red to complement a sinful chocolate cake for dessert. But the less-expensive adjacent lounge also features tasty but lighter dishes, such as wild mushroom risotto, tacos filled with pulled pork, and curried shrimp with a ginger lime sauce.

The Perfect Wife Restaurant & Tavern, 2594 Depot St. (Rtes. 11 & 30), Manchester; (802) 362-2817; http://perfectwife .com; $$$. Chef Amy Chamberlain takes a wifely (or maybe that's motherly) interest in her customers. Really. The restaurant menu notes, "Be assured that every entree will come with fresh veggies. Make sure you eat them." And she's not rushing to replace customer favorites either. The sesame-crusted yellowfin tuna over stir-fried vegetables has been a hit ever since the Perfect Wife opened in 1996. The long-time favorite appetizer here is Chamberlain's ver-sion of moo shu duck: roasted, glazed duck rolled in a crispy-skinned sesame pancake and served with chopped spring onions and hoisin sauce. She also tries to include a vegetarian entree also suitable for diners with wheat and dairy allergies. The airy restaurant boasts both a stone-walled dining room and a greenhouse garden room. The tavern, on the other hand, is a nice cozy bar with a big outdoor patio for the summer months. The food is a bit more casual but includes Chamberlain's trio of sliders (which she describes as "poppable sandwiches"): a cheeseburger, a crab cake with remoulade, and grilled chicken with herb aioli. The tavern also hosts live music on most weekends. In both venues, Chamberlain's menu advises that if you eat all your vegetables, you deserve to order dessert. Yes, dear.

Putney Diner, 82 Main St., Putney; (802) 387-5433; $. This slice of Americana manages to hold its own against the more upscale and sophisticated **Front Porch Cafe** (p. 152) just across the street. Other than the addition of a breakfast burrito and a Cajun skillet (grilled onion, potatoes, peppers, and Cajun seasoning on a platter with two eggs over easy, melted cheese, and toast), the menu could be straight out of 1959. Meat with your eggs? Choose steak, ham, kielbasa, sausage, or bacon. You'll probably smell the cinnamon rolls before you even open the door. Putney Diner may not be a "real" lunch-car diner, but it's a great place to stop for homemade pies and freshly brewed coffee.

Putney Inn, Exit 4, I-91, Putney; (802) 387-5517; www.putneyinn .com; $$$. It's easy to see where Executive Chef Ron Ange's loyalties lie. Before he lists any items on the menu, he lists the "contributors": a veritable who's who of cheesemakers, produce and fruit farms, dairies, and smokehouses. His version of New American food results in dishes with *terroir*—from the Vermont baked onion and apple soup with cheddar cheese to the grilled rib eye steak from grass-fed beef. Even the corned-beef Reuben sandwich available at lunch has Boggy Meadow's baby swiss cheese melted on top.

Reluctant Panther Inn & Restaurant, 39 West Rd., Manchester Village; (802) 362-2568 or (800) 822-2331 for room reservations; www.reluctantpanther.com; $$. As a small luxury property, the Reluctant Panther complements the neighboring **Equinox** (p. 150) rather nicely. The dining room is elegant and bright for cool-weather dining, while the terrace offers a seasonal alfresco option with views across the inn's lovely gardens. The classic Continental dishes tend to be labor-intensive but richly satisfying, such as a starter of lobster and ricotta (made on premises) in a ravioli skin with a sauce of melted leeks, sweet corn cream, and a sprinkling of sturgeon caviar. Even the simple pan-seared chicken breast might come with a ragout of Tuscan sausage and white beans, along with braised black kale. The extensive wine list is filled with upscale reds.

Sonny's Blue Benn Diner, 318 North St., Bennington; (802) 442-5140; $. You don't really need a menu at this 1948 Silk City diner. Almost every dish is described on its own piece of paper taped up behind the counter. Lines routinely go out the door, but you can sometimes snag one of the counter stools—all the better to read the menu. All the classic breakfast and lunch diner grill specials are available, but the Blue Benn also serves certain plates that have become hard to find, such as creamed chipped beef on toast, or a salmon burger that is really a big version of a cake made with canned salmon and soda crackers. Desserts include the inevitable diner pies, as well as such creamy classics as tapioca, Indian pudding, and hot fudge pudding cake (aka brownie caketop pudding).

T.J. Buckley's Uptown Dining, 132 Elliot St., Brattleboro; (802) 257-4922; www.tjbuckleys.com; $$$. This extremely intimate 1927 Worcester diner has been Brattleboro's top fine-dining locavore restaurant for nearly three decades. Chef-Owner Michael Fuller and his single assistant ply their trade in the open kitchen only a few feet from the diner's five candlelit tables laid with white linens and graced with a bevy of glasses. Forget about a printed menu—the server recites the choices, which change almost daily, depending on what's available in the market and from the farmers. Expect starters like a smoked trout tartlet with chèvre, a dollop of crème fraîche, and a sprinkling of trout roe. Dinner entrees could be local beef, poultry, or venison—or even a duo of local rabbit: the loin wrapped in serrano ham, and the leg stuffed with swiss chard and a dice of double-smoked bacon. Bring cash and a lot of it. Prices are on the high side for Brattleboro and T.J. Buckley's does not take plastic. Since there are few seats, reservations are highly recommended.

Three Mountain Inn, 3732 Main St., Jamaica; (802) 874-4140; www.threemountaininn.com; $$$. The 5-course prix-fixe dinner at Three Mountain Inn could not be a more romantic affair. All three small dining rooms in the historic property have wood-burning fireplaces. Our dinner preference runs slightly to the elegant parlor, especially in cold weather when the 200-year-old marble hearth becomes the focus of the room. This is traditional American fare at its elevated best: wild rice and leek soup, grilled beef tenderloin with garlic mashed potatoes, apple tart with caramel sauce and Ben & Jerry's ice cream. If you're fortunate enough to be staying the night, Three Mountain Inn also serves a 3-course breakfast (with Vermont maple syrup, of course) as part of the room package.

A Village Back from the Brink

Like many Vermont villages, Grafton hit its high-water mark around the Civil War, when it boasted about 1,500 residents, a thriving soapstone quarry, and several woolen mills. By the Great Depression, fewer than 400 people were hanging on, and by the early 1960s, the village was in such serious decline that the Old Tavern Inn was about to go under. Enter the Windham Foundation, brainchild of Wall Street banker and philanthropist Dean Mathey. Having enjoyed an idyllic childhood visiting his aunt each summer in Grafton, Mathey set out to save the town.

Over the years the Windham Foundation has brought back the inn, now known as the **Grafton Inn** (92 Main St., Grafton; 800-843-1801; www.oldtavern.com), and relaunched cheese production. The inn is noted for its imaginative take on classic American cooking using local products. It offers casual dining in the Phelps Barn Pub, a modern addition, and homier, candlelit dining in the Old Tavern Inn, which dates from 1801. A lot of supplies come from the inn's kitchen garden and the cheese operation next door.

West Mountain Inn, 144 W. Mountain Inn Rd., Arlington; (802) 375-6516; www.westmountaininn.com; $$$$. Located high on a hill in the countryside between Arlington and Manchester, West Mountain Inn has one of the most localized menus in southern Vermont, thanks to the passions of Chef Jeff Scott. He gets all his butter, milk, and cream from Manchester's Wilcox Dairy, cheese directly from almost a dozen farmstead producers, eggs from one

The original Grafton Cooperative Cheese Company began operations in its namesake village in 1892. The company was later destroyed by fire and reincarnated in the mid-1960s as the **Grafton Village Cheese Company** (533 Townshend Rd., Grafton and 400 Linden St., Rte. 30, Brattleboro; 800-472-3866; www .graftonvillagecheese.com). The company produces about 3 million pounds of raw-milk cheddar cheese a year. The retail shop in Grafton, with cheesemaking operations visible through a window, has an old-fashioned feel that's in keeping with its quaint village setting. The more modern production facility and tasting room in Brattleboro is larger and offers a wider range of other products such as imported cheeses, wines, and local foodstuffs. Both, of course, have the full line of Grafton cheeses to sample and purchase, including aged, flavored, and maple-smoked cheddars and Grafton Duet, a pairing of cheddar and blue cheese. The top aged cheeses selected from each lot carry the Grafton Tavern label.

local farm, produce from several others. So while the fish on the menu necessarily comes from farther away, most of the rest of the ingredients are raised or at least processed within a few hours' drive of the inn. Scott's cooking holds true to the promise of his ingredients, with dishes like a slow-roasted duck risotto with smoked tomato puree, grilled chorizo, and spinach. He's fond of pairings, like his mixed grill of Vermont venison and quail, both with a blackberry merlot sauce. Most diners opt for the ridiculously reasonable 5-course prix-fixe dinner, but the components are also available a la carte if you ask. This is another spot where you might plan to spend the night after a big dinner. There are 14 elegant rooms in the historic inn, another 6 in outlying buildings.

Windham Hill Inn, 311 Lawrence Dr., West Townshend; (802) 874-4080; www.windhamhill.com; $$$$. The 160 acres of this rural retreat are the stuff of which dreams are made. This is the Vermont that Manhattanites dream about—rolling countryside with heavily laden apple trees, resplendent maples, and meadows just begging to be grazed by photogenic cows. Sixteen of the 20 rooms have fireplaces or gas stoves. Those are among the creature comforts for the overnight guests at this legendary country retreat. (Cell-phone reception is spotty, at best, and even the inn's Wi-Fi is iffy.) You come here to unwind, and perhaps to unbuckle your belt when you sit down to dinner. London-raised chef Graham Gill, who did much of his training in the kitchens of London's Savoy Group five-star hotels, brings an adept way with cold-climate cooking to the elegant menu. The cuisine might be Escoffier light as now practiced by many of the best restaurants in London and Paris, but it speaks with a Vermont accent. Shaved Parmigiano Reggiano cheese and truffle oil accompany his carpaccio of Vermont venison. He wraps Vermont pork tenderloin in prosciutto and serves it with grilled polenta, broccoli rabe, and a mustard sauce. Dinner is prix-fixe with several options, but Gill will make a tasting menu for the table with a little notice. It is also possible, if not cost-effective, to order a la carte.

Specialty Stores, Markets & Producers

Amy's Bakery Arts Cafe, 113 Main St., Brattleboro; (802) 251-1071. We usually order soup (chicken apple chowder, for example) or a salad (Vermont goat cheese with candied walnuts, fig olive tapenade, and tomatoes) when we stop for lunch so that we can save room for a square of chocolate-chip shortbread, a dense, chocolate-covered macaroon, or one of the bakery's other irresistible desserts. Diners place their orders at the counter at the front of the narrow room, then carry their trays past the open kitchen to the dining room in back where big windows look out on the Connecticut River. Amy's serves breakfast and lunch (there's also a good choice of hot and cold sandwiches) and stays open just late enough in the evening for dinnertime takeout.

Baba-A-Louis Bakery, 92 Rte. 11 West, Chester; (802) 875-4666; www.babalouisbakery.com. Baker John McLure designed the wooden building that houses the Baba-A-Louis kitchen and light-filled dining area. He also makes breads and other goodies that are worthy of the striking space with its exposed timbers and high, peaked roof. In addition to long French loaves and organic whole wheat, breads range from cheese herb to oatmeal or anadama. Sweets tend toward such classics as carrot cake, cream-cheese brownies, peanut butter cookies or maple almond squares. In the morning, people stop in for coffee and cinnamon sticky buns, but the lunch buffet is a real find. There are always a couple of soups (perhaps broccoli and winter squash), a few premade sandwiches (egg or tuna salad or mixed vegetables), along with quiche, and a panino of the day (avocado, tomato, and swiss cheese, for example). Closed Apr and Nov up to Thanksgiving.

Basketville, 8 Bellows Falls Rd., Putney; (802) 387-5509; www.basketville.com. When we stopped in to sample **Putney Mountain Winery's** fruit wines (p. 172), we discovered that this basket emporium also stocks "country kitchen essentials" such as bean pots, farm-animal-shaped cookie cutters, cheese planes, and wooden cutting boards. We're especially fond of the small ceramic bowls with a post in the center for cooking baked apples. But more ambitious cooks can pick up everything they need to make an apple pie: hand or mechanical apple peelers and corers, apple slicers, pie plates, pie crust shields, pie birds—and, for serving, pie dividers and spatulas. Basketville also stocks a large selection of local maple syrup, honey, cheeses, preserves, and other products.

Bennington Pottery, 324 County St., Bennington; (800) 205-8033; www.benningtonpotters.com. This legendary pottery combines the Arts & Crafts aesthetic of handmade pieces with sleekly Modernist lines, and sells its stoneware at the Potters Yard Factory Store. Browse the stoneware dinnerware, bakeware, and serving pieces in a selection of earthy tones. No two of the functional and beautiful pieces are exactly alike, but those that depart too far from the ideal are offered as bargain-priced factory seconds.

The Cheese House, 5187 Rte. 7A, Arlington; (802) 375-9033; www.thevermontcheesehouse.com. True to its name, this cheese-colored roadside structure sells two of its own cheeses. The Ol' Rat Trap cheddar is mild and mellow while the pungent Truck Driver Cheddar "is old enough to bite back." The shop also carries a number of cheeses from artisanal Vermont producers and fruit and grape wines from Vermont wineries.

Consider Bardwell Farm, 1333 Rte. 153, West Pawlet; (802) 645-9928; www.considerbardwellfarm.com. Consider Bardwell makes small-batch raw-milk artisanal cheeses from the farm's herd of 100 Oberhaslis goats and from the cow's milk of a nearby herd of 30 Jersey cows. The majority of the cheeses are either bloomy-rind (akin to Brie or Camembert) or washed-rind cheeses made for early consumption. The farm also produces some award-winning *tommes,* including the nutty goat's-milk Manchester, the creamy cow's-milk Pawlet, and the alpine-style aged Rupert (similar to comté and gruyère). The cheeses are available at a number of farmers' markets,

Ah-choo

For years harried urbanites have dreamed of moving to Vermont and opening a charming bed and breakfast. These days, an equal number imagine themselves living in an old farmstead and making award-winning artisanal cheese. Manhattan literary agent Angela Miller and her husband Russell Glover did just that and she wrote a book about their venture: *Hay Fever: How Chasing a Dream on a Vermont Farm Changed My Life* (John Wiley & Sons, New York, 2010). In 2001, the couple purchased the 300-plus-acre Consider Bardwell Farm, with its redbrick 1814 farmhouse and 1920s barn. The farm's namesake had established Vermont's first cheese cooperative in 1864 (it lasted into the 1930s) and soon Miller was determined to bring the property full circle. She bought the first six Oberhasli goats in 2003 and immediately launched a cheesemaking operation. Depending on your perspective, her unflinching account of her trials and triumphs might seem an inspiration—or a cautionary tale.

cheesemongers in New York and New England, and at the farm store, which is open daily all year. A small farm cafe is also open from breakfast through lunch on summer weekends.

Crazy Russian Girls Bakery, 443 Main St., Bennington; (802) 442-4688; www.crazyrussiangirlsbakery.biz. Just to clear things up, the crazy Russian girls are baker and (American-born) co-owner

Natasha Gardner, and her babushka, grandmother Irina Vadimovna Gardner. Babushka and her penchant for trying to feed the world (after nearly starving to death in Stalin's Russia) was Natasha's inspiration. She and husband Matt Littrell opened the bakery in early 2010, and they have been doing their part to satisfy the sweet teeth of folks from Bennington and beyond ever since. In addition to great Central European–style breads, the bakery has cases filled with generously proportioned sweet treats, such as a chocolate-chip studded muffin pumped full of pastry cream, the big and rich Apple Granny Oatmeal Bar, and a chocolate cookie modestly called Better Than Brad Pitt. Asked why, Natasha says it's chocolate, and it's crunchy on the outside, gooey on the inside.

Harlow's Sugar House, 563 Bellows Falls Rd., Putney; (802) 387-5852; www.vermontsugar.com. The Harlow family began making maple syrup in 1927 with the sap from a few hundred buckets. Today they have 13,000 taps and use a sophisticated and fuel-efficient system of reverse osmosis to remove water from the sap before boiling it down. The evaporator is often operating on weekends so that visitors can see it in action. The Harlows also make maple candies and cream and press cider from their own apples. Their homemade maple walnut crunch is a favorite with visitors who enjoy the shop's old-time feel as well as the opportunity to pick their own strawberries, blueberries, raspberries, and apples. Open Mar through Dec.

Hildene Farm Signature Cheese, 1005 Hildene Rd., Manchester; (802) 362-1788; www.hildene.org. Hildene, the Robert Todd Lincoln estate, is a lot more than the grand house of the son of a president. Some 412 acres remain of the original 500, and they're safely tucked into a conservation trust. When Hildene museum was reconsidering its mission a few years ago, they decided they owed it to the memory of the Lincoln family and to the children of Vermont to demonstrate and encourage sustainable agriculture. Check in first at the visitors' center and sign up to tour the cheesemaking operation or watch the milking. Hildene is home to about five dozen Nubian does. The goats are a small, gentle breed and love attention. They also produce the milk for a great deal of fresh chèvre as well as a goat's milk Havarti-type firm cheese. When the does are pregnant, roughly between November and March, the facility purchases cows' milk from local farms to make a bovine version of the Havarti. Cheeses are for sale in the museum store.

Honora Winery, 201 Rte. 112, Jacksonville; (802) 368-2226; www.honorawinery.com. Founded in the 1990s, Honora grows several varieties of cold-climate French-American hybrid grapes developed for Minnesota and Wisconsin and uses them to produce blended estate wines and an occasional estate ice wine. The Jacksonville vineyard site is also popular for weddings and similarly festive events. Honora's major production, however, consists of wines made from vinifera grapes imported mostly from the West Coast. The

Manchester tasting room is a popular stop for guests staying next door at the **Equinox** (p. 150). There is also a tasting room and shop at 3609 Main St., Manchester Center, (802) 362-8008.

It's All About the Bean, 139 W. Main St., Bennington; (802) 442-8822; www.itsallaboutthebean.net. This roomy yet warm and welcoming coffee shop occupies an odd space on the hillside west of town back among the low-rent motels. But they roast their own beans, producing a "Bennington blend" with a solid middle of Central American and Brazilian coffees, and the toasted aroma of African beans. The shop has a lot of excellent baked goods as well as a selection of panini for lunch, ensuring a steady flow of customers.

The Kitchen Store at J.K. Adams, 1430 Rte. 30, Dorset; (802) 362-4422; www.thekitchensoreonline.com. The J.K. Adams wood-working company was established in 1944 and now uses about 1,000 board feet of hardwoods (birch, beech, oak, maple, and ash) each day to create a range of kitchenware items. On weekdays you might be able to watch the manufacturing process from a catwalk above the factory floor. The cutting boards, cheese trays, sushi boards, carving platters, wine racks, knife blocks, barbecue carts, and other products are for sale in the large shop in the same building. In fact, the Kitchen Store offers J.K. Adams products at a 25 percent discount (some seconds are reduced even more). The shop also has a wide range of bakeware, small electric appliances, cookware, glassware, linens, and fun little gadgets. If you are looking for a classy gift, many of the wood products can be custom monogrammed.

Kitchen Sync, 110 Main St., Brattleboro; (802) 257-7044. The entrance to this small kitchenware shop is through adjacent Vermont Artisan (106 Main St.) which counts beautiful wooden bowls, cheese slicers, spoons, spatulas, and cutting and serving boards among its handcrafted goods. They are a nice complement to Kitchen Sync's fine knives, rainbow-colored dinnerware, tagines, and Provençal-style table linens. If you can't resist buying Vermont's cheddar cheeses, you might want to check out the shop's nice selection of fondue pots, forks, and divided serving plates.

Lawrence's Smoke Shop, 653 Rte. 30, Townshend; (802) 365-7372; www.lawrencessmokeshop.com. Lawrence's doesn't smoke its meats and cheeses on the premises, so you don't smell the shop before you see it. Bacon, both cob-smoked and peppered, is the biggest seller, but Lawrence's also offers some more unusual products such as smoked boneless *magret* duck breast, venison summer sausage, Vermont apple wine sausage, and whiskey fennel sausage made with Jack Daniels. A number of other local products round out the shop's offerings, including an extensive selection of **Grafton Village** cheeses (p. 161) with samples laid out under a counter-weighted glass dome.

Mocha Joe's, 82 Main St., Brattleboro; (802) 257-5637; www
.mochajoes.com. Company founder Pierre Capy is one of those
coffee fanatics who had a Saul-on-the-road-to-Tarsus conversion to
coffee fanaticism when he tasted one of George Howell's fabulous
cups at Coffee Connection in Harvard Square. When Howell sold to
Starbucks, Capy began roasting his own beans and emulating his
model by dealing directly with coffee farmers. Good vibes from
selling Fair Trade, Direct Trade, and Rainforest Alliance products
are all well and good, but the proof of quality is in the cup. The
coffee is superbly roasted to match the place of origin, so a cup
of Ethiopian is full of winey, blueberry notes, a Kenyan of roasted
peanuts, a Brazilian of the lovely ashen aftertaste of walnuts. This
shop is just the iceberg's tip: Mocha Joe's ships all over the country.

Powers Market, Lincoln Square, 9 Main St., North Bennington;
(802) 442-6821; www.powersmarket.com. Clearly the folks of North
Bennington have their priorities. This marvelous old country store
inside a structure with massive brick columns is devoted to the
essentials. That is to say, the back half of the store consists
of bottles of wine, six-packs of craft brews, and all the
crackers and snacks to go with them. The front
half is a friendly bakery-cafe with big puffy
muffins, toothsome cookies, and meat and vegetarian sandwiches. You have to love a place
that serves grilled chèvre sandwiches as well as
peanut butter and bacon on whole wheat.

Putney Mountain Winery Tasting Room, Basketville, 8 Bellows Falls Rd., Putney; (802) 387-5925; www.putneywine.com. Putney Mountain makes fruit wines—no grapes—and does so very well. Only the cranberries come from outside Vermont (Cape Cod). Winemaker Charlie Dodge has focused successfully on retaining the fruit flavors in most of the final products, and his luscious apple-maple wine is a winner—a fruit wine that is truly superb with spiced or heavily herbed food (think turkey with sage stuffing, or a chicken curry). The Simply Rhubarb is a revelation. Produced with organic rhubarb from **Dwight Miller & Son Orchard** (p. 177), it's a crisp and elegant white wine that pairs well with shellfish and especially with strong-flavored fish like bluefish or mackerel. Fruit wines are often considered a novelty, but these are real table wines to accompany good food.

Saxtons River Distillery, 485 W. River Rd., Brattleboro; (802) 246-1128; www.saplingliqueur.com. Christian Stromberg drew on his Lithuanian heritage to create his own maple liqueur. "We made honey liqueur," he says, "but it was my idea to experiment with maple." After working out of his barn for about four years, he opened this production facility and tasting room in June 2011. "Basically it's me, hand-bottling with a machine," he says, and the bottles in which he puts the liqueur make for a gorgeous presentation. He makes 10,000 bottles a year. The corn-based alcohol comes from a distiller in New York. Stromberg adds the maple syrup as both sweetener and flavor ingredient. The finished liqueur, he says, is very good for mixed drinks, especially maple Manhattans. "You can add it to tea or coffee or on ice cream," he says. "You can put it in anything you want to sweeten and add a little boost, like hot chocolate or egg nog."

Twilight Tea Lounge, 41 Main St., Brattleboro; (802) 254-8887; www.twilighttealounge.com. This friendly shop might be the most laid-back place in famously laid-back Brattleboro. Once you've made your choice from among about 170 black, green, white, and oolong teas, herbal teas, and blends, you can relax with a piece of pastry and enjoy the small selection of books, games, and tarot cards left for customers to use. Store blends of herbal and caffeinated teas range from Cool Sunny Afternoon (mu tan white tea, green rooibos, spearmint, chamomile, and lemon balm) to Winter Solstice Antlers (green mate, rooibos, lemongrass, and licorice root). Not enough choices? Customers can also create their own blends of two or three ingredients.

Vermont Country Deli, 436 Western Ave., Brattleboro; (802) 257-9254; www.vermontcountrydeli.com. Vermont products seem especially well-suited to the comfort foods offered at this food emporium housed in a 100-year-old post-and-beam building. Vermont cheddar, for example, figures prominently in sandwich choices, such as turkey, cheddar, and cranberry sauce or roast beef, cheddar, and horseradish as well as in baked mac and cheese. Maple makes its appearance in the deli case with maple-glazed turkey meatballs and maple barbecue pulled pork or chicken wings. Apple cider flavors soups and apples fill crumb top pies. But the deli has an international flair as well with pot stickers and eggrolls, linzer tarts and tiramisu, tomato tortellini and German potato salad.

Vermont Country Store, 657 Main St., Weston; (802) 824-3184; www.vermontcountrystore.com. The Orton family opened their first country store in Weston in 1946 and added another in Rockingham in 1967. It's really not surprising that they would need more room for their overwhelming inventory of foodstuffs and hard-to-find gadgets. Among the offbeat items for cooks, you might find squirt-less grapefruit knives, nonstick doughnut pans, classic squirrel nutcrackers, pig-shaped cast-iron bacon presses, and Rolla Roaster camping forks for charring hotdogs or marshmallows over an open fire. And you won't go hungry while you peruse the gadgets or take a stroll down memory lane, better known as the retro toy aisles. The stores provide generous samples of their cheeses, salsas, dips, fruit butters, pretzels, cookies, and tarts. Don't overlook the classic pickle barrel or the modest Vermont Common Crackers, a country store staple first made in the early 19th century. The Rockingham location is at 1292 Rockingham Rd., Rockingham (802-463-2224).

Vermont Kitchen Supply, 4712 Main St. (Rte. 7A), Manchester Center; (802) 362-0111; www.vermontkitchensupply.com. This store for cooking enthusiasts may be tucked into the outlet clothing stores of Manchester Center, but there's nothing of the close-out or outlet here. Goods are full price, but generally worth it. In addition to the well-curated selections of small appliances and French cast iron, you'll also find square and round restaurant tableware, a great selection of dried mushrooms and chile peppers, and a full line of ecologically sensitive (and good-smelling) Caldrea liquid soaps.

Vermont Shepherd Cheese, 281 Patch Farm Rd., Putney; (802) 387-4473; www.vermontshepherd.com. When you pass a herd of sheep grazing on a hillside you'll know that you're heading in the right direction. And when you reach an impossibly cute yellow building with a red door, you'll know that you have arrived. Inside, there's a glass case full of the various ribbons that David and Yesenia Ielpi Major have won, including best of show in the American Cheese Society competition and Best of Class in the US Championship Cheese Contest. A basket is heaped full of yarn spun from the fleece of their herd. The counters are covered with jars of local honey ("try drizzling on the cheese," a sign advises) and tomato marmalade to go with the cheese. (Or "Be Creative," another sign exhorts.) The main reason for visiting, though, is to purchase the cheese, which you'll find in pre-cut wedges inside the refrigerator in the corner. It's a little pricey, but since it's some of the best aged sheep's milk cheese in North America, it's worth it.

Weston Village Store, Rte. 100, Weston; (802) 824-5477. Often overshadowed by the younger and flashier **Vermont Country Store** across the street (p. 174), the Weston Village Store opened for business in 1891. Its wide front porch, pressed tin ceiling, and worn wooden floors exude a taciturn New England charm while merchandise leans toward the classic and local: maple syrup, sturdy pottery, sampler packs of Long Trail beer, cheeses, and a wide variety of fudge flavors, including seasonal favorite pumpkin pie.

Farmstands & Pick Your Own

Apple Barn & Country Bake Shop, 604 Rte. 7, Bennington; (802) 447-7780; www.theapplebarn.com. If it's picking season, you're likely to be assaulted by the seductive aroma of apple cider doughnuts when you walk in the door. As much a bake shop as a farmstand, the Apple Barn offers PYO August into October, and a whole lot of culinary specialties from locally made jams and relishes to caramel wrappers for making caramel apples. The cookies are gigantic, the pies sky-high, and those cider doughnuts—irresistible. Open May through Nov.

Dutton Berry Farm, Rte. 9, West Brattleboro; (802) 254-0254; Rte. 30, Newfane; (802) 365-4168; and Rtes. 11/30, Manchester; (802) 362-3083; www.duttonberryfarm.com. Paul Dutton grew up on a dairy farm but his own interests tended toward berries. He and wife Wendy began growing strawberries in 1982 and have branched out to apples and a full range of vegetables which are available in their farmstands. The kitchen turns out breads, fruit pies, and other baked goods, as well as fudge and a few veggie-based entrees such as eggplant parmigiana. They even make pizza dough that shoppers can take home and load up with their favorite vegetable toppings. The farmstands also have greenhouses and covered rows where the Duttons grow bedding plants.

Dwight Miller & Son Orchard, 511 Miller Rd., East Dummerston; (802) 254-9111. Late spring frosts make it a touch-and-go business to grow peaches in Vermont, but the Miller family is up to the challenge. Their first peach trees were planted in 1895, just 24 years after they started growing apples. A pioneer among Vermont fruit growers, the farm switched to all organic practices in recent years. The family now cultivates about 70 varieties of organic apples, 20 varieties of peaches, and a dozen varieties of pears, along with strawberries, raspberries, and blueberries.

They also sell their own eggs, pasture-raised organic pork and chicken, and tiny organic pumpkins perfect for pie. Open July through late Dec.

Fair Winds Farm, 511 Upper Dummerston Rd., Brattleboro; (802) 254-9067; www.fairwindsfarm.org. When visitors pull into the parking area at Fair Winds Farm, they may catch sight of several draft horses grazing in a pasture. The Bailey family works their

42-acre farm entirely with horse- and manpower. Morning glories climb the side of their rough wooden farm store where visitors can reach into the refrigerators for regular and jumbo eggs, grass-fed chickens and lamb, and goat meat. Inquire about horse-drawn hay and sleigh rides.

Green Mountain Orchards & Farm Store, 130 W. Hill Rd., Putney; (802) 387-5851; www.greenmtorchards.com. If you're a PYO buff, you can keep busy through the growing season at Green Mountain Orchards—from blueberries and raspberries to sweet corn, then on to peaches, plums, apples, and pumpkins. You can even cut a Christmas tree if you stop in during the holiday season for some fresh-pressed cider, jams and jellies, or an apple pie. The kitchen also turns out excellent cider doughnuts with a slightly crunchy exterior coated with granulated sugar. The farmstand shares a big red barn with several antique cars and trucks. Open mid-July to early May.

Harlow Farm, 117 Deep Root Dr., Westminster; (802) 722-3515; www.harlowfarm.com. If you believe that it's best not to shop for food on an empty stomach, stop first at the farmstand's Loco Cafe for an omelet, bowl of soup, or baked good (including a number of gluten-free options). But you will still find it difficult to resist the beautiful produce grown on this 150-acre organic farm—one of the first and largest in the state. The Harlow family feeds excess vegetables to their cattle and pigs and sells beef, pork, sausage, ham, and bacon, along with eggs from their free-range chickens. Their produce also finds it way into a range of jams, pickles, relishes, salsas, and chutneys. Open May through early Dec.

Scott Farm, 707 Kipling Rd., Dummerston; (802) 254-6868; www .scottfarmvermont.com. The 626-acre Scott Farm is part of Landmark Trust USA which rescues and restores historic properties. It's easy to see why this beautiful hillside farm with more than 20 historic structures was deserving of such attention. In fact, it's so full of character that parts of the movie *Cider House Rules* were filmed here. The farm grows raspberries, blueberries, gooseberries, peaches, nectarines, and pears. But it is known for its 70 varieties of apples, including many heirlooms which visitors can select to put together their own mixed bag. For those who want to pick their own, a sign directs them to "pick the apple by bending it upwards with a twist of the wrist." Homemade apple treats include strudel and pie made with heirloom Calville Blanc d'Hiver and Reine des Reinette apples, cider reduction syrup, and a butter crust. The property's 100-year-old sugarhouse and 170-year-old farmhouse are available for overnight rentals.

Farm Stay

Shearer Hill Farm B&B, Shearer Hill Rd., Wilmington; (802) 464-3253; www.shearerhillfarm.com. Guests start the day with fresh muffins and Patti Pusey's baked apples, served with the farm's own maple syrup. In the spring, Bill Pusey taps the maple trees on the property and makes between 40 and 50 gallons of syrup. Guests are welcome to help gather syrup or stoke the fire in the evaporator in the 80-year-old sugarhouse. The 6 guest rooms are divided between the main farm house and a carriage house. Several can accommodate families and the Puseys love to introduce children to their cows.

Farmers' Markets

Bellows Falls Farmers' Market, Waypoint Center, Bellows Falls. Fri from 4 to 7 p.m., late May through mid-October.

Brattleboro Area Farmers' Market, Downtown Brattleboro. Wed from 10 a.m. to 2 p.m., early May to late October.

Brattleboro Area Farmers' Market, Rte. 9, West Brattleboro. Sat from 9 a.m. to 2 p.m., early May to late October.

Bennington Walloomsac Farmers' Market, Bennington Station at River St. Park, Bennington. Tues from 3:30 to 6 p.m. and Sat from 10 a.m. to 1 p.m., May through October.

Dorset Farmers' Market, Williams General Store, Rte. 30, Dorset. Sun from 10 a.m. to 2 p.m., mid-May through early October.

Londonderry West River Farmers' Market, Rtes. 11E and 100N, Londonderry. Sat from 9 a.m. to 1 p.m., late May to early October.

Manchester Farmers' Market, Adams Park, Rte. 7A North, Manchester. Thurs from 3 to 6 p.m., June to early October.

Marlboro Farmers' Market, Elementary School, Rte. 9, Marlboro. Sat from 10 a.m. to 1 p.m., late May through October.

Putney Farmers' Market, Carol Brown Way, Putney. Sun from 11 a.m. to 2 p.m., early May to early October.

Townshend Common Farmers' Market, Rtes. 30 and 35, Townshend. Thurs from 3:30 to 6:30 p.m., early June to mid-October.

Wilmington Farmers' Market, 17 W. Main St., Wilmington. Sun 10 a.m. to 3 p.m., late May to early October.

Deerfield Valley Blueberry Festival, www.vermontblueberry .com. The Mount Snow region towns of Wilmington, Whitingham, and Dover celebrate the blueberry harvest with 10 days of activities in July and August that include blueberry picking, pie-eating contests, jam-making, blueberry bake sales, and blueberry-themed dinners in local restaurants.

Deerfield Valley Farmers' Day Fair, www.dvfair.com. This mid-August celebration of country life held in Wilmington includes a watermelon seed-spitting contest for kids only, but adults can join them in the pie-eating competition.

Famous Apple Pie Festival, held at Dummerston Congregational Church (32 Park Laughton Rd., 802-257-0544). This one-day event in early October features 1,500 apple pies along with homemade ice cream, fresh doughnuts, apple cider, coffee, and cheddar cheese.

Guilford Fair, www.guilfordfairvt.com. This early September event features an ice cream–eating contest and a chicken barbecue along with dog agility and sheep shearing demonstrations.

Southern Vermont Garlic & Herb Festival, www.lovegarlic .com. "Vermont Stinks!" proclaim the organizers of this early September event held in Bennington. About 100 vendors offer garlic bulbs and braids and unexpected garlic-infused foods such as ice cream and jelly. Cooking demonstrations provide new ideas for using garlic and a Wine and Beer Garden lets festival-goers choose their favorite quaff to complement the "stinking rose."

Strolling of the Heifers, www.strollingoftheheifers.com. A parade of flower-bedecked heifers down Brattleboro's Main Street is the highlight of this early June event which also includes a celebrity milking contest and sampling of local cheeses and other products.

Vermont Life Wine & Harvest Festival, www.thevermont festival.com. Timed to late September foliage season, this Mount Snow valley event showcases Vermont cheeses, wines, and other specialty foods and also gives local artists and artisans a chance to display their work.

Whitingham Maple Festival, www.whitingham-maplefest.us. In addition to sugarhouse tours, this 2-day event in mid-March also features a pancake breakfast, sugar on snow ham dinner, and maple recipe contest.

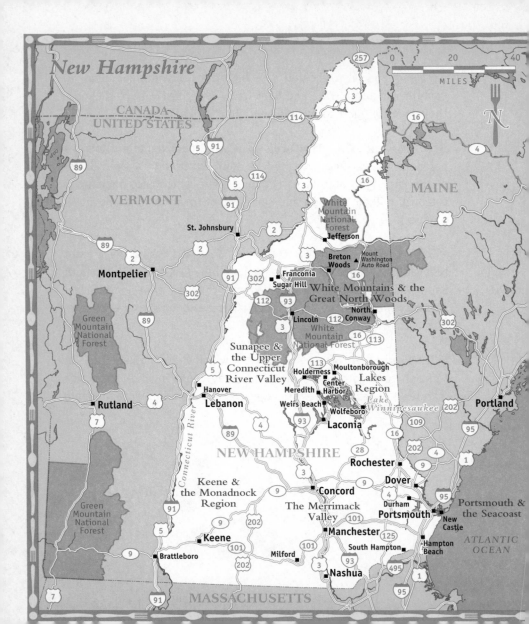

New Hampshire

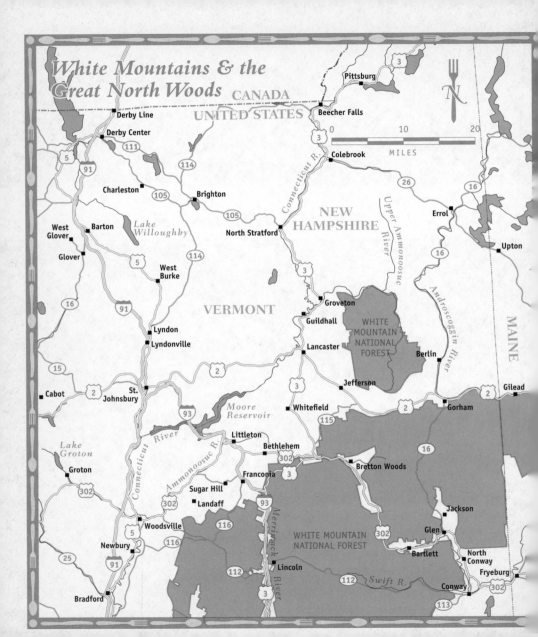

White Mountains & the Great North Woods

CANADA
UNITED STATES

Pittsburg

Beecher Falls

Derby Line

Derby Center

111

114

Charleston

105

Brighton

Colebrook

3

26

16

Errol

NEW HAMPSHIRE

Upper Ammonoosuc River

16

Upton

West Glover

Barton

Lake Willoughby

105

North Stratford

3

Glover

114

16

West Burke

91

VERMONT

Groveton

Guildhall

WHITE MOUNTAIN NATIONAL FOREST

Berlin

Androscoggin River

MAINE

Lyndon

Lyndonville

Lancaster

2

Jefferson

3

Gilead

15

Cabot

2

St. Johnsbury

Moore Reservoir

Whitefield

115

2

Gorham

93

Littleton

16

Connecticut River

Lake Groton

Bethlehem

302

Bretton Woods

Groton

302

Franconia

3

Ammonoosuc R.

Sugar Hill

Jackson

116

Landaff

93

Glen

302

Woodsville

116

WHITE MOUNTAIN NATIONAL FOREST

Bartlett

North Conway

5

Newbury

Merrimack River

112

Lincoln

Swift R.

Conway

Fryeburg

302

25

Bradford

3

113

0 10 20 MILES

White Mountains & the Great North Woods

It sometimes seems that the farther north you go in New Hampshire, the more time people spend outdoors. This chapter details the dining and food specialties of the most northerly part of the state, where people tend to see themselves as a breed apart: those who live "above the notches," as they refer to the north-south passes between the peaks of the White Mountains. This is the land of legendary sporting camps for hunting big game and landing big fish. It is the countryside of alpine hikers and, most of all, of alpine skiers. Those activities definitely help work up an appetite.

The White Mountains have another, less rugged tradition as the Switzerland of America, where East Coast urbanites came to escape the heat of the cities in favor of the clean air—and wholesome farm food—of the mountains. Grand mountain resorts sprang up in northern New Hampshire during the 19th century, sometimes resembling immense cruise ships grounded on mountaintops like Noah's ark coming to rest on Mount Ararat. A handful of them still persist, and eating is still a major factor of the resort experience. Two of the grandest hotels—the Mountain View Grand and the Omni Mount Washington—are featured in this chapter. A third, The Balsams, is not because its future was uncertain at the time this volume went to press.

Foodie Faves

Adair Country Inn & Restaurant, 80 Guider Lane, Bethlehem; (603) 444-2600; www.adairinn.com; $$$. With just 9 rooms and suites and 11 tables in the dining room, it's natural that Adair's dinners are open to nonguests. (We should add that if you're staying here, you'd be foolish not to dine at Adair at least once.) Chef Orlo Coots favors New England ingredients and contemporary New England preparations. He smokes his own meats and churns his own ice cream. The menu changes seasonally, with roasted lamb loin as his spring-summer specialty and crispy duck from Brome Lake in Quebec's Eastern Townships a feature in the fall. The menus are always prix fixe, but diners can choose from 2 to 5 courses.

The Hill's Top BBQ, 644 Rtes. 16 and 302, Bartlett; (603) 383-8101; $$. A pig weathervane on the roof signals drivers to turn in at this super casual barbecue joint with red-and-white-checked cloths on the tables and a big-screen TV on the wall. Hill's serves the barbecue classics of pulled pork, chicken, brisket, and baby back and St. Louis ribs. Each table is equipped with an array of sauces in squeeze bottles. The only thing missing is Carolina vinegar sauce. Follow the advice of the waitress and mix the hot, sweet, and smoky together for the meat and use the spicy mayonnaise-based sauce for the fries. Hill's also serves a delicious family-recipe fire-roasted corn chowder.

Inn at Thorn Hill, Thorn Hill Rd., Jackson Village; (603) 383-4242; (800) 289-8990; www.innatthornhill.com; $$$. There's a marvelously improvisational quality to the dining room of the Inn at Thorn Hill. Chef Rich Schmitt only exaggerates a little when he says, "Whatever comes in the back door is what is on the menu." Because he buys a lot of produce from local farmers and even gardeners, he's ready to scrap a routine salad if, say, a bag of golden beets arrives in time for him to roast them and pair with a local pungent cheese. He changes the menu almost every night, and tells his suppliers, "Surprise me—just bring me what you've got." As a result, the menu has such notations as "today's soup" and "today's salad." Rich's wife, McKaella Schmitt, is the pastry chef and follows her husband's lead in offering "today's fruit crisp" on the dessert menu. We would consider committing a serious crime for another taste of her butterscotch pudding served in a Mason jar with a sprinkle of sea salt and a piece of rosemary shortbread.

Libby's Bistro and SAALT Pub, 111 Main St., Gorham; (603) 466-5330; www.libbysbistro.net; $$–$$$. Liz Jackson is famed for her stints as Julia Child's right-hand woman on the cooking doyenne's 1994–98 shows, *In Julia's Kitchen with Master Chefs* and *Baking with Julia*. She and husband Steve have put Gorham on the culinary map with their bistro and the even more casual downstairs pub. The dining duet occupy an old redbrick building in the center of town. Enter through the gardens on the left for the bistro, on the street on the right for the pub. The dining room, with its North Country Victorian decor, serves American bistro fare such as porcini and asparagus risotto or crab cakes with fresh corn and green salad. The pub menu leans toward pastas, pizzas, and one-pot stews and casseroles. During the winter, Jackson also offers a series of 3-hour cooking classes that conclude with a sit-down dinner and wine.

Littleton Diner, 145 Main St., Littleton; (603) 444-3994; www.littletondiner.com; $. A diner has sat on this spot since 1930 and the current 1940 Sterling Diner with 12 stools and 8 wooden booths is a favorite with presidential candidates who want to bask in its down-home charm. It's also a favorite with pancake lovers who can order buttermilk, whole wheat, or buckwheat pancakes made with stone ground flour from the **Littleton Grist Mill** (see p. 204). The pancakes are served all day, but you have to pay a little extra for New Hampshire maple syrup.

Moat Mountain Smoke House & Brewing Co., 3378 White Mountain Hwy. (Rte. 16), North Conway; (603) 356-6381; www .moatmountain.com; $$. What do skiers like to eat and drink? Barbecue and beer, of course, and Moat Mountain delivers both in spades. The rollicking restaurant (with a brewery beneath) always seems to be full. Smoke infuses almost everything on the menu, from the blackened catfish to the Carolina-style smoked pork butt, to smoked ribs slathered in Kansas City–style sweet and tangy tomato-based sauce. Most of the meats are available as sandwiches or as entree plates. Even some of the pizzas are topped with barbecue. Beers run the gamut from the signature American Pale Ale called Iron Mike to a thick Square Tail Stout full of richly caramelized chocolate and coffee malts.

Peg's Restaurant, 99 Main St., North Woodstock; (603) 745-2740; $. Peg's serves breakfast and lunch only, but gets an early start on the day by opening at 5:30 a.m. For breakfast, pancakes, French toast, and homemade Belgian waffles are perfect for sopping up Fadden's maple syrup (see p. 199). But for a breakfast to last all day, opt for the Hungry Man's Special of three eggs with ham, bacon, or sausage, home fries or corned-beef hash, toast, and a short stack. A hot turkey sandwich with gravy is the lunch specialty, but soups, salads, and club sandwiches are also available. No credit cards.

Polly's Pancake Parlor, 672 Rte. 117, Sugar Hill; (603) 823-5575; www.pollyspancakeparlor.com; $. In 1938 Polly and Wilfred Dexter converted an old carriage shed into a small restaurant to serve waffles, pancakes, and French toast with their own maple syrup. Polly's remains a family-owned business and is such a local institution that the James Beard Foundation has recognized it as one of "America's Classics," noted for their "timeless appeal" and "quality food that reflects the character of their communities." Check it for yourself with a six-pancake sampler with a choice of five batters (plain, buckwheat, whole wheat, cornmeal, oatmeal buttermilk) and four add-ins (blueberry, walnut, coconut, chocolate chip). All orders are served with maple syrup, maple spread, and granulated maple sugar. Other breakfast dishes, along with lunchtime sandwiches, salads, and homemade baked beans are also available. Polly's serves breakfast and lunch only and is open early May through late Nov. A gift shop with maple products, pancake mixes, and other items is open year-round.

Rainbow Grille and Tavern, 609 Beach Rd., Pittsburg; (603) 538-9556; www.talltimber.com; $$. There's a frontier quality to the Tall Timber Lodge, which opened in 1946 mainly as a sporting camp for fishermen and hunters. Times change and tastes evolve. The lodge's dining room is now a destination for travelers in the

Connecticut Lakes region. Among the best bets are the several preparations of rainbow trout and the nightly wild game specials.

Sugar Hill Inn, 116 Rte. 117, Sugar Hill; (603) 823-5621; (800) 548-4748; www.sugarhillinn.com; $$$. Plan on making an evening of it when you dine at the Sugar Hill Inn. Reservations are staggered so the kitchen can keep pace, but once you sit down the table is yours for the night. That's good, because dinner is a 4-course prix-fixe affair, and Chef Val Fortin tends to amplify the number of items you actually eat by dividing some courses into multiple tastes. For example, he might serve a trio of soups, or offer "duck three ways" (sautéed breast, confit leg, and ravioli filled with *foie gras* mousse). The excellent wine list roams the world, with especially strong representation of California, Oregon, and France.

Sunny Day Diner, Rte. 3, Lincoln; (603) 745-4833; $. OK, we're suckers for classic American diners, and this all-aluminum Streamline-style 1958 Masters is as much a classic as the automotive tailfins of the same era. Blue plate specials include such standards as Salisbury steak, a hot turkey sandwich, and what the diner calls "Filet of Meatloaf." Breakfast is the more important meal here, and some of the offerings stray from the conventional. We like the Salmon Stack—a piece of freshly poached salmon on top of broccoli, scrambled eggs, and toast. They boast that their hollandaise is made on premises. For a supersweet breakfast, try the french toast made with banana bread. No credit cards.

Waterwheel Breakfast House, 1955 Presidential Hwy. (Rte. 2), Jefferson; (603) 586-4313; www.waterwheelnh.com; $. Like most breakfast and lunch places in the North Country, the Waterwheel serves pancakes, but is equally well-known for its "Sinn-Full" french toast, a breakfast special made with homemade cinnamon buns. Waterwheel's soups are so popular that the attached gift shop sells them as mixes (New England pea, broccoli and cheddar, pumpkin and pasta) along with maple products and other local treats.

Woodstock Inn Station & Brewery, 135 Main St., North Woodstock; (603) 745-3951; www.woodstockinnnh.com; $$. We recommend going into the pub side of this complex in a former train station and sampling some (or all) of the six beers before you ever look at the menu. A pint of Pemi Pale Ale brewed on the premises will put you in the proper frame of mind to decipher the groaning puns on the food list. Meat between bread is found under "Sandwiched Between the Tracks," while the "Cattle Car" heading describes the burger variations. Dinner entrees are known as the "Main Line." Tours of the seven-barrel brewpub are offered daily. If you like the style, most of the beers are available to take home in growlers.

Mountain View Grand, Mountain View Rd., Whitefield; (866) 484-3843; www.mountainviewgrand.com; $$$. This vast white-trimmed yellow resort hotel has grown from a more modest 1865 structure to the hilltop grand hotel of today. A striking restoration begun in the early 21st century has brought the property back to its heyday, and the arrival of Brian Aspell as executive chef in 2011 elevated the entire dining program. At one time the Mountain View Grand was a self-sustaining inn, thanks to operating the largest farm in the White Mountains. The resort still gets fully half of its summer produce from farms within a 10-mile radius. Aspell ranges a little farther for his fish, but much of the meat comes from northern New Hampshire and Vermont. "Once you're north of the notches," he says, referring to White-Mountains passageways of Franconia and Crawford Notches, "we think less of state distinctions. We're all North Country together." The resort has expanded its rooms for casual dining from Aspell's contemporary American bistro menu, but gastronomes should chat with the chef in advance about a tasting menu in the romantic wine cellar. Do try to stick to small portions, as Aspell's enthusiasm for the extraordinary flavor of, say, fresh strawberries or perfectly fattened duck leads him to prepare exuberant plates that are so good that it is impossible not to eat every bite. Sommelier and cellar manager Richard Wood has assembled an extremely good range of wines at excellent prices, with a bias toward value rather than any particular region. See Chef Aspell's recipe for **Chilled Brandywine Heirloom Tomato and Cilantro Cooler** on p. 356.

Omni Mount Washington Resort, 310 Mount Washington Hotel Rd., Bretton Woods; (603) 278-1000; www.omnihotels.com; $$$$. The venerable Mount Washington opened in 1902, and generations of guests have marveled at the mountain landscape, the Tiffany art glass, and the orchestral accompaniment as they supped in high style in the large, glittering dining room. Chef Ed Swetz runs the resort's kitchen now. He frames a grand expression of American fine dining in the menu for all guests, but loves nothing more than to consult with guests to prepare a special tasting menu, which the resort calls a Golden Sash Dinner. Not only can Swetz use the opportunity to audition dishes that he's considering for the main menu, he gets to lavish the extra time it takes for some of the fine touches. For example, he may grill and then chill hearts of romaine lettuce and combine them with seared tuna loin, roasted onions, a few half-roasted tomatoes, and plate the dish to make it look like a presentation of a whole fish. Swetz has the nose of a perfume blender and the palate of brandy blender, so the flavoring of food shows great finesse. Once cauliflower is available, he might open a tasting dinner with a course of chilled puree spiced with curry (see recipe on p. 354) and served with a mushroom relish and a flurry of baby celery leaves. One never need go hungry or thirsty at the Mount Washington—there are complimentary wine tastings several times a week, full tea every afternoon. When things slow down a bit in spring and fall, the resort also offers some cooking classes and special culinary weekends.

The Wentworth, 1 Carter Notch Rd., Jackson Village; (603) 383-9700; (800) 637-0013; www.thewentworth.com; $$$. The smallest of the White Mountain grand hotels at only 51 rooms, the Wentworth is really more of a large, rather barny country village inn from 1820 that also happens to have a golf course and access to 150 kilometers of cross-country ski trails. Chef Brian Gazda oversees the kitchen, and because his dining room is smaller than those at the other grand hotels, he is able to buy more food locally without overwhelming the farmers. There's a classical elegance about dining here, from the formality of the dining room to the modern updates on international standards. It's a quick drive from the Portland, Maine, fish pier to Jackson, and it shows in Gazda's reliance on fresh New England cod, bass, and flounder—which he typically pairs with vegetables in sides like a fava bean and shrimp succotash or a *ragù* of green peas, pearl onions, and porcini mushrooms.

Specialty Stores, Markets & Producers

Abbey Cellars, 78 Main St., Lincoln; (603) 745-9463; www .abbeycellarsnh.com. The New Hampshire state liquor stores tend to dominate the wine trade, but every so often we find a small shop like this one that specializes in picking out top-quality wines at $15–$40 and stocks a line of international and local artisanal cheeses to match. It's almost worth stopping just for the selection of Belgian lambic beers and the bulk olive oil and balsamic vinegar (bring your own bottle).

Bishop's Homemade, 183 Cottage St., Littleton; (603) 444-6039; www.bishopshomemadeicecream.com. It's easy to recognize Bishop's by the big cutout of an ice cream cone topped with a scrumptious scoop of purple ice cream. It's mounted on the side of the tall gray building with purple shutters. Take a cue from that bold color choice and order a scoop of Bishop's signature black raspberry flavor. Ice cream is made fresh daily and flavors tend to rotate, but you might also find apple and spice, rum raisin, mocha Oreo, green tea, or a "fun flavor" such as banana cream pie. Closed Nov through Mar.

Chutters, 43 Main St., Littleton; (603) 444-5787; www.chutters .com. A yellow measuring tape runs the entire 112-foot length of Chutters' candy counter, which claims the Guinness World Record for longest in the world. That means more than 12 feet of jelly beans alone, more than 20 choices of licorice drops, and an entire zoo of gummi animals from classic bears to octopi and tarantulas. Of course there are plenty of old-time favorites including Root Beer Barrels, Spearmint Leaves, Atomic Fireballs, and Boston Baked Beans. Can't decide? Best sellers are red Swedish Fish and Vanilla Bullseyes. Kids can select from more than 30 inches of true "penny candy." Decorators with a sweet tooth should check out the separate dispensers of single color M&Ms.

Duck Soup, 106 Main St., Littleton; (603) 444-5953. This two-level kitchenware shop has been in business about 30 years and has a loyal following of locals as well as vacationers who stop in every year to peruse the large cookbook selection and drool over the beautifully designed Viking small appliances. The shop also carries a wide variety of cookware, including both the ovenware and tabletop lines by Emile Henry, and some unusual items such as colorful ceramics from Bulgaria and elegant mango-wood serving platters.

Fadden's General Store & Sugarhouse, 109 Main St., North Woodstock; (603) 745-8371. This operation was established in 1896 and the general store has the bones to prove it—with worn wooden floors and a long wooden counter that displays homemade fudge and Fadden's own maple syrup, lollipops, hard drops, taffy, and maple walnut caramels. One corner of the store has been converted to a small maple museum with historic photos depicting the process of collecting maple sap and transforming it into syrup. There's also an assemblage of well-used pails, sleds, snowshoes, and even an old evaporator. The modern sugarhouse behind the general store is open daily during maple season.

Fuller's Sugarhouse, 267 Main St., Lancaster; (603) 788-2719; www.fullerssugarhouse.com. Ed Fuller is almost apologetic when he tells visitors that the pancake mix in this emporium of local tastes is made in Vermont. All the other products, including jams, pickles, relishes, and mustards, hail from New Hampshire. The maple syrup is from the Fullers' own operation and can be purchased in diminutive half pints up to full gallons. The Fullers make Grade B, Grade A Dark Amber, Grade A Medium Amber, and Grade A Light Amber syrups. The medium amber is the most popular, but Fuller has noticed an increased interest in Grade B syrup. "It used to be considered a cooking syrup because it's dark and hearty flavored and wouldn't get lost in a recipe," Fuller says, "but more and more people are using it as table syrup." The Fullers have close to 10,000 taps in four different locations and boil their syrup in an evaporator adjacent to the shop. During sugar season, visitors can both see and smell the process in action.

Granite Cask, 6 King's Square, Whitefield; (603) 837-2224; www .granitecask.com. Pretty much anything you need to brew your own beer is available here, but the real beauty of Granite Cask is that the staff mixes beer-making supplies fresh for each customer. They offer around six dozen custom-mixed kits with the ingredients for making different style brews from an American Pale Ale to a Winter Wit double-malted wheat beer. If you're just getting started, they also stock carboys and air locks, kegs, and draft lines, and even bulk grain that you can sprout and malt yourself. For those who like to puff while quaffing their malt beverages, the shop also carries Macanudo, Punch, H. Upman, Partaga, and Monte Cristo premium cigars.

Half Baked and Fully Brewed, 187 Main St., Lincoln; (603) 745-8811. This storefront eatery offers health conscious food to suit the active, outdoorsy lifestyle of locals and visitors to this White Mountains enclave. Breakfast options range from "Power Smoothies," such as the "Brain Booster" to wraps and sandwiches, including the "Protein Starter" of lox, two eggs, tomatoes, and cheddar cheese on bread or a bagel. Panini sandwiches dominate at lunch and include numerous vegetarian options. But Half Baked has its indulgent side as well—with muffins, lava cakes, big cupcakes, and fruit and cream pies. Many of the desserts are gluten free, as are a number of the heat-and-serve takeout entrees, including eggplant parmesan and chicken pot pie.

Harman's Cheese & Country Store, 1400 Rte. 117, Sugar Hill; (603) 823-8000; www.harmanscheese.com. Located in an

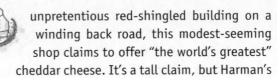

unpretentious red-shingled building on a winding back road, this modest-seeming shop claims to offer "the world's greatest" cheddar cheese. It's a tall claim, but Harman's cheddar, which is made for them in New York, uses only rich "first grass vintage" milk that is known for its sweet flavor. The cheeses are aged at least two years and sometimes up to three. Current owners, mother-and-daughter team Maxine and Brenda Aldrich, are so sure of their product that they sell it right alongside some of the region's other notable cheeses, including **Grafton Village** cheddar (p. 161) and **Crowley Cheese** (p. 128). The shop also stocks a variety of other local products including pickles, honey, mustards, jellies, and smoked meats from **Fox Country Smoke House** (p. 298).

Landaff Creamery, 546 Mill Brook Rd., Landaff; (603) 838-5560; www.landaffcreamery.com. Springvale Farms had been in Doug Erb's family for more than 50 years when he became interested in making an artisan cheese. "The dairy industry was going through a transition," he says. "We wanted to move up the food chain. The most important decision was what cheese to make." After considerable research, Erb settled on Caerphilly, a traditional Welsh cheese because "it seemed to fit what we could make" and because he couldn't find an American counterpart that he liked. He studied cheesemaking in Somerset, England, and began production on the family farm in 2009. Erb produces 10-pound wheels of the crumbly white cheese, which then goes to the caves at **Jasper Hill** in

Vermont (p. 107) for aging. On weekdays visitors are welcome to watch the cheesemaking from the windows of a viewing hallway. (You can, of course, also purchase cheese.) About half of Erb's herd of 160 Holsteins are milkers, and the cheese business provides a strong boost over selling raw milk at depressed wholesale rates. The positive customer response to his Caerphilly has encouraged him to experiment with making a second cheese. "It will be a French-style *tomme* that is washed and a vertical mold allowed to grow on it," he says. The point of a farmstead cheese, he believes, is to reflect the land where the cows are feeding. Every batch, he says, has a slightly different taste because of the type of grasses and hay in the diet of his cattle.

Le Rendezvous, 121 Main St., Colebrook; (603) 237-5150. Bakers Verlaine Daëron and Marc Ounis learned their craft in Paris and have practiced it in the little village of Colebrook since 2001. Stop in first thing in the morning and the smell of fresh baked bread will hit you as soon as you open the door and the croissants will still be warm from the oven. In addition to breads (long baguettes, country boules, soft honey loaves) and croissants (plain, choco- late, raspberry, strawberry rhubarb), the kitchen in back turns out beautiful tarts, *macarons,* and quiches for lunch. Daëron and Ounis have a particular fondness for madeleines, which they flavor with bitter almond, lemon or mocha or fill with dark Belgian chocolate. "They are usually just one flavor," says Daëron, "but we decided to make our own flavors." Comfortable chairs and couches invite patrons to linger. "We want to be cozy and comfortable so people feel like this is home," Daëron says. Their neighbors returned the favor in 2009 by launching a letter-writing campaign to help persuade the US State Department to renew Daëron's visa.

Littleton Food Co-op, 43 Bethlehem Rd., Littleton; (603) 444-2800; www.littletoncoop.org. This co-op the size of a supermarket has been known to challenge its patrons to take a weeklong pledge to eat only foods that are grown, raised, or produced within 100 miles. They prove that it's possible to eat well while eating local by stocking their shelves with local produce, cheeses, meat, poultry, and baked goods—not to mention locally produced wine, beer, and ice cream as well as locally roasted coffee.

Littleton Grist Mill, 18 Mill St., Littleton; (603) 259-3205; www.littletongristmillonline.com. Located on the banks of the Ammonoosuc River, this red clapboard grist mill was opened in 1798 and operated into the 1930s. Following a restoration in the 1990s, it is once again grinding flour, albeit with a newfangled electric grinder from 1898. It gets quite a workout creating stone-ground flours from organic grains including buckwheat, corn, wheat, rye, oats, and spelt. Visitors can check out the old wooden water wheel and gears on the lower level and listen to an audio presentation about the history of the property. For a more literal taste of history, pick up a bag of flour, a package of muffin, waffle, or pancake mix, or some steel-cut oatmeal.

Local Grocer, 3358 White Mountain Hwy. (Rtes. 16 and 302), North Conway; (603) 356-6068; www.nhlocalgrocer.com. The epicenter of the local food scene in Mount Washington Valley, Local Grocer is a natural foods shop that morphed into a supermarket and now carries produce from five local farms and sources most of its eggs, poultry, lamb, grass-fed beef, bison, and pork from area growers. The milk comes from nearby Sherman Dairy, and the cheese case is stocked with New Hampshire, Vermont, and Maine artisanal cheeses. Even the baked goods hail from a nearby organic bakery.

Maia Papaya, 2161 Main St. (Rte. 302), Bethlehem; (603) 869-9900. This colorful breakfast and lunch spot demolishes stereotypes about Bethlehem by offering two pleasant surprises: excellent espresso and vegetarian lunches. Mind you, many of the breakfast plates and the luncheon dishes have eggs or cheese or both, but there are always a number of vegan sandwiches and hearty all-veggie salads. Smoothies are made entirely with frozen fruit and juice (no dairy). Ovo-lacto diners should ask about the quiche of the day.

The Met Coffee House, 2680 White Mountain Hwy., North Conway; (603) 356-2332; www.metcoffeehouse.com. As much a social center for North Conway as any of the bars, the Met is a gem of a coffeehouse. For starters, they roast their own coffees (available by the pound, if you like). Not only do they have free Wi-Fi—they even have some house computers for checking your e-mail.

There's good local art on the walls (also for sale) and live music on occasion. Just don't plan on ordering soup and sandwiches. It's a coffeehouse, dude.

Miller's Cafe & Bakery, 16 Mill St., Littleton; (603) 444-2146; www.millerscafeandbakery.com. In nice weather, Miller's deck is a great place to take in the view of the Ammonoosuc River and Littleton Grist Mill with a cup of coffee and a slice of lemon cream pie or a chocolate gob cookie. Any time of year, the congenial cafe is a good bet for a muffin or scone for breakfast or a salad, bowl of soup or specialty flip bread sandwich (filled with pot roast, lamb, chicken, or vegetables) for lunch. Move fast if you want a slice of fruit pie. "We can hardly get them from the oven to the table," says server Donna Leavitt. Miller's is not open for dinner, but fills the evening void with a case of prepared dishes to heat and serve at home including meat loaf, sausage lasagna, chicken and biscuits, and shepherd's pie. Stop in on a Friday and you might score one of the bakery's very popular macaroons. See Miller's recipe for **Carrot Apple Thyme Soup** on p. 350.

Mount Washington Homebrew Supply, 678 Meadow St., Littleton; (603) 444-8803; www.brewbyyou.com. Located inside the Agway store at the edge of town, this home-brew supply store has all the gear and most of the ingredients any home brewer could ask, including canned and crystal malt, ground malted grains, and several varieties of hops as whole flowers or extracts. You can also purchase amber and clear glass bottles in a few sizes and good old-fashioned crown cap tabletop bottlers.

Saladino's Italian Market, 152 Main St., Gorham; (603) 466-2520; www.saladinositalianmarket.com. Saladino's bills itself as "a taste of Italy in the White Mountains," and the little storefront has about as broad a selection of Italian and Italian-American foodstuffs as you'll find north of the notches. It is a good place to purchase olive oil or vinegar in bulk, Italian cheeses and Italian-style cold cuts, dried pastas imported from Italy, and the shop's own marinara and caponata sauce, marinated mushrooms and artichokes, and olive spread. Saladino's very popular biscotti come in a range of intriguing flavors, including lemon pine nut, apricot ginger, almond anisette, and chocolate amaretto. If shopping makes you hungry, the shop serves soups, paninis, and pizza at lunchtime.

Tuckerman Brewing Co., 64 Hobbs St., Conway; (603) 447-5400; www.tuckermanbrewing.com. Tuckerman Ravine is, of course, a famous summer and fall hiking destination in the White Mountains. It is also a mecca for spring skiers seeking some of the edgiest thrills available in the East. Kirsten Neves and Nik Stanciu came to ski in 1998 and could not bear the thought of leaving. So they started a brewery, which now produces about 5,000 barrels per year. And the pair is still in Conway—thanks to their American Pale Ale, their Headwall Alt (a German-style brown ale), and their 6288 American Style Stout. (That's the height in feet of Mount Washington, in case you wondered.) Mount Washington Valley hikers and skiers drink up most of the production, although it is shipped elsewhere in New England. Once a week, Tuckerman lets people in for a brewery tour.

Wendle's Delicatessen, Cafe, and Then Some!, 297 Main St., Franconia; (603) 823-5141; http://wendlesdeli.com. Soups, sandwiches, and salads are the forte of Wendle's, which serves breakfast and lunch and does a monster business in take-out food. If you'd prefer not to eat in the car, there are a few indoor tables as well. Some of the sandwich spreads (like homemade roasted garlic mayo) are also available by the pound.

White Mountain Cider Co., Rte. 302, Glen; (603) 383-9061; www.whitemountaincider.com. This roadside complex includes a white clapboard farmhouse converted into a small restaurant and a large vertical-planked barn that functions as a store and deli. The small building tucked between the two is the cider mill, and it's central to the business here. You can also pick up a range of sweet baked goods, ready-to-heat dinners, and grilled panini sandwiches at the store and deli, but the cider doughnuts are the real draw. If you want to attempt replicating the magic at home, pick up a bag of apple cider doughnut mix.

Farmstands & Pick Your Own

Meadowstone Farm, 809 Brook Rd., Bethlehem; (603) 444-0786; www.meadowstonenh.com. A lot of customers drive the 1.5 miles from Route 302 to Meadowstone just so they can bring their kids to see real live goats and chickens. Tim Wennrich encourages visitors to walk around and get a feel for the place. There's a large shed-style farmstand at one end of the driveway where customers can select pre-picked produce, fresh eggs, and the farm's own goat cheese, then pay by the honor system. If you need help, there's a little walkie-talkie radio to call for assistance. The farm also grows herbs in a large greenhouse where you can snip your own selections.

Sherman Farm, 2679 E. Conway Rd., East Conway; (603) 939-2412; www.shermanfarmnh.com. One of the more diversified farms in the North Country, this family operation includes nearly 60 acres of row crops, a small herd of beef cattle, milking cattle, and a few dozen pigs. The family even hauls and delivers milk in glass bottles. The extensive farmstand carries their vegetables, meat, and milk as well as products from nearby farms. They also bake fresh breads on the weekends.

Farmers' Markets

Berlin Farmers' Market, Mechanic St., Berlin. Thu from 3 to 6 p.m., late June to mid-September.

Bethlehem Farmers' Market, Main St., Bethlehem. Sat from 10 a.m. to 2 p.m., May through October.

Campton Farmers' Market, off exit 28, Rte. 49, Campton. Fri from 3 to 6 p.m., late May to early October.

Colebrook Farmers' Market, Main St., Colebrook. Fri from 8 a.m. to noon, July through October.

Jackson Farmers' Market, next to Snowflake Inn Field, Jackson. Sat from 9 a.m. to 1 p.m., late June through October.

Lancaster Farmers' Market, Centennial Park, Lancaster. Sat from 9 a.m. to noon, May through October.

Lisbon Farmers' Market, N. Main St. (Rte. 302), Lisbon. Sat from 9 a.m. to noon, mid-June to early October.

Littleton Farmers' Market, Senior Center, 77 River Glen Lane, Littleton. Sun from 10 a.m. to 2 p.m., mid-June to early October.

Whitefield Farmers' Market, On the Common, Whitefield. Fri from 3 to 6 p.m., mid-June to early October.

Food Events

Annual Chocolate Festival, www.mwvskitouring.org. The Mount Washington Valley Ski Touring & Snowshoe Foundation counts on good snow cover by late February when participants follow the trails to a series of "chocolate stops," where they might indulge in cookies, brownie sundaes, chocolate-dipped strawberries and more.

Chili Challenge, www.watervillevalley.com. The folks in Waterville Valley look forward to winter at this October competition to select the best bowl of chili, a staple of hearty ski country cuisine. The annual event at Town Square also features live music.

Chowderfest, www.watervillevalley.com. Visitors get a chance to sample chowders from local restaurants and cast their votes for the recipient of the "Golden Clam" award. The late May event takes place at Waterville Valley's Town Square.

Lancaster Fair, www.lancasterfair.com. This classic agricultural fair has been held over Labor Day weekend for more than 140 years and features baking and pie-eating contests along with horse and tractor pulls, 4-H exhibitions, midway rides, and entertainment.

New England Brewfest, www.nebrewfest.com. New England's microbrewery scene has matured in recent years. About 20 gather for this one-day event held in late June at the Lincoln Village Shops in Lincoln, giving festival-goers a chance to sample and compare their products.

Oktoberfest, www.loonmountain.com. Loon Mountain in Lincoln is the site of this weekend event in early August that celebrates the fall season with German music, beer, and food, including bratwurst, knockwurst, sauerkraut, and strudel.

Lakes Region

New Hampshire's largest lake, Winnipesaukee, and scores of smaller ones nestle in a broad belt beneath the bulging belly of the White Mountains. Agriculture and animal husbandry figure less prominently in this area than perhaps any other part of Vermont and New Hampshire. In the early decades of the 19th century, many farmers abandoned this hardscrabble glacial till in favor of more easily plowed and more fertile lands on the western frontier. The dominant industry, if there is one, is leisure. As early as the 1850s, trains and steamboats brought rusticators to the Lakes Region, and even today, many New Englanders flock here to spend summer at the lake.

As a result, there are very few large farmstands in the Lakes Region, but many farmers' markets. Dining tends to be a casual affair, carried on alfresco whenever possible. Winnipesaukee, in particular, is so large that there is an experience for every taste—and a restaurant to match—from honky-tonk Weirs Beach to family-friendly Meredith to genteel Wolfeboro.

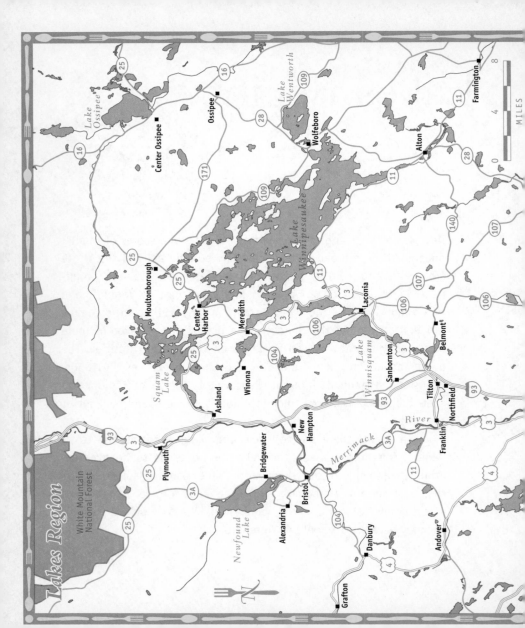

Lakes Region

White Mountain National Forest

Lake Ossipee

25

16

16

25

Center Ossipee

171

Ossipee

28

16

Lake Wentworth

109

Wolfeboro

11

Alton

28

11

Farmington

11

140

107

Lake Winnipesaukee

109

Moultonborough

25

25

Center Harbor

Meredith

3

3

106

Laconia

107

106

106

Squam Lake

3

Winona

104

Lake Winnisquam

Sanbornton

3

Belmont

107

Ashland

25

3

93

Tilton

Northfield

93

Plymouth

3

93

New Hampton

Bridgewater

Merrimack River

3A

Franklin

3

25

3A

Bristol

Alexandria

104

Danbury

4

Andover

11

4

Newfound Lake

Grafton

N

MILES

0   4   8

Camp, 298 Daniel Webster Hwy., Meredith; (603) 279-3003; www .thecman.com; $$. Part of the **Common Man** empire (p. 221), Camp is ensconced in a fully modern building in the Mill Falls complex but is decorated to look like an old-time New Hampshire lake camp. The tin roof, fieldstone fireplace, peeled wood details, and big pine tables manage to evoke an imaginary past, and, to a great extent, the food is the kind of summer fare that mom or the camp counselors used to make, including mac and cheese, pot roast, and even s'mores for dessert. It's a great place for old-timers to regale the grandkids with tales of how it really was way back when.

Common Man Ashland, 60 Main St., Ashland; (603) 968-7030; www.thecman.com; $$. The original restaurant of the **Common Man** group (p. 221) retains its droll, folksy New Hampshire character along with a rarely altered menu of simple comfort food. The hoary monologue of not-very-funny jokes that plays in the rest rooms is part of the lore of the place. It certainly encourages you to get back to the dining room in a hurry. Like the rest of the Common Men, it serves well-executed familiar food.

Coe House, Rte. 25B at Senters Market, Center Harbor; (603) 253-8617; www.coehousenh.com; $$$. Coe House might be unique in the Lakes Region, as it is an authentic historic building and the small shopping center that surrounds it is a recent encrustation. The big Victorian house has dining rooms on two levels, each with a different decor, and a single-table dining aerie in the cupola reached via a steep, narrow staircase. With incredible 360-degree views, it's perfect for a romantic dinner (think marriage proposal). Note that the restaurant tacks on a 30 percent tip for staff who have to carry the food up those precarious stairs. Other tables offer more elbow room to savor the beautifully plated American bistro fare with some nice touches. The pan-seared tuna with braised bok choy is graced with the kitchen's own tomato-ginger jam, for example. With so many of the Winnipesaukee restaurants going for the breezy, casual approach, Coe House is a soothing alternative for fine dining where you can get dressed up to eat.

Hart's Turkey Farm Restaurant, Junction Rtes. 3 and 104, Meredith; (603) 279-6212; www.hartsturkeyfarm.com; $$. The Lakes Region's king of family dining has been serving turkey dinners here since 1954, and while they don't raise their own turkeys anymore, there are more turkey dishes than you can shake a drumstick at. That includes the classic with sliced meat, gravy, stuffing, and cranberry sauce, as well as turkey tempura, fried turkey nuggets with duck sauce, turkey livers sautéed with bacon and onions, and bowls of turkey chili and turkey vegetable soup. The menu also nods to steaks, chops, and ham as well as fried and broiled seafood, but most diners come for the gobbler.

Inn on Newfound Lake, 1030 Mayhew Tpk., Bridgewater; (603) 744-9111 or (800) 745-7990 for room reservations; www.newfound lake.com; $$$. The 28-room lakeside inn welcomes guests all year, but the restaurant may be at its best in the summer when you can dine outdoors at one end of the grand wraparound porch. The menu is perfect for families, as it runs the gamut from elegant (grilled filet mignon, salmon and asparagus in puff pastry) to more casual items like grilled meat loaf, a burger with fries, and fresh pasta tossed with cheese, prosciutto, and seasonal vegetables.

Kitchen Cravings, 15 Airport Rd., Gilford; (603) 528-0001; www .kitchencravingsnh.com; $$. Despite the peculiar airport location, Kitchen Cravings has earned an almost fanatical following among Lakes Region folk for bold breakfast plates (puffy soufflé-style omelets, eggs nested in bread and grilled . . .) as well as salads, chowders, and burgers. The kitchen prepares no fewer than 11 variations of eggs Benedict as well as a very popular lobster macaroni and cheese. The walls covered with nostalgic photos of lakeside summer fun make Kitchen Cravings seem like it's been around for generations.

Lago, 1 Rte. 25, Meredith; (603) 279-2253; www.thecman.com; $$. This Meredith collaboration between the Common Man folk and the Inn at Bay Point departs from the usual Common Man menus to emulate summer-at-the-lake Italian style—as if Winnipesaukee were Lake Como. The Italian dishes lean more to northern and central Italy, which translates as lots of light salad vegetables and roasted meats and fish. One of the tastier dishes that works especially well with Granite State provender is the risotto with apple and bacon. A special pleasure of dining at Lago is sitting outside on the dockside deck sipping a Campari and soda while wrapped mysteriously in Gucci sunglasses.

Lakehouse Grille, Church Landing, Meredith; (603) 279-5221; www.thecman.com; $$$. The name is a little misleading—this superb grill is located inside a modern events and functions building that is part of the Inns & Spas at Mill Falls complex. The Adirondack-style decor, however, emulates the name, and the food is modern American steak-house fare. Apparently believing that good things come in threes, the restaurant offers a tuna trio appetizer of sashimi with jasmine rice, seared with green onion salad, and tartare with corn chips. Keeping with the theme, the duck trio entree includes a spiced breast, a confit leg, and *foie gras*. The wine list is strong on California Cabernet Sauvignon. The polished bar is a great place to nurse an afternoon drink.

Main Street Station, 105 Main St., Plymouth; (603) 536-7577; $. Even die-hard patrons of Main Street Station are a little confused about its origins, as the decor suggests a past life as a railroad car. Truth is, the front section of this venerable (since 1946) dining establishment just across the street from Plymouth State University is a Worcester Lunch Car Co. vehicle, #793 to be exact. It retains its lunch-counter stool seating and booths along the front windows. Breakfast is the main dish of the day and you can almost imagine the waitresses calling out "Adam and Eve on a raft—wreck 'em!" for an order of scrambled eggs and toast. A few evenings a week the diner also serves dinner with such classics as country-fried steak or liver and onions.

O Steaks & Seafood, Lake Opechee Inn and Spa, 62 Doris Ray Court, Lakeport; (603) 524-9373; www.opecheeinn.com; $$$. The location on the shore of Lake Opechee at the edge of town is unbeatable. In fact, there's even a nice outdoor covered patio for alfresco dining with lake views. True to its name, the restaurant features steaks, chops, ribs, and racks of lamb, along with a more limited selection of seafood. Best bets, honestly, are the meats. Should you feel the need for a little surf with the turf, all the steaks can be garnished with a crab cake or with lobster, asparagus, and hollandaise sauce.

The Restaurant 03894 INC, 37 N. Main St., Wolfeboro: (603) 569-3000; www.therestaurant03894.com; $$. Wolfeboro dining has traditionally been very schizophrenic—either beachy fried food or über-traditional Continental fare. But dining's new millennium arrived with The Restaurant and its snappy New American fare and emphasis on fresh, local food and regional microbrews. The dishes are simple—grilled pork tenderloin with peaches and a house-made bacon chutney, for example—and the prices are low by summer resort standards.

Route 104 Diner, 752 Rte. 104, New Hampton; (603) 744-0120; www.thecman.com; $. Sometimes known as "Bobby's Girl Diner," this recent diner entry from the Common Man group shares the menu and the 1950s theme decor with the ever-popular **Tilt'n Diner** (see below).

Tilt'n Diner, 61 Laconia Rd., Laconia; (603) 286-2204; www .thecman.com; $. Alex Ray planted his first diner here in Tilton in 1992 and it's been the prototype for the Common Man diners that have followed. Part of the structure is a genuine circa-1952 dining car, but subsequent additions have almost dwarfed it. The decor owes more to the *Happy Days* television show and several Hollywood movies than to authentic New England diners, but the grill-based breakfast fare (eggs, french toast, pancakes) is reliable, and regulars swear by the macaroni and cheese and the meat-loaf plates. On Wednesday evening in the summer, local classic-car aficionados bring their rides to the diner for Cruise Night.

Union Diner, 1331 Union Ave., Laconia; (603) 524-6744; www .theuniondiner.com; $. Sort of the anti-Common Man, this ancient diner with 6 booths and 17 stools has been engulfed by a strip-mall building. In addition to all the grill classics, it also serves surprisingly sophisticated soups (lobster stew or turkey barley soup, for example) and usually features a couple of fruit and at least one custard pie. If the diner gets crowded, there's an attached dining

THE COMMON TOUCH

CIA-trained cook Alex Ray probably had no idea that he was launching an empire when he opened the first Common Man restaurant in Ashland in 1972. Spurred by enthusiastic response, the chain has evolved into 18 restaurants, two inns, a company store, and a movie theater. We imagine the business plan goes something like this: If you build them, they will come. The formula remains pretty much the same today as it was at the beginning: decor that evokes nostalgia for simpler times, lots of food that grandma used to make, and a few Big Night Out dishes like roast prime rib, rack of lamb, and baked stuffed shrimp. Comfort food faves remain the baked mac and cheese, crab cakes, and the baked apple dessert.

The Common Man has even developed a kind of mystique over the years, especially among young Granite Staters who can't remember a world without it. Ray and company recognized this, and in 2007 opened the **Common Man Company Store** (59 Main St., Ashland; 603-968-3559; www.thecman.com) for fans who yearn for the Common touch at home. This fun, old-style general store has a full line of food products including soup (lentil and vegetable or country corn chowder), rice (wild rice pilaf with cranberries or risotto with mushrooms), pasta sauces, pickles, fruit spreads, and salsas. There's also homemade fudge and complimentary cups of coffee to keep you wired while you shop.

room to absorb the overflow. Union Diner welcomes cyclists during Loudon's Motorcycle Week.

Landmark

Castle in the Clouds Carriage House Cafe & Patio, 455 Old Mountain Rd., Rte. 171, Moultonborough; (603) 476-5900; www .castleintheclouds.org; $$$. The main reason to visit Castle in the Clouds is for the magnificent views, and the best way to enjoy them is on the patio with a tasty lunch. The menu is both hearty in flavor and restrained in style—sandwiches like a lobster melt on French bread, a *croque madame,* or a portobello mushroom "burger," or entrees such as baked chicken or haddock. Add a glass of Sauvignon Blanc and soak in the panorama.

Specialty Stores, Markets & Producers

Agape Homestead Farm, 40 Rte. 16B, Center Ossipee; (603) 539-4456. Kevin and Janna Straughan leave a calculator on the counter so that customers can total up their purchases at this honor-system farmstand furnished with an old stove and wooden hutches stocked with fabric-topped jars of jams and jellies. The Straughans also sell the farm's raw goat's milk, cheeses (including feta and marinated chèvre), pasture-raised chicken, granola, and baked goods.

Bonnie Brae Farms, 601 Daniel Webster Hwy., Plymouth; (603) 536-3880; www.bonniebraefarms.com. There's a very good chance that if you have eaten venison in a central New Hampshire restaurant, that red deer came from Bonnie Brae. Henry and Bruce Ahern have raised the deer on this well-fenced farm since 1994. At any one time, they have from 225 to 300 head, and cannot meet demand, especially from the restaurant trade. It's a good idea to call ahead before stopping to determine if any frozen cuts are available for purchase. Velvet antler (a dietary supplement especially favored in various Asian medical traditions) is usually readily available.

Butternuts Good Dishes, 12 Railroad Ave., Wolfeboro; (603) 569-6869; www.butternutsgooddishes.com. If you don't feel like cooking, you can pick up local cheeses and a variety of freshly prepared foods such as curried chicken or roasted vegetable salad, lasagna or butternut risotto. But the selection of herbs, oils, and spices and range of cookware in this combination deli and kitchen store will almost certainly inspire you to head to the stove. In addition to Le Creuset and Staub cookware, Butternuts carries a range of small appliances and knives, and a great selection of baking pans, including scone pans, mini madeleine pans, and nonstick popover pans. Lots of clever gadgets make for fun browsing.

Cornucopia Bakery, 26 Central Square, Bristol; (603) 217-0005; www.thecornucopiabakery.com. "I'm a nutritionist," says Audrey Pellegrino, "and many of my clients have food allergies. I wanted a place for people to come and relax and have healthier foods." The solution was this storefront cafe in a downtown building that over the years had served as a restaurant, hotel, and brothel, but now features comfortable couches and small tables. "Health is so related to food," says Pellegrino, who developed recipes for a tempting array of baked goods (including many that are gluten free). "People are always asking for the recipe for my gluten-free carrot cupcakes," she says. To make for one-stop shopping, Pellegrino shares the space with Sara Shattuck, proprietor of Blue Skies Natural Foods, a purveyor of bulk grains, teas, spices, and a small selection of products from local farms. On the lower level, a deli offers lunchtime soups and sandwiches and a once-a-month Sunday jazz brunch. Pellegrino also offers cooking classes for children and adults that might range from tailgate dishes to gluten-free breads. See Cornucopia's recipe for **Orange Polenta Cake** on p. 363.

Heritage Farm Pancake House, 15 Parker Hill Rd., Sanbornton; (603) 524-5400; www.heritagefarmpancakehouse.com. This rustic restaurant with wooden walls, doily-topped tables, and mismatched chairs has a relaxed, homey feel. Big breakfasts—pancakes, eggs, bacon, and home fries—are served family style. And since the dining room is attached to the sugarhouse, there is no shortage of pure maple syrup. After the meal, the kids can check out the donkey, horse, cows, pigs, rabbits, chickens, and goats in the little petting farm out back. Open early Mar through late Dec.

Hermit Woods Winery, 56 Taylor Rd., Sanbornton; (603) 253-7968; www.hermitwoods.com. This tiny boutique winery focuses principally on a wide variety of fruit wines (including tomato wine!) made with their own and other local fruit. The signature wine is a tangy, semisweet crabapple vinted from fruit from heirloom Dolgo trees. The young winery, which opened to the public in 2010, also imports wine grapes from California and South America to make a limited number of traditional red wines. Open June through Oct.

Kellerhaus, Rte. 3, Weirs Beach; (603) 366-4466; www.kellerhaus .com. Company founder Otto G. Keller began working in the candy business in Laconia in 1906 and was clearly a clever man. In the 1920s, he figured out how to make ice cream year-round, using ice harvested from Lake Winnipesaukee. The family business relocated to this gracious estate on a hill overlooking the lake in 1966 and is now under the enthusiastic stewardship of Mary Ellen and Dave Dutton, who share Otto's can-do attitude. "We make 101 different varieties of candy," says Mary Ellen, including old-fashioned sugary fudge, peanut brittle, butter crunch, caramello kisses, and sugar mints. They even make ribbon candy on Otto's original candy crimper from 1896. "Nobody makes it anymore," says Mary Ellen. "It has to be cold and dry, with less than 30 percent humidity." Dave makes all the ice cream in 1920s machines and still uses the Kellers' recipes for the fudge and chocolate sauces and smooth marshmallow topping on the extremely popular Sundae Buffet.

Lee's Candy Kitchen, Mill Falls Marketplace, Meredith; (603) 279-5173; www.leescandykitchen.com. On rainy days at the lake, Lee's 40-foot "Candy Corral" is one of the busiest places in town. "Kids love it," says Kathy Fagan, who runs the shop with her husband Gerry. Three different commercial kitchens provide the Fagans with a full range of chocolates. "Nonpareils and butter crunch are the biggest sellers," says Kathy. "We are all about retro candy." But the Fagans don't ignore taste trends. "Bacon and chocolate is a huge item now," Kathy notes. "We can't keep our chocolate and bacon bars in stock."

The Mill Fudge Factory & Ice Cream Cafe, 2 Central St., Bristol; (603) 744-0405; www.themillfudgefactory.com. Right in downtown Bristol, this 1767 grist mill has been converted to a sweets emporium. In addition to fudge standards like chocolate and penuche, the Mill turns out an imaginative range of flavors including cappuccino, maple whisky, and strawberry fields forever (penuche with strawberries and white chocolate). So it's not surprising that there are equally clever "swirl-in" combos available for the homemade ice creams, including kid-favorite "s'mores" with graham crackers, marshmallows, and chocolate chips in vanilla ice cream. If you believe in eating your meal before having dessert, sandwiches, salads, and other light fare are available in the cafe. Fudge is available by mail-order all year or at the cafe, which is open Apr through Dec.

Mountain View Manna, 765 Rte. 3, Winnisquam; (603) 968-7042. Former long-haul truckers Bob and Judith Ulrich now operate a commercial bakery in the basement of their home and turn out about 100 loaves of bread a day. The Ulriches are especially proud of their maple walnut loaves, but other options include oatmeal molasses, garlic basil, cranberry orange, and Asiago cheddar. In addition to 1- and 2-pound loaves, the Ulriches bake dinner rolls, hamburger rolls, French braids, and bread bowls for serving soup.

Sandwich Creamery, 134 Hannah Rd., North Sandwich; (603) 284-6675; www.sandwichcreamery.com. If you want to try the cheeses you purchase from the honor-system farmstand, there are a few benches and picnic tables out front amid pretty gardens. The creamery's cheeses will almost make you think you're in Europe: farmhouse cheddar, French-style brie and coulommier, and Jersey jack (first made in California by Spanish monks). The ice creams, however, are all American. You can dig into a pint of maple walnut, pumpkin or cinnamon with the flat, paper-wrapped wooden spoons that the creamery leaves on hand. Contented cows and goats graze nearby.

Stone Gate Vineyard, 27 David Lewis Rd., Gilford; (603) 524-4348; www.stonegatevineyard.com. Located just two miles from Lake Winnipesaukee, Stone Gate enjoys the ameliorating lake effects on central New Hampshire's harsh climate. Jane and Peter Ellis grow a mix of American varietals, first-generation French-American hybrids like Marechal Foch and Seyval, and some of the more successful cold-climate wine grapes like Leon Millot and Frontenac. The vineyards are lovely, and the tasting room is a handsome operation that bustles with curious drinkers on weekend afternoons. Open June through early Nov.

Via Lactea, 366 Stoneham Rd., Brookfield; (603) 522-3626; www.vialacteafarm.com. Family beagles Abby and Lily make sure you don't come or go unannounced when you wend your way up a series of back roads to the Via Lactea farm store. Both soft (chèvre and feta) and hard cheeses carry the Brookfield Dairy Goat Milk Products label, and in season the farm also makes  both traditional and Greek-style yogurt from goat's milk. All the products are available at the farm store, along with fresh eggs from their own hens. The Brookfield Dairy goat's milk Gouda is a marvelously nutty cheese despite its nearly ghostly pallor. Open Mar through Dec.

Winnipesaukee Chocolates, 53A Main St., Wolfeboro; (603) 569-4831; www.winnipesaukeechocolates.com. When Sally Cornwell and Jonathan Walpole were courting, he learned to make chocolate truffles to surprise her on Valentine's Day. Years later, artisanal chocolates are their livelihood, and Walpole still seems to invest as much care into his candy as he did to win over his sweetheart. (She said yes.) Their principal line consists of variously flavored chocolate bars, including a heavenly one of dark chocolate and crystallized ginger.

Farmstands & Pick Your Own

Beans & Greens Farmstand, 245 Intervale Rd., Gilford; (603) 293-2853; www.beansandgreensfarm.com. Beans and greens are really just the tip of the iceberg at this farmstand where fresh picked fruits and vegetables fill the bins; pickles, preserves, jams, salsas, and honeys line the shelves; and pasture-raised chicken, grass-fed beef, local eggs, and cheese fill the refrigerators. Beans and Greens also has a very busy bakery that turns out molasses cookies, apple caramel nut pies, raspberry turnovers, and an array of breads that are used for sandwiches at the small deli. In the fall, children can fuel up on a peanut butter and jelly panini before they tackle the farm's giant corn maze. Open early May through Oct.

Cardigan Mountain Orchard, 1540 Mount Cardigan Rd., Alexandria; (603) 744-2248; www.cardiganmountainorchard.com. Even if you don't want to pick a peck of McIntosh, Cortland, or Macoun apples, you're welcome to take a stroll through the orchards and select one ripe, red apple for a snack. The orchard actually contains more than 15 varieties of apples, some of which are blended into apple cider. In addition to pumpkin whoopie pies and other baked goods, Cardigan Mountain also offers a few healthy snacks including granola bars, trail mix, and dried apple slices. Open Labor Day to Thanksgiving.

DeVylder Farm, 563 Pleasant Valley Rd., Wolfeboro; (603) 569-4110. This pretty farm specializes in both annual and perennial bedding plants from May through early June. Come fall, it offers pick-your-own pumpkins and chrysanthemums, as well as apples from trees on dwarf stock. DeVylder also makes apple cider in the fall and offers its own line of preserves and relishes, including the old-time New England standby, piccalilli. Open May through Oct.

Moulton Farm, Quarry Rd. (off Rte. 25), Meredith; (603) 279-3915; www.moultonfarm.com. Moulton Farm is the type of place that gives us hope for the future of New England agriculture. The cattle and then dairy farm, established in the 1890s, had been out of production for about 20 years when the Moulton family put it to new use growing produce. The land is now in perpetual con-

servation. The Moultons constructed their farmstand in 1990 and now fill it with gorgeous fruits and vegetables, artisan breads, beautiful pies, apple fritters, and their own jams, pickles, relishes, and spreads. The farm chef and lead field grower even offer occasional cooking demonstrations. Open May through Dec.

Surowiec Farm, 53 Perley Hill Rd., Sanbornton; (603) 286-4069; www.surowiecfarm.com. Though Surowiec Farm sits far back from the road, it's easy to spot the tall, white barn with distinctive green roof. The former dairy farm now grows vegetables, fruits, berries, herbs, and flowers. In the fall, customers can pick their own apples and pumpkins, then stop in the farmstand for potatoes, roasting onions, and squashes, along with honey, maple syrup, and all sorts of salad dressings, pickles, preserves, and marmalades. For a quick treat when you return home with your apples, pick up a package of apple crisp mix and a jar of creamy caramel topping. Open late June through Oct.

Farmers' Markets

Barrington Farmers' Market, Rtes. 9 and 125, Barrington. Sat from 9 a.m. to 1 p.m., June through September.

Farmington Farmers' Market, Central and Main Streets, Farmington. Sat from 8:30 a.m. to 12:30 p.m., May through October.

Gilmanton Farmers' Market, Academy at Gilmanton 4 Corners. Wed from 3 to 6 p.m., July through October.

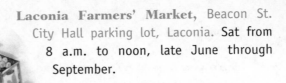

Laconia Farmers' Market, Beacon St. City Hall parking lot, Laconia. **Sat from 8 a.m. to noon, late June through September.**

Laconia Main Street Outdoor Marketplace, municipal parking lot between Main and Pleasant Streets, Laconia. **Thurs from 3 to 7 p.m., May through October.**

New Durham Farmers' Market, off Depot Rd. next to Post Office, New Durham. **Sat from 9 a.m. to 1 p.m., May through October.**

New Hampton Stone Gardens Farmers' Market, 1012 Straits Rd., New Hampton. **Mon from 3 to 6 p.m., June through September.**

Newfound Farmers' Market, Lake St., Bristol. **Sat from 10 a.m. to 1 p.m., May through October.**

Ossipee Farmers' Market, Main St. Park, Moultonville Rd., Center Ossipee. **Tues from 10 a.m. to 2 p.m., late June through August.**

Pittsfield Sunrise Farmers' Market, River Rd. at intersection of Rte. 28, Pittsfield. **Fri from 3 to 6 p.m., June through Oct.**

Plymouth Community Farmers' Market, 263 Highland St., Plymouth. Thurs from 3 to 6 p.m., June through early September.

Sanbornton Farmers' Market, Rte. 132, Sanbornton. Fri from 3 to 6 p.m., late June to early October.

Sandwich Farmers' Market, Town Green, Center Sandwich. Sat from 9 a.m. to noon, May through November.

Tamworth Farmers' Market, Unitarian Church in the Village, Tamworth. Sat 9 a.m. to noon, June through October.

Tilton Farmers' Market, Exit 20 at Tanger Outlets, Tilton. Wed from 3 to 6 p.m., late June to late September.

Wakefield Farmers' Market, corner of Rte. 16 and Wakefield Rd., Wakefield. Sat from 9 a.m. to 3 p.m., late May to early October.

Wolfeboro Area Farmers' Market, Clark Park, Wolfeboro. Thurs from 12:30 to 4:30 p.m., mid June to early October.

Food Events

Belknap County 4-H Fair, www.bc4hfair.org. The only nonprofit 4-H fair in New Hampshire, this mid-August event in Belmont celebrates the next generation of farmers with competitions for rural youth ages 5–18 in areas as diverse as animal husbandry and heritage skills (like weaving rush chair seats).

Sandwich Fair, www.thesandwichfair.com. This early October agriculture fair in Center Sandwich originated in the 1890s and still honors the farm traditions with exhibitions and competitions to select the top baked and canned goods, along with vegetables and fruits, and dairy, maple, and honey products.

Sunapee & the Upper Connecticut River Valley

The foliage in these parts often lasts longer than anywhere else in New Hampshire—a tip-off to the northern region's unusually long growing season. Blessed with extensive hillside pastures, the district also has a concentration of farms that raise meat animals. Many of them sell cuts from their cattle, pigs, chickens, and bison through farm stores. Indeed, several of these farms appear on the menu credits of farm-to-fork restaurants all over New England.

Dartmouth in the Upper Valley and Colby-Sawyer College near Lake Sunapee give the area a cosmopolitan worldliness uncommon in farm country. The presence of large numbers of professionals throughout the region helps support several ambitious restaurants, which in turn help support many of the farmers. All in all, the synergy makes Sunapee and the Upper Valley a very good place to eat.

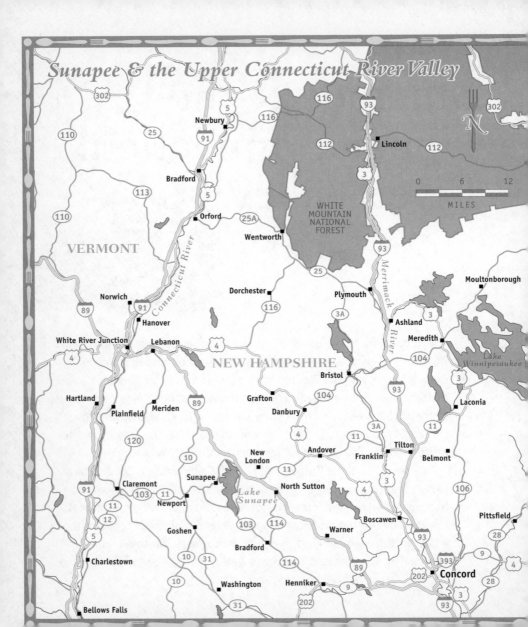

Ariana's Restaurant, Bunten Farmhouse, 1322 Rte. 10, Orford; (603) 353-4405; www.arianasrestaurant.com; $$. Chris and Bruce Balch started this farmhouse restaurant, and in 2011 turned it over to Chef Martin Murphy so they could devote themselves fulltime to their herd of rare Devon cattle. Dining here is about as close to the land as you can get—and equally close to the large open kitchen. In fact you can eat at the bar and chat with the chef. A typical fall menu has a crispy duck leg with butternut squash and a cider glaze, medallions of smoked pork (smoked on premises) with sweet-potato gratin, and pan-roasted steak with a red-wine mushroom glaze. By contrast, in high summer, the menu is redolent with heirloom tomatoes, fresh corn, and bright veggies. Come winter, expect a cassoulet with local veal, homemade pork sausage, and duck confit. Murphy also serves Sunday brunch. It's easy to miss the restaurant, so drive slowly as you get close.

Bradford Junction, 2370 Rte. 114, Bradford; (603) 938-2424; $. The railroading connection at this roadside diner is a little vague, but on weekends overflow diners can grab a table in the attached authentic caboose. This spot just down the road from the junction of Rtes. 103 and 114 is a classic New Hamsphire greasy spoon with hardcore country music blaring on the radio, pickup trucks and SUVs parked outside, and a menu of all the egg, pancake, and french toast classics. We're partial to the Speed Buggy Special: a short stack of french toast with two eggs and ham, bacon, or sausage.

Common Man, 21 Water St., Claremont; (603) 542-6171; www.thecman.com; $$. Located in the completely renovated redbrick Monadnock Mills #2 (1853) and #6 (1915), this Common Man is easily one of the handsomest of the group (p. 221), and has proved a dining magnet for the Claremont area. The menu is conventional Common Man fare—comfort food with some added steaks and chops—but the open, bright space with a huge stone fireplace in the middle of the room turns a simple meal into an occasion. There is also a Common Man Inn in the same building complex.

Daddypop's Tumble Inn Diner, 1 Main St., Claremont; (603) 542-0074; $. A vintage red-and-white enamel diner, the Tumble Inn is grafted to the back of the Bond Auto Parts building just off Claremont's central square. The authentic 1941 Worcester Lunch Car still has its gorgeous blue-and-yellow mosaic floor, the counter with a dozen red stools, and eight wood and red-vinyl booths. Serving breakfast all day and a grill menu at lunchtime, the Tumble Inn is a blast from the past, right down to the heavy crockery coffee mugs and the flapjack specials.

Flying Goose Brewpub and Grille, 40 Andover Rd., New London; (603) 526-6899; www.flyinggoose.com; $. New Hampshire's first solar-powered brewery serves wraps, salads, and some serious burgers (with blue cheese and hickory-smoked bacon, for example) as a foil to a dozen standard ales and another five seasonal brews—all of them on tap. If there's a style of beer you favor, you'll probably find it at the Flying Goose. Moreover, all 17 (and the nonalcoholic root beer) are available in growlers to go. Every few weeks the brewpub hosts a Thursday evening acoustic concert with touring singer-songwriters.

Foothills of Warner, 15 E. Main St., Warner; (603) 456-2140; $$. It doesn't get homier than this family-run breakfast and lunch eatery. A line of wooden rocking chairs and a checkerboard balanced on a barrel hold down the front porch. Inside, each place at the nine-stool counter is set with a big stoneware mug waiting to be filled with coffee. Foothills serves breakfast all day, with choices ranging from omelets or steak and eggs to biscuits with gravy or platter-sized pancakes. The big cinnamon buns, served warm with a sticky glaze, are a local favorite. At lunch, there are also salads and sandwiches, as well as a large kids' menu that even includes fried mac 'n cheese bites. Foothills bakes its own breads, along with a small assortment of cookies and muffins.

Home Hill Country Inn & Restaurant, 703 River Rd., Plainfield; (603) 675-6165; www.homehillinn.com; $$$. **Despite belonging to**

Select Registry of fine lodgings, Home Hill is one of the better-kept secrets of the Upper Valley. The grand Federal-style home was constructed in 1818 a short distance from the Connecticut River banks, and now features 11 guest rooms. Chef Peter Varkonyi reaches out to farmers on both sides of the river for as much of his meat and produce as possible. "On this road alone," he says, "I can count on buying milk, squash, and apples." That's in the fall. In the summer he can also get tomatoes, peppers, lettuce, peas, beans, and corn. He cures his own duck breast, serving it in the fall with sweet potato spaetzle, bacon, pomegranate and pistachio relish, and a duck demi-glace. Varkonyi also offers a Sunday brunch that goes beyond multiple variations of eggs Benedict to include a lobster roll, grilled strip steak, and pan-seared halibut. Some of the same dishes, along with baby back ribs, house-made bratwurst, and a killer burger, are available at dinnertime on the pub menu.

Inn at Pleasant Lake, 853 Pleasant St, New London; (603) 526-6271; www.innatpleasantlake.com; $$$$. Chef-Owner Brian MacKenzie prepares an elegant New American 5-course prix-fixe meal five nights a week at this waterfront inn. The evening begins with a cocktail reception during which MacKenzie greets the diners, explains the menu he has chosen for the evening, and offers them a choice of meat or fish for the entree course. Seasonality rules: The spring soup might be "Essence of Asparagus," a summer version a roasted tomato and onion bisque, and fall a wild mushroom bisque. MacKenzie is also a believer in rich desserts, from a Grand Marnier crème brûlée one night to a dark chocolate Chambord bavarian another.

Lou's, 30 S. Main St., Hanover; (603) 643-3321; www.lousrestaurant.net; $. Every college town has a Lou's—or ought to. It's the downtown bakery–cum–sandwich shop that always has big cookies and sweet bars for casual munching as well as pies and cakes for special occasions. The booths and tables fill at breakfast for simple egg dishes and muffins, at lunchtime for grilled sandwiches, soups, and salads. None of the food is haute cuisine, but it's all well prepared and ready in a hurry.

Rockwell's at the Inn, New London Inn, 353 Main St., New London; (603) 526-2791; www.rockwellsattheinn.com; $$$. Chef de Cuisine Jeff Lewis offers diners a choice of the cozy tavern or the elegant dining room at this venerable hostelry that opened in 1792. Tavern dishes are wonderfully straightforward New American comfort food—everything from lemon roasted chicken or steak-frites to a grilled and chilled salmon club sandwich or rosemary meat loaf with "really good gravy" (as the menu puts it). The dining room menu has a little more polish—truffle oil on the fries, veal sweetbreads with fresh spring ramps, a rosemary-roasted filet mignon with bacon rösti potatoes and a horseradish crust.

Seven Barrel Brewery, Rte. 12A, West Lebanon; (603) 298-5566; www.7barrel.com; $. One of New Hampshire's pioneer brewpubs (it opened in 1994), Seven Barrel leans toward the British side of the beer taste scale, especially with the murky black stout and the classic red. While the strip-mall location might seem a bit odd, it's so pubby inside that you'll forget about the sea of blacktop. The British slant continues into the food, so in addition to the usual burgers and sandwiches, you can always get a plate of local cheeses, a cock-a-leekie pie (essentially a chicken potpie with leeks), or a Toad in the Hole—North Country Maple pork sausage, sautéed onions, and mild cheddar baked in puff pastry. It's especially good with the cleanly hoppy Champion Reserve IPA.

Landmark

Hanover Inn, Main St., Hanover; (603) 643-4300; www.hanoverinn .com; $$$. Simply *the* place for visiting Dartmouth parents and dignitaries, the Hanover Inn has dominated downtown Hanover since 1780. Surprisingly, the inn has eschewed formal dining in favor of a breezier, more casual style in the lounge-y Zins. Executive Chef Justin Dain actively seeks out products from Upper Valley farms and foragers. During mushroom season, he often offers tortellini stuffed with leeks and locally foraged wild mushrooms, for example. He is equally fond of serving roasted Vermont guinea hen with fava beans, local bacon, and fingerling potatoes. During the summer, lunchtime salads are exuberant bowls of the best greens and other produce from the Upper Valley.

Specialty Stores, Markets & Producers

Board & Basket, Shaw's Powerhouse Plaza, 10 Benning St., West Lebanon; (603) 298-5813; www.boardandbasket.com. The in-store kitchen at Board & Basket often hosts visiting chefs whose demonstrations might feature seasonal ingredients or cooking techniques particularly suited to some of the cookware lines or small appliances available for sale. But along with a full array of national and international brands, Board & Basket also features a number of products with New Hampshire or Vermont provenance, such as tablecloths and napkins woven in Vermont and whimsical maple cutting boards shaped like pigs or chickens.

Co-op Food Store, 45 South Park St., Hanover; (603) 643-2667; and 12 Centerra Pkwy. (Rte. 120), Lebanon; (603) 643-4889; www.coopfoodstore.coop. Founded in 1936 in Hanover, this co-op has grown over the decades to serve as a national model of customer-oriented buying power. By 1996, the co-op had grown so large that the members voted to open a second store in Lebanon. A third store opened across the river in White River Junction, Vermont (p. 136), when the Co-op absorbed the Upper Valley Food Co-op in

2010. The co-op carries a high concentration of local products—from farm produce and meats to baked goods and even local maple syrup. Regional artisanal cheeses, yogurts, and butters are all well represented, and the stores carry an extensive line of **King Arthur Flour** (p. 126) products. Staples from brown rice to pastry flour are available in bulk.

Garfields Smokehouse, 163 Main St., Meriden; (603) 469-3225; www.garfieldssmokehouse.com. The sister operation to Taylor Brothers Sugarhouse (see p. 247) across the road cold-smokes some of the Taylor Brothers cheeses along with an aged sharp cheddar. Using both hardwoods and corn cobs, Garfields also smokes bacon, ham, breakfast sausage, and pepperoni. The smokehouse products are widely available at grocers and farm stores in south-central New Hampshire and Vermont.

Haunting Whisper Vineyards, 77 Oak Ridge Dr., Danbury; (603) 768-5506; www.hauntingwhisper.net. It's a far cry from the computer router business where Eric used to work, but Erin and Eric Wiswall realized their bucolic dream of starting a winery in the middle of the New Hampshire countryside, planting their initial vines in 2005 and opening to the public in 2008. At this point, their own cold-climate grapes produce only about 10 percent of the wine. The remainder is made from Chilean grapes. The self-taught winemakers have refined their techniques and are experimenting with cold-climate varietals like Frontenac, for example, to make a Pinot

Noir–style wine. As the vines mature, new wines will be added to the stable. The attractive tasting room can accommodate substantial groups, but the rural location means that it's rarely crowded. Open May through Dec.

Main Street Kitchens, 24 S. Main St., Hanover; (603) 643-9100; www.main-street-kitchens.com. This well-stocked shop does an especially good business in Cuisinart appliances and usually offers discounts to match "big box store" prices on items such as mixers, food processors, and espresso machines. But the buyer also clearly has a soft spot for quirky gadgets, such as the "olivator" to inject flavor into olives or the "cherry chomper" to push pits out of cherries. There's even a deluxe nutcracker and squeeze-style citrus juicers, which are said to yield 20 percent more juice.

Morano Gelato, 57 S. Main St., Hanover; (603) 643-4233; www.moranogelato.com. With its sleek, minimalist design and big espresso machine behind the counter, Morano Gelato would look right at home in an Italian city. In fact, Morgan Morano learned the art of making dense and creamy gelato in Italy before opening her college-town shop. Her gelato is made fresh in small batches every day. Production concludes about 2 p.m. and popular flavors tend to sell out by 8:30 p.m. or so. Be forewarned if you have your heart set on a scoop of pistachio, dark chocolate or *fior di latte*.

North Country Smokehouse, 471 Sullivan St., Claremont; (800) 258-4304; www.ncsmokehouse.com. You would hardly realize it when you drive up to modest roadside North Country Smokehouse, but Mike Satzow claims that his business—established in 1912 by his grandfather from Russia—is the largest producer of smoked meats in the country. Not only does he have a catalog and ship retail across the country, Satzow supplies ham, bacon, and sausage to a couple of cruise lines and innumerable restaurants. In fact, he smokes 15 tons of bacon a week. The bacon is smoked with apple wood, but he is as likely to use maple or hickory for other products. We're partial to his smoked hot dogs, which he modestly calls "the finest hot dogs made in New Hampshire and Vermont." (As close as we can tell, they're the only ones.) All the products (including smoked Hudson Valley duck) are available at the smokehouse.

PT Farm, 15 Petticoat Lane, North Haverhill; (603) 787-2248; www.newenglandmeat.com. If you've dined at a farm-to-fork restaurant anywhere in a 75-mile radius, chances are you have eaten some of PT Farm's grass-fed beef. In addition to cattle, the farm also produces some pork and chicken. Although most of the meat goes to restaurants and fresh meat counters at places like the **Co-op Food Store** (p. 243), some of it ends up in the freezer at the small farm store. It's one of the few places where you can reliably find veal bones and shanks for making classic demi-glace.

Robie Farm & Store, 25 Rte. 10, Piermont; (603) 272-4872; www.robiefarm.com. The Robie family has farmed in the Connecticut River Valley since 1870, and although their honor-system farm store is modest in size, the family's commitment to the land and to their animals is huge. They sell antibiotic- and hormone-free beef from their own herd (including marrowbones and organ meats) and breakfast sausage made from their own pigs. The Robies pasture-graze their herd of Holstein and Jersey cattle and sell raw milk and cream and their own ice cream made with 16 percent cream. Sixth-generation farmer Mark Robie has begun artisanal cheesemaking, transferring still-warm raw milk into the cheese vat and later aging the cheeses on wooden shelves right at the farm. His small but select line includes Toma, an Italian Alpine-style cheese (which is also available smoked); Swaledale, which is reminiscent of a clothbound English farmhouse cheese; and "Manch-vegas," a cow's-milk adaptation of Manchego, a Spanish sheep's-milk cheese.

Taylor Brothers Sugarhouse & Creamery, 166 Main St., Meriden; (603) 469-3182; www.taylorbrotherssugarhouse.com. The maple business is tradition in the Taylor family, though this modern sugarhouse with its gift-shop component wasn't added until 2002. In 2009, the dairy farmers also started making cheese on-site. The Mill Hollow is a Gouda-style, while Evelyn's Jack is a semihard Jack style that gets sharper with age. The store also sells the products of **Garfields Smokehouse** (p. 244), another family operation across the street.

D Acres of New Hampshire, 218 Streeter Woods Rd., Dorchester; (603) 786-2366; www.dacres.org. As you drive down the woods road to simply find D Acres, you might encounter one of the farm's projects: using pigs to clear the forest for planting. This certified organic farm does a lot of things the old-fashioned way, in part as a protest against what they perceive as a Walmart-dominated world. The farmers even allow camping and run a small hostel with occasional yoga classes. In the '60s, the place might have been mistaken for a commune, but the D Acres farmers work far harder. The name of the farm is actually an acronym: Development Aimed at Creating Rural Ecological Society. Ideology aside, D Acres cultivates a garden with all sorts of greens, squashes, eggplant, broccoli, carrots, beets, turnips, and other veggies. Some of that food feeds people on the farm, some goes into breakfast and dinner for the hostel guests, and some is delivered to monthly bulk orders The rest is available for sale from the refrigerator.

Eccardt Farm, 2766 E. Washington Rd., Washington; (603) 495-3157. The farm store at this third-generation dairy farm was opened to offer the farm's own raw milk (available in both glass and plastic) but has since expanded to carry cuts of the family's own grass-fed, USDA-certified beef. The meat is vaccum-packed and flash frozen, so be sure to bring a cooler. Eccardt also has a wide variety of lamb and pork cuts, as well as eggs from neighboring Spring Meadow

Farm and an assortment of vegetables in season. Don't be surprised if a school bus is parked out front. The farm is a popular outing for school field trips.

Poverty Lane Orchards & Farnum Hill Ciders, 98 Poverty Lane, Lebanon; (603) 448-1511; www.povertylaneorchards.com. Something of a throwback farm, Poverty Lane grows a number of heirloom apples for the specialty retail trade as well as acres of bittersweet and bittersharp apples to make great fermented cider. The orchards have a limited PYO operation in September and October. You can taste both apples and cider at the farm store, which is only open from September into early November. You can also find the Farnum Hill ciders in restaurants and a number of grocery and package stores throughout New England. The Extra Dry is a particularly good companion to spicy Asian fare.

Riverview Farm, 141 River Rd., Plainfield; (603) 298-8519; www .riverviewnh.com. Perched on a hillside above the Connecticut River, Paul and Nancy Franklin's Riverview Farm really lives up to its name. Views across the grass and down to the river are particularly striking in the fall when the Franklins open their fields and orchards for apple, pumpkin, and fall raspberry picking. Their farmstand features their own cider and fruit jams, pies made at **Home Hill Country Inn** (p. 239) from Riverview's fruit, local maple syrup, and honey extracted from hives placed all around the Upper Valley. On weekends, pickers can fuel up on Nancy's homemade doughnuts. Open late Aug (for blueberry picking) through Oct.

Spring Ledge Farm, 37 Main St., New London; (603) 526-6253; www.springledgefarm.com. Every New England gardener who has studied seed catalogs all winter while impatiently waiting for spring will envy Greg Berger who gets to plant tomato seeds in his greenhouses in February no matter how much snow is on the ground. His farmstand presents the bounty of the growing season from luscious strawberries in June through squashes and pumpkins in the fall. Berger's loyal employees seem to have a culinary bent and have developed a number of recipes that are posted as handouts near their primary ingredients, from broccoli and cauliflower to potatoes and onions. Open mid-Apr through late Dec.

Windy Ridge Orchard, Rte. 116, North Haverhill; (603) 787-6377; www.windyridgeorchard.com. "We hope you had bushels of fun," reads a sign at this orchard that does, indeed, sit on a ridge with views of the Connecticut River Valley. And it would be hard not to have a good time with pumpkins and 18 varieties of apples to pick, cider and fruit wines to taste, nature trails to walk, and a playground and petting animals for the kids. The orchard's Cider House Cafe is a good place to take a break with an apple cider doughnut or a slice of apple pie with cheddar cheese. All the sandwiches are named for apple varieties, such as the Cortland, a mix of turkey, cheddar cheese, and apple with maple mayonnaise.

Yankee Farmer's Market, 360 Rte. 103 East, Warner; (603) 456-2833; www.yankeefarmersmarket.com. It's pretty easy to guess the main product at this farm. If you don't see the penned bison wandering around next to the driveway, you can't miss the massive mounted head in the shop. That bison, by the way, was named Grindel and he was a pet who died a natural death. The 20-acre farm supports 60 to 100 head of bison and the market also has two other farms not far away. Proprietor Eric Emery likes to point out that bison meat "has three times less fat than chicken." He has a hard time keeping up with demand from New England restaurants, so most of the meat available at the shop is summer sausage, jerky, or ground buffalo. He also sells **Misty Knoll** chicken (p. 47), free-range turkeys, local eggs, and ostrich meat from a Massachusetts farm. Visitors are welcome to walk around and see the buffalo. See the Yankee Farmer's Market's recipe for **Bison Chili** on p. 353.

Farmers' Markets

Bradford Farmers' Market, Community Center, Main St., Bradford. Thurs from 3 to 6 p.m., June to mid-October.

Canaan Farmers' Market, Rtes. 4 and 118, downtown Canaan. Sun from 10 a.m. to 1 p.m., May through October.

Claremont Farmers' Market, Broad St. Park, Claremont. Thurs from 4 to 7 p.m., June to early October.

Cornish Farmers' Market, Rte. 100, Cornish Flat. Sat from 9 a.m. to 1 p.m., May through October.

Enfield Farmers' Market, Huse Park, Main St. (Rte. 4), Enfield. Sat from 10 a.m. to 1 p.m., July through Oct.

Goshen Farmers' Market, Center Commons, Goshen. Sat from 10 a.m. to 1 p.m., mid-June through September.

Hanover Farmers' Market, The Green, Hanover. Wed. from 3 to 6 p.m., June to mid-October.

Lebanon Farmers' Market, Colburn Park, Lebanon. Thurs from 4 to 7 p.m., June through September.

Lebanon Winter Farmers' Market, Lebanon United Methodist Church, 18 School St., Lebanon. Third Sat of month from 10 a.m. to 1 p.m., November to April.

Market on the Green, Town Green, New London. Wed from 3 to 6 p.m., June through September.

Newbury Farmers' Artisans' Market, Rte. 103, Newbury. Fri from 3 to 6 p.m., July to early October.

Newport Farmers' Market, Town Common, Newport. Fri from 3 to 6 p.m., June through October.

Warner Area Farmers' Market, Town Hall lawn, Warner. Sat from 9 a.m. to 1 p.m., June through October.

Wilmot Farmers' Market, Town Green, Wilmot. Sat from 9 a.m. to noon, June through September.

Food Events

Cornish Fair, www.cornishnhfair.com. This family-oriented agricultural fair takes place in mid-August and includes a farmers' market as well as entertainment and 4-H livestock competitions.

North Haverhill Fair, www.nohaverhillfair.com. A baking contest and 4-H shows are among the events at this late July fair that also features live music, a demolition derby, and rodeo.

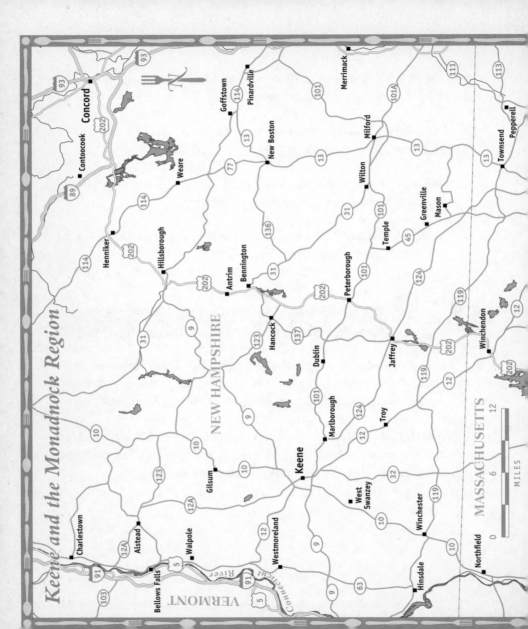

Keene and the Monadnock Region

Keene & the Monadnock Region

This southwestern corner of New Hampshire takes its name from the second most-climbed mountain in the world, Mount Monadnock. In turn, the mountain is named for the Abenaki word for "isolated mountain." Geologists took the New Hampshire hill as a model of an ancient mountain that remains long after its range has been eroded away and applied the term to similar formations around the world. The important thing about a monadnock is that it rises in isolation from a plain. While there are some gentle hills in the Monadnock Region, it too is mostly flat.

As early as the 18th century, farmers began tilling that flat land, and the region remains strongly agricultural. The country folk have had to contend with an influx of urban intelligentsia to the area around Peterborough every summer since the MacDowell Colony was established in 1906, and Keene State College has made its former farm-market town a magnet for scholars and professionals who support a small but strong group of fine restaurants.

The Monadnock Region continues west to the Connecticut River, where some of New Hampshire's most fertile farms are found. In a short stretch, visitors will discover dairy cheeses, heirloom apples, fine country dining, and even a farm-stay B&B.

Foodie Faves

Elm City Brewing, 222 West St., Keene; (603) 355-3335; www.elmcitybrewing.com; $. The setting inside the Old Colony Marketplace may not be the most atmospheric for a brewpub, but master brewer Bill Dunn's skill with a mash tun (the vessel in which the ingredients are steeped before fermenting) makes up for the mall-like surroundings. The standard bearer for Elm City is Keene Kolsch, a light-bodied golden German-style ale with more pronounced malt than hops. In fact, apart from a big, black porter and a heavily roasted Irish stout, most of Dunn's ales are on the light side. The restaurant side of the pub serves both the usual pub-grub suspects and inventive comfort food that complement the ales. Order the grilled pork loin with baked walnut and brown sugar crust topped with a sweet maple cream sauce and pair it with Dunn's American Pale Ale, which has the bitter bite to balance out the sweetness.

Hancock Inn, 33 Main St., Hancock; (603) 525-3318; www .hancockinn.com; $$$. This hostelry has been functioning as an inn since 1789, giving good cause to the claim that it is New Hampshire's oldest continuously operating inn. There's a definite Colonial-Federal air about the place, despite the 19th-century Greek Revival entrance. Fittingly, there are a few old-fashioned dishes on the otherwise New American dining menu. The most prominent of them is a winner in any age: Shaker Cranberry Pot Roast. You'll find a strong local accent to the food. The meat loaf is made with beef and pork from **PT Farm** in North Haverhill (p. 246), the chicken potpie uses poultry from **Misty Knoll** (p. 47), and **Grafton** cheddar (p. 161) adorns the cheeseburger.

L.A. Burdick Cafe, 47 Main St., Walpole; (603) 756-9058; www .burdickchocolate.com; $$$. After establishing an exquisite chocolate shop (see p. 266), Burdick opened a little cafe (how else to serve hot chocolate?) that has swelled to a full-scale restaurant that serves lunch and dinner and has a limited bistro menu for the gap between meals. Lunch includes classics such as quiche lorraine and steamed mussels, while dinner is a little heartier: steak-frites, pan-roasted duck breast . . . The fare is French enough to suggest you are in Paris, or at least Montreal. Likewise, the French dominate the nicely chosen, reasonably priced wine list. Sunday brunch is wildly popular.

Lindy's Diner, 19 Gilbo Ave., Keene; (603) 352-4273; www.lindys diner.com; $. We can't vouch for the claim that candidates who skip eating at Lindy's always lose the presidential primary, but we do know that an awful lot of people just passing through Keene make a point of eating at this 1961 Paramount diner. Both Bushes, Bill Clinton, and Barack Obama all campaigned here. The fare is diner classic—every known variant of eggs, baked macaroni and cheese, meat loaf, homemade baked beans, country-fried chicken, and homemade lasagna and eggplant parm. In a nod to local Polish farmers, you can order your eggs with kielbasa rather than bacon or sausage. Lindy's also goes a little beyond the usual by offering oysters—stewed, fried, or in a po' boy sandwich. One of the more unusual specials you might encounter is New England–style fried pickled tripe. Unlike most northern New England diners, Lindy's stays open late enough for an early supper. Cash only.

Luca's Mediterranean Cafe, 10 Central Sq., Keene; (603) 358-3335; www.lucascafe.com; $$$. Gianluca Paris happens to favor the cooking of three of our favorite countries: France, Italy, and Spain. And his Mediterranean Cafe reflects them all, with Italy and its fresh-ingredient cuisine coming to the fore in the summer and the French stealing the show in cooler weather. His favorite appetizer, for example, consists of crêpes stacked quesadilla style with caramelized onions and brie and sauced with a port-apple reduction. The brie is imported—but the rest of the ingredients tend to come from area farms. Likewise, he uses local lamb for his lamb loin chops dusted with *herbes de Provence* and served with a tart cherry and port wine glaze. While Luca loves to cook those big fine-dining dinners, he also looks after the budget diner. His adjacent Luca's Market, which normally sells ready-to-heat meals, turns into a spaghetti house on Friday and Saturday nights. Pick a pasta, pick a sauce—it's all at one low price. His favorite pasta dish? "I make a Bolognese sauce with dark meat chicken instead of veal. Put it on cavatappi and it's one of my favorite meals."

Mile Away Restaurant, 52 Federal Hill Rd., Milford; (603) 673-3904; www.mileawayrestaurant.com; $$$. Founded in the 1960s by a pair of Swiss chefs, Mile Away almost instantly became the Special Occasion restaurant in this corner of New Hampshire. And why not? The Swiss and Austrian specialties such as several styles of schnitzel were hard to find elsewhere, and classic Escoffier dishes like Tournedos Henry IV (small broiled filet mignons on artichoke bottoms with béarnaise sauce) signaled European fine dining. The Swiss sold the place in 1994, but the menu still recapitulates the greatest hits of Continental dining and the 100-seat old barn remains a major destination. Dishes are priced either as an entree or as part of a 4-course meal. Some appetizers—like escargots, bacon-wrapped scallops, French onion soup, or lobster bisque—carry a surcharge. As you might guess, Mile Away is also popular for weddings and family reunions.

Parker's Maple Barn Restaurant, 1316 Brookline Rd., Mason; (603) 878-2308; www.parkersmaplebarn.com; $. A 19th-century barn with an exposed beam ceiling gives an appropriately rustic vibe to this country-style restaurant that serves breakfast all day and offers plenty of options (pancakes, waffles, french toast) to soak up Parker's own maple syrup. That syrup also makes an appearance on the lunch menu, in the form of maple baked beans and the enormously popular maple ribs, which are cooked for several hours with maple syrup. Parker's is a BYOB establishment, though you might prefer a maple frappé or maple coffee (made with maple-infused beans). Also on the property, the Corn Crib Gift Shop sells Parker's maple syrup, taffy, peanut clusters, and fudge, along with jams and other food products including a large selection of hot sauces. Open mid-Feb through late Dec.

Peterborough Diner, 10 Depot St., Peterborough; (603) 924-6710; www.peterboroughdiner.com; $. This 1950 Worcester Lunch Car diner still sports its exterior dark green enamel panels with creamy yellow trim and a dizzying turquoise and beige tile pattern on the inside. Although the claim grows more dubious by the year, some regulars profess to have been on hand when the diner was delivered on a flatbed truck the same year it was built. In the same spot ever since, the diner is a fixture in downtown Peterborough. The kitchen still makes a soup from scratch every day and offers blue plate specials of open-faced turkey or roast beef sandwiches as well as grilled liver and onions and a chopped sirloin, aka Salisbury steak.

The diner is also one of the last places where you can find grapenut custard pie on a regular basis. The menu for children is one of the most extensive we've encountered, and there's even a small toy section where young ones can amuse themselves while their parents eat in peace.

Pickity Place, 248 Nutting Hill Rd., Mason; (603) 878-1151; www .pickityplace.com; $$$. If Pickity Place looks familiar, you're probably dating yourself. The red 1786 cottage was Elizabeth Orton Jones's model for her illustrations in the 1948 Little Golden Books edition of *Little Red Riding Hood*. Temporal dislocation is the aim at Pickity Place, with its acres of gardens, greenhouse, herbal gift shop, and "Red Riding Hood Museum." Three seatings a day are offered for the luncheon, which includes soup, salad, special bread, entree, and dessert. Every course features herbs or edible flowers grown on the premises, and a vegetarian entree is always available. The location at the end of a winding dirt road only adds to the Red Riding Hood feel. (What big teeth you have, grandma!)

Pit Stop Smokehouse, 1041 Rte. 12, Westmoreland; (603) 399-9010; www.pitstopsmokehouse.com; $$. The smoker beside this small restaurant can be a little finicky in the rain, but it doesn't mind the cold weather at all. So Pit Stop is open year-round and has become something of a haven for snowmobilers traveling on the nearby trails. For a change of pace, try the Smoke Show Pizza topped with barbecue sauce, pulled pork, roasted peppers, onions, and chile peppers. Purists can stick to the brisket, St. Louis ribs, or pulled pork or chicken with a choice of original Tennessee-style or spicy chipotle barbecue sauce.

Red Arrow Diner, 63 Union Sq., Milford; (603) 249-9222; www .redarrowdiner.com; $. The street-level portion of this casual restaurant is constructed to resemble the original **Red Arrow Diner** in Manchester (p. 290), and it has the look down pat: a long counter with stools and upholstered booths in a side dining room. The menu features the same comfort food classics as the Manchester location.

Stuart & John's Sugar House, 19 Rte. 63, Westmoreland; (603) 399-4486; www.stuartandjohnssugarhouse.com; $. The eponymous owners began making maple syrup back in 1974 when Stuart Adams was in the 8th grade and John Matthews was in the 10th. They're still at it, and have added 5-day-a-week breakfast and lunch service to the property. Breakfast emphasizes pancakes, waffles, and french toast—all with real maple syrup, of course—and lunch is big on burgers and sandwiches. In the summer, the Sugar House stays open into the evenings serving fried seafood and **Blake's Ice Cream** (p. 296), including a maple frappé.

Vendetta, 43 Central Sq., Keene; (603) 282-0233; $$. This bar with a great selection of craft brews forces us to reexamine our reluctance to order seafood more than 50 miles from the coast— especially raw seafood. But the use of local farm vegetables and fresh fish and nori from the Maine coast (not that far away) makes for some of northern New England's best sushi. There are also some pizzas, nachos, and the like, but the sushi is the big attraction. We suggest one of the wheat beers to go with it.

Specialty Stores, Markets & Producers

Ava Marie Chocolates, 43 Grove St., Peterborough; (603) 924-5993; www.avamariechocolates.com. When Susan Mazzone and her family moved to New Hampshire, she found that she missed the artisanal chocolates that she had enjoyed in upstate New York. So she took matters into her own hands and started a chocolate-making business out of her home. It's now grown into this chocolate boutique in Peterborough's Grove Village Shops. Ava Marie is known for its pecan turtles with dark or milk chocolate and caramel and for stunning hand-painted chocolates flavored with cinnamon, orange, mint, or dark espresso. It the fall, Mazzone offers her caramel acorns, a milk chocolate shell filled with caramel and topped with a dark chocolate cap. The shop also serves Richardson's ice cream with homemade waffle cones.

Bakery 42, 46 Main St., Antrim; (603) 588-4242. Between Tuesday and Saturday, baker Cindy Crockett creates more than a dozen different types of bread, from French boules to ciabatta loaves. She also makes scones and muffins daily and surprises regular customers with other little treats each day. In addition to cookies, brownies, cupcakes, and a variety of bars, she makes clever little cake bites. At two or three bites apiece, the cranberry orange or mocha cake morsels are just enough to satisfy a craving for something sweet.

Ben's Sugar Shack, 83 Webster Hwy., Temple; (603) 562-6595; www.bensmaplesyrup.com. A preschool field trip to a sugar shack set 5-year-old Ben Fisk on his career path. "I fell in love with it," he says. "My dad made me a homemade evaporator and then later bought me a bigger one and built a sugarhouse for me as a Christmas present." Now in his 20s, Fisk taps 10,000 trees and makes more than 3,000 gallons of syrup a year. He and his several employees also make maple cream and maple candy in the small production area next to the evaporator. In 2011, he captured the blue ribbons for his syrup, cream, and candy at the Cheshire Fair.

Boggy Meadow Farm, 13 Boggy Meadow Lane, Walpole; (603) 657-3300; www.boggymeadowfarm.com. We'll attest that the farm is well named. Every time we have ever visited some of the meadows were half-flooded and the driveway was something of a mire. But we keep going back to get the cheeses at the source. The herd of gentle Holsteins (and a few Jerseys) produce fabulous raw-milk alpine-style farmstead cheeses. The Baby Swiss is popular and widely available in groceries and farmstands. The Fiddlehead Tomme is much harder to come by. A natural rind cheese similar to the French Tomme de Savoie, it is aged at least 6 months and develops a rich, nutty tang. The honor-system farm store also carries a few smoked sausages and some maple syrup.

Central Square Ice Cream Shoppe, 5 W. Main St., Hillsborough; (603) 464-3881; www.centralsquare icecream.com. This old-fashioned ice cream parlor is just the place to hop on a stool at the long counter and order an ice cream soda or banana split or a slice of pie or cobbler a la mode. All the ice cream is made daily and flavors vary with season (from strawberry to pumpkin) and whim (from ginger to gummi bear). Open June through Sept.

German John's Bakery, 5 W. Main St., Hillsborough; (603) 464-5079; www.germanjohnsbakery.net. As the name suggests, this bakery specializes in hearty German-style sourdough breads including hazelnut rye, whole wheat sourdough, and corn rye with caraway. But in addition to the breads, customers line up out the door for soft southern German–style pretzels and for *schnecken*— breakfast pastries filled with cheese and fruit or with cinnamon, raisins, and walnuts. Even more German specialties are available on weekends only, such as apple strudel or chocolate pear cake. German John's also stocks German mustards, vinegars, and honeys and a whole range of sausages and *wursts*.

The Good Loaf, 75 Mont Vernon Rd., Milford; (603) 672-1500; www.thegoodloaf.com. Linda Shortt's artisanal bread bakery is an

example of what might have happened if bakers who learned their craft from the *Tassajara Bread Book* grew up and traveled the world breaking (and baking) bread. The loaves here are huge and healthful—black olive bread, walnut bread, seeded multigrain sourdough, oatmeal loaves, cinnamon buns, and even focaccia. Check the bakery cases for scones and muffins, too. If you have your heart set on a particular bread, get there early before it's all gone.

Hayward's Ice Cream Stand, 383 Elm St., Milford; (603) 672-8383; www.haywardsicecream.com. This takeout-window location carries the same wonderful homemade ice cream as **Hayward's** in Nashua (p. 301). Opened in 2001, it sits at the edge of what used to be the Hayward dairy farm.

L.A. Burdick Chocolate Shop, 47 Main St., Walpole; (603) 756-9058; www.burdickchocolate.com. It can be hard to separate the chocolate shop from the **L.A. Burdick Cafe** (p. 257) at the Walpole original, as they share the same storefront. As the name suggests, the shop holds all those artisanal confections that Larry Burdick and his staff create. Burdick got his own start in the trade working in a chocolate shop in Bern, Switzerland. The firm's chocolate lives up to that heritage with a range of bon-bons, creams, truffles, and other specialties. One of our favorites is a divine piece called Pavé Glacé—a melt-in-your mouth buttery cube of ground hazelnuts and dark chocolate with a hint of saffron.

Morning Star Maple, 1596 Main St. (Rte. 101), Dublin; (603) 563-9218. "We try anything with maple," says Karen Keurulainen, who runs the sugarhouse and gift shop with her husband John. In addition to maple syrup, her offerings include maple candy, sugar, and creams, as well as maple drops, maple caramel corn, and maple granola. For gifts, you can select syrup in a variety of pretty clear glass bottles. Open late Feb through Dec.

Orchard Hill Breadworks, 121 Old Settlers Rd., East Alstead; (603) 835-7845; www.orchardhillbreadworks.com. Noah Elbers launched this iconic country bread bakery in the family barn in 1997, and it's still there—turning out beautiful whole wheat, country, 4-Seed Sunny Flax, French, and olive-rosemary loaves on Tuesday, Thursday, and Saturday. The self-service farmstand–cum–bakery store is open daily.

The Sausage Source, 3 Henniker St., Hillsborough; (603) 464-6275; www.sausagesource.com. If you don't subscribe to the old adage that it's best not to observe laws or sausage being made, this shop is for you. Rick and Kathie Brown stock everything you need for making sausage, including meat grinders, sausage-stuffing machines, and smokers. They also have sausage casings and their own seasoning blends for breakfast sausages; ready-made Polish, German, or Italian-style sausages; spicy Cajun sausages; and more. More interested in dried meats? The Browns can set you up to make your own jerky.

Walpole Creamery, 532 Main St., Walpole; (603) 445-5700; www .walpolecreamery.com. Walpole Creamery's ice cream starts with fresh milk from a nearby farm and the best way to get the true taste of New Hampshire dairy is to stick with the simple but elegant sweet cream flavor. For other local tastes, try maple walnut with New Hampshire syrup, or strawberry or blueberry when the berries are in season. For those with more eclectic tastes, Walpole also offers chocolate and peanut butter, chocolate and mint, caramel cashew chip, and a host of other flavors. Open May through Oct.

Walpole Grocery, 47 Main St., Walpole; (603) 756-9098. More a gourmet shop than a grocery store, this tiny establishment in the same complex as **L.A. Burdick** (p. 257) stocks local produce, local milk in glass bottles, and a wonderful array of local, national, and international cheeses. For a great picnic, supplement the cheeses with a loaf of bread, a selection of pâtés and terrines and some Montreal smoked brisket. The wine and beer offerings are small but highly select.

Walpole Mountain View Winery at Barnett Hill Vineyard, 114 Barnett Hill Rd., Walpole; (603) 756-3948; www.bhvineyard .com. Virginia Carter's little winery is planted with more than two dozen varieties of cold-hardy French-American hybrid grapes developed in Minnesota and Wisconsin and one older hardy hybrid bred in France, Seyval Blanc. The bulk of the juice ends up in the signature Barnett Hill white and blush blends. Her most celebrated wine is a La Crosse white varietal. Visitors to the tasting room get to sample six wines after buying a logo wine glass.

Ye Goodie Shoppe, 49 Main St., Keene; (603) 352-0326; www.yegoodieshoppe.com. Confectioner Jason Smart usually works in the kitchen on weekdays between 10 a.m. and 2 p.m. and you can watch him through a big window. His shop has been serving Keene's sweet tooth since 1931 and in keeping with that venerable history he makes old standards such as buttercrunch, and even Jordan crackers (an old-fashioned soda cracker) dipped in chocolate. He also makes luscious chocolate-dipped fruits, truffles, and cashew or pecan turtles with dark or milk chocolate. One of Smart's most popular new creations is the "Mayan," a rich square of dark chocolate with cinnamon, nutmeg, and cayenne pepper.

Your Kitchen Store, 20 Main St., Keene; (603) 352-1626; www.yourkitchenstore.com. Last time we visited, a browsing couple admitted to us that the shop is one of their favorite Saturday outings. "We can't wait to come here," they said as they marveled over the asparagus peelers, corn strippers, avocado slicers, and carrot curlers. The shop does have a marvelous range of gadgets including the whimsical Joie egg-themed line of breakfast utensils. But this is a shop for serious cooks with a full range of cookware, small appliances, and baking pans. There's a kitchen in the rear for cooking classes and a select inventory of international food products including Spanish saffron, Italian rices and truffle oils, and Mexican and Thai sauces.

Farmstands & Pick Your Own

Alyson's Orchard, 19 Alyson's Lane, Walpole; (603) 756-9800; www.alysonsorchard.com. This hilltop spot is a favorite with apple pickers who are lured by the 50 or so varieties of apples (about half are heirloom)—and the beautiful views. The orchard, which was established on a glacial drumlin by Bob and Susan Jasse in the 1980s, also grows peaches, pears, plums, grapes, and berries. On weekends, don't be surprised to find wedding parties posing for photos while hungry pickers chow down on barbecue from **Pit Stop Smokehouse** (p. 261). Alyson's also sponsors a number of fun weekend events, such as peach and apple festivals, heirloom apple tastings or pumpkin carving demonstrations. The orchards are open all year, especially for guests at the overnight accommodations, and the farmstand opens up in August and stays open on the honor system through Thanksgiving.

High Hopes Orchard, 582 Glebe Rd., Westmoreland; (603) 399-4305; www.highhopesorchard.com. Principally an apple orchard, High Hopes also sells raspberries and blueberries across the summer at area farmers' markets. Head to the farm in July for PYO raspberries, in August for PYO blueberries.

Lull Farm, 165 Rte. 13 South, Milford; (603) 673-3119; www.lullfarmllc.com. The slightly smaller version of the Hollis farmstand (see p. 309) carries the same amazing variety of produce and baked goods. Farmer Dave Ord has a reputation for getting a little carried away. He grows about 10 varieties of hot peppers and a dozen or so varieties of eggplants. But he really goes overboard with tomatoes, harvesting about 80 different heirloom varieties over the course of a season. Customers can also pick their own strawberries, blueberries, apples, and raspberries. Open April through mid-January.

Old Ciderpress Farm, 119 Thompson Rd., Westmoreland; (603) 399-7210. About a decade ago, Marius Hauri, who is originally from Switzerland, and his American wife Angie, bought this old farm and set about reviving the orchard. "Now we have 70 varieties of rare and heirloom apples," he says. The Hauris allow people to pick their own, but the real attraction is the 1870 cider press that Hauri relocated to the property and installed in a custom-designed building. "It's 11 feet tall and weighs 2,000 pounds," says Hauri. "People enjoy watching; it's a little spectacle." While Hauri is scrupulous about cleanliness, he "throws the recipes out the window," pressing his apples as they become ripe, making for a different cider with every batch. "It's like a trip through fall," he says. The Hauris also

HOLDING ON TO OLD-FASHIONED APPLES

Back in the 19th century, New England orchards were covered in dozens of apple varieties. As shipping improved and the food distribution network went national—and then international—many growers cut back to a few profitable varieties like McIntosh and Red Delicious. Many of the hundreds of apple varieties that enlivened New England pies and ciders were almost lost. Since apples do not grow true from seed (only grafting can guarantee the propagation of a specific variety), once the old trees have died, no one can grow that apple again. But many New Hampshire and Vermont orchardists are determined to make sure that doesn't happen. Every time you bite into a piece of their fruit, you're tasting history. Here are a few heirloom apple varieties favored by specialty growers:

harvest small edible chestnuts. "They are very sweet," he says. "We are trying to get people back into roasting them." The farm is open mid-Aug through Nov. Hauri presses cider on an irregular schedule which includes most weekends in Oct.

Stonewall Farm, 242 Chesterfield Rd., Keene; (603) 357-7278; www.stonewallfarm.org. This agricultural education center is a great place to take children, who tend to get a kick out of visiting

Baldwin: Grown in northeastern Massachusetts well before the American Revolution, this sweet-tart green apple with a maroon blush was the first widely grown commercial apple in the US. It remains a popular apple for pies, cider, and eating out of hand.

Belle de Boskoop: A Dutch apple developed in the 1850s, it has extremely firm, dense flesh that holds its shape even after cooking.

Black Sheepnose (aka Black Gilliflower): Shaped rather like a cone (hence the name), this dry-flesh apple is sweet and distinctive. It is a good choice for open-faced tarts. When ripe, it looks almost purple.

Cox's Orange Pippin: Originally from England, this small, dry, rather orange apple makes a pear-scented pie.

Farmeuse: Extremely sweet, this dessert apple is probably a French-Canadian parent of the McIntosh.

Wolf River: Apple fanciers divide on this apple, as it is on the tart and soft side. Individual fruits are huge, sometimes weighing a pound or more. It is particularly suited for drying or for making cider or applesauce.

the sheep, llama, ducks, and chickens in the small animal barn or watching the 4:30 milking (a.m. or p.m.—your choice) in the dairy barn. The farm also has extensive hiking trails and many families like to picnic on the grounds. All across the summer into fall, the Farm Stand (in the sugar-house) has produce for sale, and PYO vegetables are also available.

Farm Stay

Inn at Valley Farms, 633 Wentworth Rd., Walpole; (603) 756-2856; www.innatvalleyfarms.com. This 105-acre organic farm offers 3 romantic B&B rooms in the inn, as well as a pair of cozy cottages and a whole farmhouse where breakfast basics are stocked in the kitchen. Guests can help gather fresh warm eggs from the hen house and visit with the pastured pigs, beef cattle, and cashmere goats. During the growing season, guests may also pick veggies and edible flowers from the organic gardens. Even nonguests can stop by to visit the farm store on Wednesday and Saturday to purchase beef, pork, chicken, fresh eggs, and garlic.

Farmers' Markets

The Farmers' Market of Keene, Main St., Keene. Tues and Sat from 9 a.m. to 2 p.m. early May to late October.

Hancock Farmers' Market, Main St., Hancock. Sat from 9 a.m. to noon, late May to early October.

Hillsborough Farmers' Market, Butler Park, corner Main and Central Streets, Hillsborough. Sat from 9 a.m. to noon, July through September.

Jaffrey Farmers' Market, Old Sharon Rd., off Rte. 202, Jaffrey. Sat from 9 a.m. to noon, mid-July to late September.

Milford Farmers' Market, Granite Town Plaza, Elm St., Milford. Sat from 9 a.m. to noon, June through October.

Peterborough Farmers' Market, Depot Sq., Peterborough. Wed from 3 to 6 p.m., May through October.

Rindge Farmers' and Crafters' Market, West Rindge Common Park, Rindge. Thurs from 3 to 6 p.m., May through October.

Temple Farmers' Market, Town Common, Temple. Sun from 11 a.m. to 2 p.m., May through October.

Walpole Farmers' Market, Town Common, Walpole. Fri from 4 to 7 p.m. May through October.

Walpole Winter Farmers' Market, Town Common, Walpole. Third Sat of month 11 a.m. to 2 p.m., November through April.

 Food Events

Cheshire Fair, www.cheshirefair.com. This annual event in early August focuses on 4-H competitions, but there's always plenty of food to go around at the fairgrounds in Swanzey.

Keene Pumpkin Festival, www.pumpkinfestival.com. Huge displays of lighted jack-o-lanterns are the main attraction at this community-oriented late-October event. But food vendors offer all kinds of specialties—from warm cider to hot soup—to ward off the chill of autumn.

Schnitzelfest, www.schnitzelfest.com. An oom-pah band provides the musical accompaniment to Hillsborough's late September German fest, complete with schnitzel, bratwurst, knackwurst, homemade German potato salad, sauerkraut, beer and wine, and desserts.

Concord, Manchester, Nashua & the Merrimack Valley

The cities of Concord, Manchester, and Nashua share a common legacy of massive redbrick buildings along the banks of the Merrimack River. In the 19th century, the mills were a magnet for manpower, concentrating the population in the three river cities. The cotton and woolen industries have departed, but the mill buildings remain as the characteristic downtown architecture. Many of them now house some of the cities' best restaurants.

Before the river was harnessed for industry, the Merrimack also created a fertile valley for agriculture. When the Shakers planted their first 3-acre vegetable garden in Canterbury in 1795, they

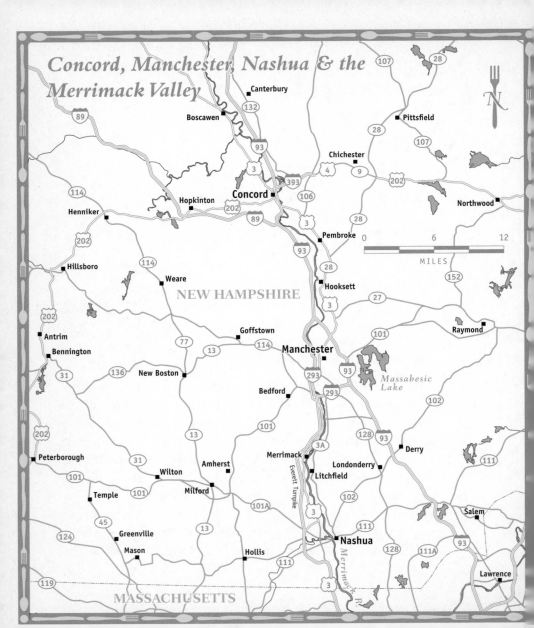

chose the spot because it was productive land. Even with the pressure to construct suburban housing, farming remains a key enterprise all up and down the valley—placing the source of great fresh food close to the consumer. This section of New Hampshire may well have the best balance of restaurants and farms, not to mention nearly two dozen farmers' markets.

Foodie Faves

Arnie's Place, 164 Loudon Rd., Concord; (603) 228-3225; www .arniesplace.com; $. It's most fun to visit Arnie's on Tuesday evening from May through Columbus Day when the Lone Wolf Car Club convenes in the parking lot for classic-car cruise nights. But any time is a good bet for St. Louis–style barbecued spareribs, a pulled pork or chicken barbecue sandwich, or a char-grilled burger, an annual contender for best in the city. Arnie's occupies a 1960s Dairy Queen building and keeps the faith by making more than 60 flavors of ice cream on the premises. Open mid-Feb through mid-Oct.

Barley House Restaurant & Tavern, 132 N. Main St., Concord; (603) 228-6363; www.thebarleyhouse.com; $$. Located across the street from the State Capitol, the Barley House jockeys with Arnie's Place for "best burger" in local polls. As befits a pub favored by legislators—even notoriously frugal ones like New Hampshire's—there is plenty of pork on the menu. Even the crab sliders have bacon, and the pulled pork shows up on quesadillas and on a bun as a sandwich. The pub has trademarked the "Dublin Burger," a concoction where the meat is rolled in cracked black pepper and is served with whiskey gravy, blue cheese, and crispy onions. In case you had not guessed, there's a nice selection of Irish whiskeys on the back bar.

Bavaria German Restaurant, Granite Hill Plaza, 1461 Hooksett Rd., Hooksett; (603) 836-5280; www.bavaria-nh.com; $$. When Chef Anton Berger and his wife Monika moved to the US in 2010, they opened this strip-mall restaurant serving big portions of authentic Bavarian food at phenomenally good prices. The decor evokes their homeland with white walls decorated with copper cooking utensils and a shelf of beer steins behind the bar. The traditional dishes run the gamut from soup (potato soup with vegetables and bacon) to *Jägerschnitzel* (a lean pork cutlet topped with mushroom cream sauce). We love the fact that many of the grilled entrees are accompanied by homemade spaetzle. One of the popular sausage specialties is *Currywurst,* a grilled sausage with a spicy sauce of onion, curry, and ketchup as good as any you could find on the streets of Munich.

Bedford Village Inn, 2 Olde Bedford Way, Bedford; (603) 472-2001; www.bedfordvillageinn.com; $$$$. This picturesque countryside inn just off Route 101 west of Manchester is a quadrennial hangout of politicians and reporters during New Hampshire presidential primary season, but the restaurant, tavern, and wine bar make it a good stop anytime. Located in the multiply-renovated farmhouse of the property, the kitchen is under the enthusiastic guidance of Chef Benjamin Knack, a Hell's Kitchen season seven contender. Tavern diners might choose a duck quesadilla with confit duck leg, pepper jack cheese, and a little side of pickled Napa cabbage as a starter, and flip a coin whether to wallow in the creamy richness of the New Orleans Mac n' Cheese (with creole chicken and andouille sasuage) or the meaty grilled skirt steak with roasted garlic hash. The dining menu presents similarly intense flavors in a dressier format. Do not miss Knack's perfect gnocchi, which might be fried in butter and served with confit duck, figs, and shaved cheese. Knack keeps halibut on the menu most of the year, switching between Atlantic and Pacific fish as the seasons shift. Typical late summer or fall accompaniments might include a bed of tiny beech mushrooms and a mixed tangle of curried spaghetti squash and Jonah crab meat. Upstairs, Corks wine bar serves small, medium, and full pours of premium wines and offers thematic flights to explore the wines of a single region, different styles of winemaking with the same grapes, or seasonal concepts (good wines with turkey, for example).

Black Forest Cafe & Bakery, 212 Rte. 101, Amherst; (603) 672-0500; www.theblackforestcafe.com; $. It's hard to tell which side of Black Forest does the bigger business—the sit-down cafe or the take-out bakery. The food is an innovative reinvention of casual American classics. For example, the "Backyard Barbecue" section of the menu offers a juicy half-pound burger with a side of dill potato salad, while the "From the Bread Box" sandwich list includes a fried green tomato sandwich with fresh spinach and jack cheese. The house chicken salad contains grapes and walnuts. Even the soups are a little different—like lemon chicken with brown rice. On the bakery side, pies are of the amazing, high-rising variety, while many customers come in just for the cookies (peanut butter, molasses, or lemon meltaways) or the caramel-walnut or apricot-almond sweet bars. To top things off, the coffee comes from **A&E Roastery** (see p. 294).

Chez Vachon, 136 Kelley St., Manchester; (603) 625-9660; www.chezvachon.com; $. Franco-American pride reigns at Chez Vachon, where "Chinese Pie" (the Quebecois version of shepherd's pie known in French as *pâté Chinois*) is one of the weekly specials, and more than a dozen different pies are available all the time. Chez Vachon also specializes in *poutine,* the French-Canadian dish of french fries topped with cheese curds and gravy. *Poutine* is available plain or topped with a choice of hamburger, hot dog, Italian sausage, turkey, bacon, link sausage, kielbasa, ham, steak tips, or chicken tenders. As if that were not enough choice, diners can substitute beef gravy or spaghetti sauce for the usual chicken gravy.

The Colosseum, 264 N. Broadway, Salem; (603) 898-1190; www.thecolosseumrestaurant.com; $$. When Annibale Todesca decided to open this southern Italian restaurant in 1987, he made the commitment to shop for fresh ingredients daily in Boston. Fortunately, that's easy from this highway-side location just north of the Massachusetts border. The restaurant's old-country bent is most apparent in the antipasti, including Todesca's seafood-stuffed mushrooms. Marinara sauce appears on the most popular plates, including the eggplant *alla Romana* (panfried eggplant stuffed with ricotta and grated cheese, then baked in fresh marinara with melted cheese). The fettuccine pasta is made on premises, but most others are not.

Cotton, 75 Arms St., Manchester; (603) 622-5488; www.cotton food.com; $$. Easily the sleekest place in town, Cotton raised the bar for contemporary dining and drinking in Manchester when it opened in the Historic Millyard in 2000. All black and white and glass all over, the design epitomizes a certain New American bistro look with all the clarity (and punch) of a martini. Martinis, in fact, are the bar specialty, and if you simply can't choose, you can order a sampler of three small glasses: a Raspberry Cosmo, an Orange Crush, and a Lemon Drop. They're all made with infused Hangar One vodka. Thanks to a nitrogen preservation system, the wine list is even better. Cotton offers 40 choices by the glass, overwhelmingly from California. Chef-Owner Jeffrey Paige offers a delicious menu of what might be called the New Comfort Food—plates like wood-grilled salmon, lamb sirloin with an almond-mint pesto, butternut squash ravioli in a sage–brown butter sauce, and that old standby designed to warm the cockles of every diner's heart, Retro Meatloaf with whipped potatoes and mushroom gravy.

Common Man, 25 Water St., Concord; (603) 228-3463; www.thecman.com; $$. Serving the same comfort-food menu as most **Common Man** restaurants (p. 221), this version has the added draw of an expanded bar, known as Doc's Primary Pub.

Crepes Island, 81 Hanover St., Manchester; (603) 232-0994; www.crepesisland.com; $. "I'm from Thailand and we have crepes everywhere," says Alice Kultawanach as she expertly spins batter on the griddle in her little storefront shop. Her Thai-style crepes are thinner and crisper than their French cousins and feature fillings that are more unfamiliar to Western tastes. When first-time customers order a "Bangkok Delight," Kultawanach gives them a taste of the dried shredded pork that she mixes with corn, cheddar cheese, Thai chili paste, and spicy mayonnaise for the filling. "It's a little salty," she says, "but Asian people love it." We can see why. But Kultawanach also offers less challenging savory crepes (ham and pineapple, or a BLT, for example), sweet crepes (including one with green tea ice cream, strawberries, red bean paste, and chocolate syrup), and several noodle soups. She also serves bubble teas and fruit smoothies.

Greenwood's at Canterbury Shaker Village, 288 Shaker Rd., Canterbury; (603) 783-4283; www.shakers.org/greenwoods.html; $$. Canterbury Shaker Village was founded on this beautiful hilltop site in 1792 and at its peak was home to about 300 people. It's now a museum dedicated to exploring the lifestyle and beliefs of the celibate sect that embraced hard work and a simple way of life. For all who subscribe to the notion that food reveals character (or anyone who is simply hungry) a stop at Greenwood's is essential. Located on the site of a 19th-century blacksmith shop, the restaurant is furnished with long maple tables and straight-back chairs with woven seats and backs. The kitchen prepares the simple, hearty food that nourished the farming community, including chicken potpie, Shaker Fish and Eggs (baked haddock, eggs, potatoes, and cream), and a traditional meat loaf made with ground beef and pork. If you want to bring a taste of the Shaker kitchen home, the museum store stocks mixes for soups, pancakes, and baked beans, along with dried herb mixes, and vinegars, jellies, and mustards from other local producers. Open mid-May through Oct and select weekends in Nov and Dec.

Hanover Street Chophouse, 149 Hanover St., Manchester; (603) 644-2467; www.hanoverstreetchophouse.com; $$$. Posh and polished with tufted leather banquettes and lots of cove lighting, this upscale steak house has the look down pat. Executive Chef Stuart Cameron has the chops to go with the looks. (He also has the steaks—along with rack of lamb, swordfish, whole chicken, and pork loin.) Sides are classics, such as tater tots, creamed spinach, and steamed asparagus topped with hollandaise. The largely Californian wine list concentrates, naturally enough, on the kind of giant fruit-bomb reds beloved by wine guru Robert Parker.

Intervale Farm Pancake House, 931 Flanders Rd. (at Rte. 114), Intervale; (603) 428-7196; $. Built in the chalet style popular in ski country, the pancake house sits right at the turnoff to Pat's Peak and opens at 5:30 a.m. so that winter skiers or summer hikers can fuel up on pancakes, french toast, or waffles with Intervale's own maple syrup before hitting the mountain. For those who want some protein, the Hungry Man Breakfast includes three eggs, two pancakes, two slices of bacon and links of sausage, toast, and home fries. Omelets, breakfast sandwiches, and burritos are equally filling. Intervale is particularly busy during maple syrup season, when they boil their syrup in an attached room. The take-out window does a big summer business in ice cream.

KC's Rib Shack, 837 Second St., Manchester; (603) 627-7427; www.ribshack.net; $$. Barbecue aficionados take note: KC's serves all its sauces on the side. To the initiated, that means that the meat has to be marinated or dry-rubbed a day ahead of cooking and then slow-roasted over a smoky fire. Co-owner Kevin Cornish is an amateur BBQ fan who got the bug so bad that after years of trying to replicate all the classic regional styles, he opened his own restaurant to serve those he likes best. Thus, his pulled pork is North Carolina style, his brisket speaks with a Texas accent, and his ribs have a St. Louis pedigree. The chicken is just good old smoky charcoal-broiled chicken. Add in baked beans, dirty rice, a beany chili, sweet cornbread, and plenty of beer, and you have the makings of a Southern-style pig-out.

Martha's Exchange Restaurant & Brewing Co., 185 Main St., Nashua; (603) 883-8781; www.marthas-exchange.com; $. While the brewery pumps out more than two dozen different ales across the year, the one that's always on tap is Volstead '33, a pale German ale with a slightly bitter finish and prickly carbonation. Most of the beers, in fact, run to the light side. On Thursdays, Martha's Exchange taps a cask-conditioned ale—a smoother, more mellow version of the original beer as it would be pulled straight from conditioning tanks. The food menu is surprisingly eclectic, ranging from bowls of jambalaya doused in marinara sauce to haddock sautéed with a mango-pineapple sauce to balsamic grilled tilapia. For something lighter, there are always salads and pizzas.

Milly's Tavern, 500 N. Commercial St., Manchester; (603) 625-4444; www.millystavern.com; $. Manchester's only microbrewery is the only one it needs. Brewmaster Peter Telge and his assistant "Scuba" Steve Souza heat the brew kettles with open fire, which tends to caramelize the sugars, giving all of Milly's 18 beers a family signature. The tavern is a must-visit for fans of craft brews. Telge's oatmeal stout is one of the best we have ever tasted anywhere (and that includes at a certain plant in Dublin). The caramelization of the sugars in Bo's Scotch Ale gives this high-alcohol version (9.5 percent) a flavor that can only be described as porter meets butterscotch. The seasonal Chocolate Porter has an interesting local angle—it's brewed with black and chocolate malts, and with real chocolate from **Van Otis Chocolates** (see p. 305).

MT's Local Kitchen & Wine Bar, 212 Main St., Nashua; (603) 595-9334; www.mtslocal.com; $$$. Give it to Michael Buckley. When the economy went south and more and more customers skipped a full meal in favor of pizza and a glass of wine at the bar, he overhauled his upscale New American restaurant, Michael Timothy, and reinvented it as this casual bistro with simpler food and a great wine bar. Sure, some of the favorite dishes remain on the menu, such as the seared duck breast and the wood-grilled filet mignon, but a lot of plates change daily depending on the produce from **Lull Farm** (p. 309) or the availability of certain sausages from **North Country Smoke House** (p. 245). The sheer hominess of some dishes—braised beef and mushrooms with spaghetti, or slow-cooked pot roast—could have you lingering over dinner with a nice bottle of red.

Newick's Lobster House, 317 Loudon Rd., Concord; (603) 225-2424; www.newicks.com; $$. The Dover institution (p. 322) opened this Concord branch in 2007, serving all the same coastal classics—baked, boiled, broiled, and steamed, but, alas, without the harbor view.

900 Degrees, 50 Dow St., Manchester; (603) 641-0900; www.900degrees.com; $$. There are other Italian (or Italian-American) dishes available at this sleek pizzeria, but why would you order anything but the thin-crust, Neapolitan-style pies? We are purists, so we favor the Margherita (tomato sauce, fresh basil, mozzarella) but American traditionalists might prefer the House Pie topped with pepperoni, sausage, provolone, mozzarella, tomato sauce, oregano, and garlic. The martini list is extensive.

Peddler's Daughter, 48 Main St., Nashua; (603) 821-7535; www.thepeddlersdaugher.com; $$. Guinness is only one of almost 20 beers on tap at this friendly pub with live music on weekend nights and a deck overlooking the Nashua River for outdoor dining on sunny days. The kitchen turns out classics like bangers and mash and Guinness braised beef stew, but also takes some liberties with the Irish culinary canon in such dishes as a corned-beef quesadilla or the "Irish Breakfast Burger," with aged cheddar cheese, an egg cooked sunny-side up, bacon, and tomato.

Puritan, 245 Hooksett Rd., Manchester; (603) 623-3182; www .puritanbackroom.com; $. This Manchester institution, opened in 1917, claims to be the birthplace of now ubiquitous "chicken tenders." We can't vouch for their claim. But after years of experience it's no surprise that Puritan turns out a lightly-breaded, nongreasy, all-white-meat tender, which is a good benchmark for all others. The Puritan takeout counter is the best place to try them. Purists prefer the plain (served with a thin sweet-and-sour sauce), but spicy, coconut, and Buffalo-style tenders are also available. You can order them alone or as a dinner with fries and onion rings. Buffalo tenders are also served atop a pizza. Breakfast eggs and baked goods and soups, salads, sandwiches, and fried fish dinners are also available. In addition, Puritan makes its own ice cream—including Baklava, which is flavored with cinnamon, honey, and walnuts and honors the founders' Greek roots. Most of the same food is also available in the sit-down restaurant, entered from the back.

Red Arrow 24 Hour Diner, 61 Lowell St., Manchester; (603) 626-1118; www.redarrowdiner.com; $. The last survivor of five Red Arrow diners in Manchester, this location has been slinging hash since 1922. While the exterior is a low brick and concrete building rather than a classic dining car, the interior is long and narrow, with red-upholstered stools lined up at the counter and five booths around the corner. The whole menu is served 24/7, so one member of the party can get eggs and pancakes while the other has a French-Canadian pork pie "just like Meremere's." It's one of the last places actually serving American chop suey. The Red Arrow also does all its own baking on premises, including the whoopie pies (chocolate all the time, pumpkin in the fall, red velvet when the spirit moves). The baker also makes a homemade sponge cake roll filled with white cream, i.e., a homemade Twinkie. You can't beat that for retro.

Republic, 1069 Elm St., Manchester; (603) 666-3723; www.republic cafe.com; $$. It's a coffee shop. No, it's a wine bar. No, it's a Mediterranean restaurant. No, it's a breakfast joint. The identity of Republic may be a bit schizophrenic, but it's a popular hangout from morning into early evening. Grab a latte in the morning, a crepe in the afternoon, a glass of Pinot after work, or a bowl of red lentil stew in the evening. A long list of local farms and suppliers is prominently posted. Republic emulates the great bar-cafes of Europe—the place you go when you're not at home.

Saffron Bistro, 80 Main St., Nashua; (603) 883-2100; www.the saffronbistro.com; $$$. Warm and welcoming, Saffron is not half as exotic as its name suggests. In fact, Chef Joseph Drift turns out solid American bistro food that gives a nod to all the gourmet influences of the last few decades. We had thought escargots would be a hard sell, but the signature appetizer of snails in a creamy saffron sauce on puff pastry is a perennial favorite. Drift's steak-frites plate, on the other hand, veers more down-home American than French, since the hanger steak (a typically tough cut) is tenderized by steeping it in a bourbon–brown sugar marinade and the crisp potatoes come with a healthy side of sautéed baby spinach. The most popular main dish is the linguine tossed with generous portions of shrimp and lobster and brightened with lemon and cherry tomatoes. Diners who want to keep it all-American (and inexpensive) can opt for a bacon-cheddar burger on a brioche bun with a crisp pickle and a choice of shoestring potatoes or onion rings.

Stella Blu, 70 E. Pearl St., Nashua; (603) 578-5557; www.stella blu-nh.com; $$. With a sprightly bar menu highlighted by lots of high-alcohol sweet concoctions and a food menu of salty, savory small plates inspired by a variety of cuisines, Stella Blu covers the culinary waterfront. These are bar-food bites (fish tacos, pita and hummus, buffalo wings) that clearly hit the mark with the clientele. The more meal-like plates are on the "Main Street USA" section of the 30-plate menu, offering protein-intense fare like Kobe sliders, a lobster mac 'n' cheese spring roll, pulled pork and fennel slaw on jalapeño-cheddar cornbread, and a beer-braised beef short rib with a root-vegetable purée. The kitchen piles a lot of flavors into each small dish. The "shrimp and grits," for example, spikes the grits with habañero pepper and smoked Gouda cheese, and the dish arrives with a sliver of crisp deep-fried prosciutto on top. The all-veggie "Farmer's Market" section of the menu has some pretty terrific plates, like grilled brussels sprouts with olive oil and sea salt, and Szechuan green beans in a spicy garlic sauce. (These change a lot with the seasons.) Stella Blu also offers a tweaked version of the menu with 20 gluten-free plates.

Surf, 207 Main St., Nashua; (603) 595-9293; www.surfseafood .com; $. Michael Buckley of **MT's Local Kitchen & Wine Bar** (p. 288) also has a way with fish. At his popular seafood restaurant right across the street, the raw bar ranges from oysters to sashimi, and the entrees represent spice combos from around the world. Scallops, for example, star in a Moroccan dish with couscous, seared spinach, and North African spices. Buckley does a Jamaican twist on salmon—searing the fish and serving it over black beans and rice with mango salsa and blood-orange puree.

Tuscan Kitchen, 67 Main St., Salem; (603) 952-4875; www .tuscan-kitchen.com; $$$. Aspiring to cover all the Italian bases, Tuscan Kitchen makes its own fresh pasta and breads and serves thin-crust pizzas ranging from the basic Margherita (mozzarella, tomato, and basil) to the elaborate Ficchi (fig balsamic reduction, fresh rosemary, fresh local *burrata,* and thinly sliced Parma ham). Pastas are available as a first course or as a main entree. (Our vote goes to the pappardelle noodles with a wild boar *ragù.*) The wood grill gets a workout with meat options, including a grilled lamb chop served with minted gnocchi.

Woodman's Seafood & Grill, 454 Rte. 3A, Litchfield; (603) 262-1980; www.woodmans.com; $$. We know that it seems odd to find a clam shack in New Hampshire farm country. Opened in 2009, the kitchen is under the watchful eyes of the Woodman family and turns out the same fried clams, clam cakes, clam chowder, and other specialties that have made the original Essex, Massachusetts, location a destination for seafood lovers since 1914. The location in Mel's Funway Park, with its batting cage, mini-golf, and go-karts, makes for a nice family outing.

Specialty Stores, Markets & Producers

A&E Roastery, 135 Rte. 101A, Amherst; (603) 578-3338; www.aeroastery.com. You have to love a coffee roaster that just does its own thing very well and doesn't try to overreach. The cafe here is stocked with baked goods from other small area bakeries and ice cream from a small local maker. The coffee is why you come, though. A&E roasts six Central and South American coffees, three African, and three Pacific (including Hawaiian Kona). Each is handled a little differently, drawing out the native flavors. Most are sold in 12-ounce bags. A&E not only roasts coffee expertly; its baristas know how to handle all the variations possible from an espresso machine.

Abigail's Bakery, 352 S. Sugar Hill Rd., Weare; (603) 724-6544; www.abigailsbakery.com. Stop in before noon on Monday through Thursday and one of the bakers will dust the flour from her hands and help you select a warm loaf of bread made from recipes handed down through three generations of owner Jenny Chartier's family. This rustic bakery is known for its whole-grain breads, including anadama, stone-ground honey whole wheat, and cinnamon raisin swirl, a real breakfast treat. Chartier and her fellow bakers also make a number of gluten-free breads using millet and sweet brown rice. Abigail's is a bit off the beaten path, but you can also catch the bakers at the Friday farmers' market in Weare and the Saturday market in Concord, where they also bring a variety of muffins, scones, sticky buns, and eagerly anticipated raspberry almond squares.

Angela's Pasta and Cheese Shop, 815 Chestnut St., Manchester; (603) 625-9544; www.angelaspastaandcheese.com. Open the door to this storefront *salumeria* and the aroma of simmering garlic and tomatoes will tell you that you are in the right place. The kitchen turns out a veritable feast of sauces (pesto, marinara, alfredo), homemade pastas (grilled vegetable or shrimp, scallop, and fennel ravioli), salads (white beans in vinaigrette, marinated chèvre with olive oil, cranberries, and garlic) and prepared dishes (lasagna with meat sauce, chicken with artichokes, eggplant and olives). The cheese case is stocked with more than 50 top choices from around the world and Angela's is generous with its samples. There's also a well-curated selection of Italian and a few California wines.

Barb's Beer Emporium, 27 Buttrick Rd., Londonderry; (603) 425-6480; and 249 Sheep Davis Rd., Concord; (603) 369-4501; www.barbsbeeremporium.com. When we walk into either outlet of Barb's—especially the Londonderry branch with its beer cave—we're reminded that the ancient Egyptians stuffed fresh hops in their bed pillows, believing that the aroma would stimulate amazing dreams. Barb's has a beer selection beyond our dreams, getting in all the North American craft beers and a number of fairly obscure European and British brews as well. Of course, you can always get cases of Bud and Miller for the big game. All we can say is . . . *prost!*

Blake's Creamery, 353 S. Main St., Manchester; (603) 669-0220 and 53 Hooksett Rd., Manchester; (603) 627-1110; www.blakes icecream.com. Blake's Creamery was established in 1900 and now makes more than 80 flavors of ice cream, frozen yogurt, sherbet, and sorbet. The extremely popular ice cream, including such signature flavors as caramel peanut butter, walnut fudge, and strawberry cheesecake, is available throughout the state. But it's fun to stop into one of the restaurants, grab a seat at the counter, and dig into a banana split. Blake's also makes old-fashioned ice cream sodas, complete with a requisite sidecar (a scoop of ice cream hanging off the lip of the glass).

The Craft of Mass-Market Beer

Granite Staters are known for their fondness for malt beverages, which helps explain the preponderance of craft breweries in the state. But New Hampshire is also home to the northeast operations of one of the American beer giants, Anheuser-Busch.

The company's brewery on the edge of the town of Merrimack may be the smallest of its production facilities, but the New Hampshire operation can still produce up to 22 million 12-ounce cans and bottles each week. Free tours give a basic overview and include a visit to the Clydesdale horse stable.

For a more in-depth look at brewery operations, the **Beermaster Tour** ($25, reservations required) takes visitors behind the scenes to follow every step of the process from fermentation and aging through bottling. It also includes a taste of 21-day-old beer straight from the lagering tanks at the perfect temperature of 38°F and more extensive sampling in the tasting room.

Anheuser-Busch Brewery, 221 Daniel Webster Hwy., Merrimack; (603) 595-1202; www.budweisertours.com.

Butter's Fine Food and Wine, 70 N. Main St., Concord; (603) 225-5995; www.buttersfinefood.com. It's hard to characterize the merchandise at Butter's, but we think of it as the shop that stocks what we like to eat and drink. The cheese case, for example, is not only strong on New England artisan cheeses. It also holds a number of excellent French, Spanish, and Italian cheeses. The charcuterie extends from local smokehouse products to wonderful Italian salamis with just the right shade of white casings. The wine offerings are very un–Granite State and nicely suited to the cheeses and charcuterie.

Candia Vineyards, 702 High St., Hooksett; (603) 867-9751; www.candiavineyards.com. Open since 1999, Candia makes grape wines exclusively, though not all from its own fruit. Winemaker Bob Dabrowski runs the daily tastings himself (call first to make sure he's around), and is particularly proud of his Frontenac red and his off-dry Diamond white. Candia is one of the few wineries growing Diamond, a late–19th century cross between Concord and Iona that is very cold-hardy and very productive.

Chichester Country Store, Rte. 28 at Main St., Chichester; (603) 798-5081; www.chichestercountrystore.com. Established in 1847, this country store with a welcoming front porch is too picturesque to pass up. The selection of local cheeses and maple products is fairly limited. But it's worth stopping for the store's own apple cider doughnuts, which are crunchy on the outside and light in the middle. They come plain, dusted with cinnamon sugar or plain sugar, or with blueberries. Best of all is the plain doughnut with a lightly sweet maple syrup glaze.

Fox Country Smoke House, 164 Brier Bush Rd., Canterbury; (603) 339-4409; www.foxcountrysmokehouse.com. Established in

1969 to service area farmers, this wonderfully atmospheric smoke-house in the woods cold-smokes a huge array of meats, including hams, several types of kielbasa, beef sausage, beef-pork-garlic sausage, St. Louis–style pork ribs, and Cabot cheeses. You can also buy smoked beef bones for your dog. And then there are the different styles of bacon. While Fox Country products are sold in many gourmet shops and farmstands, the advantage to visiting is that you can pick out the exact cut that suits your fancy. For example, we tend to buy extra-lean, unsliced bacon to cut into seasoning pieces, almost like you'd use Tyrolean speck.

Frederick's Pastries, 109 Rte. 101A, Amherst, and 25 S. River Rd., Bedford; (603) 647-2253; www.pastry.net. Frederick's is known for its celebratory cakes and it's not unusual to see a bride-to-be consulting with the bakers about her dream wedding cake. A strawberry mousse torte, Boston cream pie, or Black Forest cheese-cake would be perfect for a birthday or anniversary party. Smaller treats such as chocolate dipped macaroons, chocolate Grand Marnier bars, or rasp-berry shortbread cookies are just right for a mini-celebration.

Free Range Fish and Lobster, 885 Second St., Manchester; (603) 518-5585; www.freerangefish.com. This fishmonger is principally a wholesaler of Maine lobster, but since they're dealing with the fishermen anyway, they always have a good array of current wild-caught fish and farmed clams, oysters, and mussels. It's some of the freshest lobster in Manchester.

Fulchino Vineyard, 187 Pine Hill Rd., Hollis; (603) 438-5984; www.fulchinovineyard.com. Al Fulchino is nothing if not enthusiastic. A home winemaker for 30 years, he planted a vineyard of cold-climate grapes adjacent to his bedding-plant nursery and started making wine for sale in 2010. Al calls it a boutique winery, but it's almost the definition of a garage winery. Production takes place mostly in carboys in a small building literally steps from the vines. Fulchino makes two dozen different wines. Only a few are varietals—the rest are proprietary blends that he will not reveal. There's no worry about Fulchino wines seeing too much oak. They're bottled as soon as the fermentation finishes and offered for sale. Oddly enough, although he breaks many of the rules of fine wine-making, Fulchino makes some very interesting wines.

Granite State Candy Shoppe & Ice Cream, 13 Warren St., Concord; (603) 225-2591; www.nhchocolates.com. Not surprisingly, chocolate ice cream rises to new heights at the ice cream counter of this third-generation candy maker. Among the 30 or so flavors, look for chocolate chocolate chip, chocolate Scooby-Doo (chocolate ice cream flavored with peanut butter and swirled with peanut butter sauce), and ultra chocolate (with a double dose of Dutch cocoa and dark chocolate). One of the most popular ice creams, the coconut snowflake, is modeled on the classic chocolate-dipped coconut candy. Other favorites from the candy counter include almond butter crunch, cashew and pecan caramel patties, almond and peanut nut clusters, peppermint patties, and cordial cherries. For the kids? Chocolate-dipped Twinkies.

Hayward's Ice Cream, 7 Daniel Webster Hwy., Nashua; (603) 888-4663; www.haywardsicecream.com. This small dairy operation opened its first ice cream stand window in 1940, then had to move the shop back 100 feet to make room for more parking in 1942. Some of the flavors have changed, but Hayward's has been Nashua's favorite ice cream ever since. The stand also has grilled burgers and steamed hot dogs, but the cold, sweet stuff is the main attraction. FYI, Hayward's uses 1.5 tons of jimmies per year. Open Valentine's Day through Columbus Day.

Jacques Fine European Pastries, 128 Main St., Suncook; (603) 485-4035; www.jacquespastries.com. If you can't make it to Paris, stop in this Suncook shop for a gorgeous French-style plated dessert that would be right at home in a patisserie in the City of Light. Although husband-and-wife team Jacques and Paula Despres are best known for stunning cakes that often star in magazine photo shoots, the shop always has a refrigerated case full of little gems such as pecan bourbon tarts, raspberry vanilla tarts, or chocolate passion-fruit pyramids. Son Justin practically grew up in the shop and has inherited his parents' flair for elegant style and sophisticated taste. His own line of handcrafted chocolates includes caramelized macadamia nuts in a white chocolate ganache and Maine blackberries with a dark chocolate ganache.

Madeleines, 124 N. Main St., Concord; (603) 224-5353; www
.madeleinescakes.com. Chef Paul Brown is a stickler for tradition.
"We stick to the older methods, the old-style recipes," he says as he sweeps his hand over display cases filled with quiches, croissants, and beautiful small desserts. He's particularly proud of the Mogador, a chocolate raspberry confection. "It's the best seller here and at Dalloyau," he says, referring to the esteemed Parisian confectioner established in 1682. Brown nods to his French Canadian neighbors to the north with classic *tourtières,* or meat pies, and *gorton,* a ground pork spread that he likes to serve with one of his baguettes. Soups, quiches, and sandwiches are available at lunchtime. Brown has a following for his madeleines. "If I don't have them, I'm in trouble," he says. "They are perfect for dunking in tea because they won't fall apart."

Moo's Place Homemade Ice Cream, 27 Crystal
Ave., Derry; (603) 425-0100; www.moosplace.com.
Moo's is locally famous for its ice cream which is rich and flavorful enough to stand on its own. But this seasonal ice cream stand also offers a variety of "Moovalous" sundaes, such as a banana royale or a double fudge brownie. Handmade ice cream sandwiches

might include espresso or strawberry fillings. For man's best friend, doggie cups feature a scoop of ice cream topped with mini dog biscuits. Open Apr through Oct.

Moonlight Meadery, 23 Londonderry Rd., Unit #17, Londonderry; (603) 216-2162; www.moonlightmeadery.com. Operating on the assumption that women are drawn to mead like, well, bees to honey, Michael Fairbrother had been a hobbyist mead-maker for 16 years when he opened his business in 2010 in a two-stall garage. Now Moonlight Meadery has production facilities and a tasting room in a small industrial park. Visitors are welcome to take a mini-tour of the production area and learn something about how mead is made before tasting the end result. "My mother taught me how to cook," Fairbrother says, "so I concentrate on trying to bring out flavors." His personal favorites among the more than two dozen varieties are his flagship Desire, made with blueberries, black cherries, and black currants, and his limited-edition Utopian, which is fermented and aged in Samuel Adams beer casks that he purchases from Boston Beer Company. The finished mead has a rich complexity akin to an amontillado sherry.

Stella's Fine Chocolates, Village Shoppes of Bedford, 176 Rte. 101, Bedford; (603) 472-3131; www.stellasfinechocolates .com. Stella's carries filled chocolates from several manufacturers, but makes all its own molded chocolate novelties, toffees, and barks. The butter almond toffee is the most popular, but owners Lydia Lauzier and Elaine Alexander also offer other flavors such as espresso, maple crunch, red fire, and bacon. "Guys like the bacon," says Alexander. Of the barks, Alexander is partial to the pumpkinseed with cayenne and cranberry, "It's excellent with a glass of wine." Tiny "emergency" boxes stuffed with four chocolates sit on the counter next to the cash register. "Those are for the girls," Alexander says with a smile.

Sweet Retreat, 90 Dow St., Manchester; (603) 641-2251; www .sweetretreatmanchester.com. This welcoming bakery is putting its own stamp on classic desserts like mom used to make. "We use recipes from the 1950s," says baker Lisa Johnson. "But people say they haven't had anything like it." The shop's chocolate whoopie pies are filled with real whipped cream; the Boston cream pie whoopie features a custard filling with fudge icing. Molly Merrick, daughter of owner Joanne Merrick, is the creator of the cream-filled chocolate "Mostess" cupcake and the "Pinkie," a golden cupcake filled with raspberry buttercream and topped with white chocolate ganache. Muffins, scones, croissants, and fruit turnovers are available for breakfast, while Johnson turns out quiche and pizza for lunch.

Things Are Cooking, 74 N. Main St., Concord; (603) 225-8377; www.thingsarecooking.com. This well-stocked kitchenware shop seems particularly attuned to the seasons. In the fall, for example, look for apple peelers and apple pie baking dishes, corn cutters, and food strainers for making tomato sauce. The shop has good selections of Belgian waffle, panini, and pizzelle presses; knife sets in wooden blocks, and baking pans and sheets in all sizes.

Van Otis Chocolates, 341 Elm St., Manchester; (603) 826-6847; www.vanotis.com. Smooth and creamy Swiss fudge is the foundation of this chocolate emporium that was established in 1935 and now features a complete line of filled chocolates, chocolate covered fruit and nuts, truffles, and specialty chocolate bars. Everything is made right upstairs from the shop and lots of samples are available. On hour-long factory tours visitors get a chance to participate in candymaking and take home some samples. Tours are usually offered a couple of times a week and require reservations. Van Otis also offers truffle-making classes on demand.

White Birch Brewing, 1339 Hooksett Rd., Hooksett; (603) 224-8593; www.whitebirchbrewing.com. Moving up from an itty-bitty brewery to a small craft brewery big enough to be viable is a tough transition, but White Birch made it in 2011 on the strength of the loyalty of its fans. For our money, the Belgian-style pale ale with its spicy nose and crisp, dry finish is the flagship. For a pale ale, it surprises with overtones of fresh pear and slightly gnarly esters associated with the Belgian style. The Hooksett Ale is similar, but much more dominated by West Coast hops. The Brewery Store carries bottles of the current releases and sometimes has experimental beers. You can always fill a growler to go.

White Mountain Gourmet Coffee, 15 Pleasant St., Concord; (603) 228-3317; www.wmgconline.com. We pardon WMGC for sinning against the coffee gods by making flavored roasts because they keep the equipment apart from the single-origin real roasted coffees. The roasting style tends to be medium to medium-light, which works well to bring out the high notes in their largely Central and South American beans. The shop opens bright and early (before dawn much of the year) and serves breakfast sandwiches and quiche slices all day. Heck, you can even get oatmeal made to order in the morning, sandwiches from lunchtime until closing.

Farmstands & Pick Your Own

Apple Hill Farm, 580 Mountain Rd., Concord; (603) 224-8862; www.applehillfarmnh.com. "My husband Chuck and I bought this farm straight out of school," says Diane Souther. "We farm full-time even though it's rare for farmers not to have other jobs." Diane also devotes a lot of time to baking in the open kitchen in one corner of the farmstand and usually has samples on hand. She says that her ginger molasses chews are great with a glass of milk and that she likes to blend McIntosh and Cortland apples in her pies so that "you get a good mix of soft and crunchy." She also makes jellies, preserves, and apple butter and stocks products, including cheese, bacon and wines, from other local producers. The stand offers a full range of fruits and vegetables and the Southers also have an extensive PYO operation: strawberries starting in mid-June, blueberries and raspberries starting in mid-July, and apples starting around Labor Day. Their farmstand opens in early August and closes right before Thanksgiving. See Diane's recipe for **Garden-Fresh Peach Salsa** on p. 357.

Brookdale Fruit Farm, 38 Broad St., Hollis; (603) 465-2241; www.brookdalefarms.com. At Brookdale, pick-your-own season stretches from strawberries in June through pumpkins in late October, with blueberries, raspberries, black raspberries, and apples in between. The farm's own vegetables fill the farmstand, along with a small but select assortment of other local products including Valicenti Organico's "Red Gravy," made in Hollis using local tomatoes and basil.

Brookford Farm, 250 West Rd., Canterbury; www.brookfordfarm .com. Mary Brower, the female side of one of the two couples who operate Brookford Farm, exudes confidence about farming in New Hampshire. "We used to farm in northern Russia, so we're pretty good with northern vegetables and season extensions," she explains. The move in 2012 from land on the Piscataqua River in

Rollinsford to the historic farmland in Canterbury was a challenge, since it meant restarting organic certification. The can-do spirit will serve them well as they reestablish their complete operation. Most of the vegetables are sold through CSA shares, though the general  public is welcome to shop for the excess at the farm store. The farmers also offer their own pork, grains, free-range eggs, and raw-milk dairy products. They make an aged cheddar cheese, two soft cheeses in the style of Camembert and Coulommier, a fresh feta, quark, and yogurt. See the recipe for **Brookford Farm Braised Country-Style Ribs with Star Anise and Whiskey** on p. 361.

Carter Hill Orchard, 73 Carter Hill Rd., Concord; (603) 225-2625; www.carterhillapples.com. This family-run orchard and farm store is particularly welcoming of children and coordinates with New Hampshire Audubon for raptor identification programs throughout September and October. Pick-your-own blueberries start in July, apples around Labor Day through mid-October, and raspberries in September and October. There's even cross-country skiing on groomed trails December through March.

Dimond Hill Farm, 314 Hopkinton Rd., Concord; (603) 224-0602; www.dimondhillfarm.com. A working farm since 1827, Dimond Hill sells a wide array of vegetables, from the first greens of spring to the last pumpkins of fall. Jane Presby is the sixth generation of her family to farm the land. She was the first to use high tunnels to expand the season (some of the Merrimack Valley's earliest tomatoes are grown here). In addition to produce, the farmstand carries homemade pies, breads, pancake mixes, jams, and pickles, as well as maple syrup and honey. Open May through Oct.

Lull Farm, 65 Broad St. (Rte. 130), Hollis; (603) 465-7079; www .lullfarmllc.com. Farmer Dave Ord has a reputation for getting a little carried away. He grows about 10 varieties of hot peppers and a dozen or so varieties of eggplants. But he really goes overboard with tomatoes, harvesting about 80 different heirloom varieties over the course of a season. Customers can also pick their own strawberries, blueberries, apples, and raspberries. The well-stocked farmstand features Lull Farm's own breads, jams, jellies, and preserves, along with other local products including turkey and chicken potpies and beef, chicken, or veggie Jamaican patties. Another, slightly smaller farm stand in Milford (p. 271) also carries the farm's produce and baked goods. Open April through mid-January.

Mack's Apples, 230 Mammoth Rd., Londonderry; (603) 434-7619; www.macksapples.com. Established in 1732, this 400-acre farm devotes 100 acres to more than 30 varieties of apples and invites families to make a day of picking fruit, enjoying a picnic at one of the tables scattered around the property, and walking some of the trails. For the little ones, there's also a PYO pumpkin patch next to each PYO apple orchard and a big pumpkin display at the farm market. The market opens in mid-August when the picking season gets underway with Paula Reds and remains open through the following spring. They even sponsor an apple pie baking contest early in the year with prizes for both traditional and nontraditional pies.

Meadow Ledge Farm, Rte. 129, Loudon; (603) 798-5860; www .meadowledgefarm.com. This fruit farm and country store opens up in June for pick-your-own strawberries but doesn't get into high gear until apple season. September and October weekends also feature some fancy picking by old-time musicians for a few hours after lunch to entertain the apple pickers. The farm store has hot apple cider doughnuts and homemade apple ice cream on weekends. The peach trees are young, but peaches are available from late August into September. Produce keeps rolling with pumpkins well into the fall. Open late June until Christmas.

Miles Smith Farm, 56 Whitehouse Rd., Loudon; (603) 783-5159; www.milessmithfarm.com. This picturesque hilltop farm raises Angus and Scottish Highland beef cattle in about as humane an environment as can be imagined. Co-owner Bruce Dawson is proud of his naturally raised, pasture-fed beef and advertises that his animals lead "a happy and stress-free life." Does that make a difference? We were a little dubious, but after buying and cooking his beef, we have to say that it does. It was some of the tastiest we have ever tried. Several restaurants use this beef and it is available in a few markets. But the best selection (and best price) can be found at the farm. All cuts are packaged, and those not sold right away are flash frozen.

Pustizzi Fruit Farm, 148 Corn Hill Rd., Boscawen; (603) 796-6040; www.pustizzifruitfarm.com. This small farmstand gets going in June with peas and strawberries and builds to a fall climax of apples and pumpkins. The farm's own maple syrup is sold in containers from sample to gallon-size, and fresh eggs are available at the stand when the hens are laying. Open June into November.

Wilson's Farm Stand, 144 Charles Bancroft Pkwy., Litchfield; (603) 882-5551; www.wilsonfarm.com. Like many New Hampshire farm markets, Wilson's carefully identifies the produce from its own fields. In this case, Wilson's 500 acres yield sweet butter and sugar corn, tomatoes, beans, squashes, peppers, beets, cucumbers, berries, and more. Wilson's also has an extensive line of its own jams, jellies, preserves, honey, and mixes for pancakes, bread, cakes, and even apple crisp. Treats from the bakery, including muffins, pies, shortcakes, hermits, and brownies, eliminate the need to bake at all. Open early May through mid-October.

Farmers' Markets

Amherst Farmers' Market, Village Green, Amherst. Thurs from 2:30 to 6:30 p.m., May through October.

Atkinson Farmers' Market, Community Center parking lot, 4 Main St., Atkinson. Wed from 3 to 7 p.m., June through October.

Bedford Farmers' Market, Benedictine Park, Bedford. Tues from 3 to 6 p.m., mid-June to mid-October.

Canterbury Community Farmers' Market, Elkins Library parking lot, Center Rd., Canterbury. Wed from 4 to 6:30 p.m., June through October.

Concord Farmers' Market, Capitol St., Concord. Sat from 8:30 a.m. to noon, June through October.

Contoocook Farmers' Market, Train Depot, Contoocook. Sat from 9 a.m. to noon, mid-June to mid-October.

Deerfield Farmers' Market, Deerfield Fairgrounds, Deerfield. Fri from 3 to 7 p.m., June through October.

Derry Farmers' Market, 1 W. Broadway, Derry. Wed from 3 to 7 p.m., early July to late October.

Downtown Manchester Farmers' Market, Concord and Pine streets, Manchester. Thurs from 3 to 6:30 p.m., June through October.

Henniker Farmers' Market, 931 Flanders Rd., Henniker. Wed from 3 to 6 p.m., June through October.

Hooksett Farmers' Market, 1292 Hooksett Rd., Hooksett. Wed from 4 to 7 p.m., June through September.

International Farmers' Market, 315 Pine St., Manchester. Tues from 9 a.m. to 2 p.m., July through November.

International Farmers' Market, Lafayette Park, Manchester. Wed from 9 a.m. to 2 p.m., July through November.

Main Street Bridge Farmers' Market, Main Street Bridge, Nashua. Sun from 10 a.m. to 2 p.m., June through September.

Merrimack Farmers' Market, 515 Daniel Webster Hwy., Merrimack. Wed from 3:30 to 6:30 p.m., June through September.

Nashua City Hall Farmers' Market, 229 Main St., Nashua. Fri noon to 6 p.m., June through September.

New Boston Farmers' Market, Town Common, New Boston. Sat from 9 a.m. to noon, June through October.

Northwood Farmers' Market, junction Rtes 4, 43, 202/9, Northwood. Thurs from 3 to 6:30 p.m., May through October.

Raymond Farmers' Market, 4 Essex Dr., Raymond. Tues from 3 to 6 p.m., June through September.

St. Paul Amherst Farmers' Market, 3 Craftsman Lane, Amherst. Fri from 4 to 7 p.m., June through October.

Salem Farmers' Market, 37 Lake St., Salem. Sun from noon to 4 p.m., mid-July through October.

We Are One Farmers' Market, Town center gazebo, Weare. Fri from 3:30 to 6:30 p.m., mid-June to early October.

Food Events

Manchester Restaurant Week, www.manchester-chamber.org. About 20 restaurants offer value-priced 3-course menus during the third week of October.

Nashua Feast Weeks, www.downtownnashua.org. Nashua restaurants offer special promotional menus in early April and the third week of October.

Taste of the Nation Manchester, www.strength.org/man chester. About 50 restaurants participate in this April event to help stamp out childhood hunger. A strong selection of wines ensures a perfect pairing for every chef's dish.

Portsmouth &
the Seacoast

New Hampshire's modest 18-mile coastline has an outsized impact on the quality of Granite State dining. The sliver of land spreads outward underwater to one of the richest groundfishing areas along the perimeter of the Gulf of Maine. Commercial fishermen haul a healthy catch of cod, haddock, flounder, and monkfish from nearby waters (especially around the Isles of Shoals), and the inshore zone, just off the short rocky coast, is dotted with buoys marking lobster traps on the ocean floor. Environment cleanup of the big tidal estuaries near the mouth of the Piscataqua River, known locally as Great and Little Bays, not only brought back the bald eagles to the New Hampshire coast—the same cleanup also created the conditions to cultivate beds of fat, delectable oysters.

The seacoast also has some of the richest alluvial soils in northern New England, thanks to the rich outwash plain between the foothills of the White Mountains and the coastal marshes.

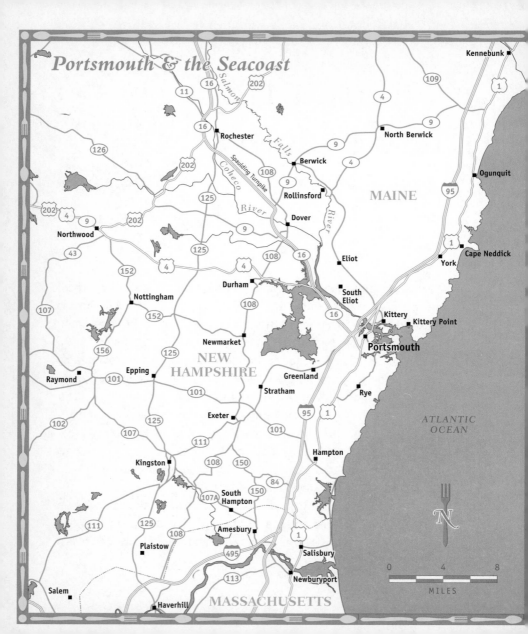

Portsmouth & the Seacoast

Kennebunk

MAINE

Ogunquit

Cape Neddick

York

Kittery
Kittery Point

Portsmouth

North Berwick

Berwick

Rollinsford

Dover

Eliot

South
Eliot

Rochester

Northwood

Durham

Nottingham

Newmarket

**NEW
HAMPSHIRE**

Epping

Raymond

Greenland

Stratham

Rye

Exeter

Kingston

Hampton

South
Hampton

Amesbury

Plaistow

Salisbury

Salem

Newburyport

Haverhill

MASSACHUSETTS

*ATLANTIC
OCEAN*

N

0   4   8
MILES

America's oldest family farm (since 1632) lies in the area, and some of New England's most productive commercial orchards are close enough to the coast that you can smell the salt air when the wind turns from the southeast. These resources translate into good eating for the whole seacoast, especially Portsmouth, the region's urban hub. It is no accident that more than half the restaurants in this chapter lie within a few blocks of each other in this hip and well-heeled city. Moreover, Portsmouth shows every sign of hatching new establishments all the time.

Foodie Faves

Black Trumpet Bistro, 29 Ceres St., Portsmouth; (603) 431-0887; www.blacktrumpetbistro.com; $$$. We like to think of Black Trumpet as simultaneously representing the best of the old and the best of the new in Portsmouth fine dining. The legendary Blue Strawberry—the first restaurant in Portsmouth worth getting snobby about—held down this space next to the harbor tugboats for many years. Chef-Owner Evan Mallet of Black Trumpet doesn't subscribe to the same gastronomic rigidity (Blue Strawberry offered one choice for each course per night, take it or leave it), but he does uphold the high culinary standards, borrowing liberally from various Mediterranean cuisines for his preparations while sourcing his fish, meat, and produce in coastal New Hampshire and Maine. The results can be fantastic, as with his Sardinian stew of cuttlefish, assorted finfish, scallops, and mussels in a tomato-mushroom broth, or a simple grilled steak with an autumnal hash of brussels sprouts and delicata squash. The old building guarantees a romantic atmosphere, which is complemented by probably the best service in Portsmouth.

Blue Moon Evolution, 8 Clifford St., Exeter; (603) 778-6850; www.bluemoonevolution.com; $$$. This restaurant shares space with the Yogalife Institute of New Hampshire, which offers classes and workshops. You could think of the meals here as fine dining for yoga enthusiasts—or at least by yoga enthusiasts. There's a light delicacy to entrees like a plate of raw vegetables or tofu marinated in a red wine *escabeche* and served with tomato and fennel salad. But carnivores and pescavores need not fear. The Buddha might not approve, but Blue Moon serves grilled and panfried fish as well as grilled pork and beef. At lunchtime, you can stop by for a wrap and organic smoothie to go.

Brazo Restaurant, 75 Pleasant St., Portsmouth; (603) 431-0050; www.brazorestaurant.com; $$$. Chef Phelps Dieck and partner Deb Week like a little drama with their food, and this full-on Latin restaurant somehow brings a common spirit to dishes drawn from Yucatecan, Cuban, Nuevo Latino, Venezuelan, and other New World cuisines. These are plates with splash and salsa—Gulf Stream cooking with New England provender and some judicious additions of Spanish ingredients and ideas. To get an idea of the fusion, try the butternut squash empanada, or a Yucatecan-style fish taco made with fresh New England cod. In late summer Dieck stuffs roasted poblano peppers with a mix of corn, chorizo, rice, onion, and cilantro and tops it off with a half lobster. It's like a Maine lobster bake went to Mexico. You can even get churros (fried dough tossed in cinnamon and sugar) for dessert.

Cava Tapas and Wine Bar, 10 Commercial Alley, Portsmouth; (603) 319-1575; www.cavatapasandwinebar.com; $$. We travel and eat a lot in Spain and are often disappointed with American restaurants that bill themselves as tapas bars. But Chef-Proprietor Greg Sessler of this exceedingly cool bar-restaurant in a back alley of Portsmouth's most touristic neighborhood gets it all right—from an heirloom tomato gazpacho served with a white corn soup shooter to authentic *patatas bravas* (fried potatoes with spicy bravas sauce) to a seared slice of yellowfin tuna mounted on a morsel of watermelon. The kitchen even does some hearty Spanish entrees, such as seared beef sirloin rubbed with star anise. The wine list is long on Spanish imports, including Catalan sparklers (cavas), bracing Albariños from Galicia's Rias Baixas, and bold but quaffable Toro reds. Adjusting to an American rather than Spanish schedule, drinks and tapas are offered in the late afternoon, with dinner service beginning at 5 p.m.

Gilley's PM Lunch, 175 Fleet St., Portsmouth; (603) 431-6343; www.gilleyspmlunch.com; $. Gilley's is a piece of history. The mobile lunch cart was built by the Worcester Lunch Car Company in 1940 and was towed into Market Square every evening to serve hungry workers. Permanently settled on Fleet Street since 1974, Gilley's is the only one of five such carts still in business. Slide the door open any time between 11 a.m. and 2:30 a.m., order at the counter and grab one of eight stools in the original oak and porcelain interior. Breakfast items, hamburgers, and sandwiches are available, but the Gilley's classic is a steamed hot dog. There's an art to ordering. Ask for the "works" if you want mustard, relish, and onions on your dog. Ask for "loaded" if you also want to add ketchup. Ask for "everything" and the server will pile on mayonnaise and pickle as well. It's messy but good.

Holy Grail, 64 Main St., Epping; (603) 679-9559; www.theholy grailpub.com; $$. David and Maureen Kennedy channeled their Irish roots when they set about converting an 1890s church building into a convivial pub. Though not as cozy as a traditional "local," the Holy Grail gains a literal sense of grace from its pew-like booths and striking stained glass windows. In addition to standard pub grub, the menu features a number of Irish classics such as Guinness beef stew, corned beef, and bangers with the mashed potato–cabbage–scallion mix called colcannon. The bar gets fancy with Irish coffee, offering both an original style with Jameson's and Bailey's and a "grand" with Bushmills, Grand Marnier, and Bailey's.

Jumpin' Jay's Fish Cafe, 150 Congress St., Portsmouth; (603) 766-3474; www.jumpinjays.com; $$$. For those who grew up on the coast and believe that fish should ideally be eaten outdoors when the weather permits, Jumpin' Jay's has its own rooftop garden. The motto here is "The finest in fresh seafood from around the world and around the corner," and they're serious about it. A raw bar dominates the room, serving a couple of different New Hampshire oysters in season alongside others from Cape Cod; Damariscotta, Maine; Long Island Sound; and the Chesapeake Bay. Origins are carefully indicated, so if you prefer wild-caught American shrimp, you can skip the jumbo Vietnamese variety. Widely praised for their crab cakes, Jumpin' Jay's also does a mean *salade niçoise* with grilled yellowfin tuna, a perky haddock piccata with local fish, and a rich San Francisco–style cioppino.

Moe's Italian Sandwich, 22 Daniel St., Portsmouth; (603) 436-2327; www.moesitaliansandwiches.com; $. Moe's is a Portsmouth fixture for a quick and filling lunch. "But it's never too early for a Moe's," says Taylor Bistany, of the extended Pagano family that launched the sandwich shop in 1959. "We serve them for breakfast at 8:30 a.m.," she says, "and when people return from winter in Florida, this is their first stop." Moe's "original" consists of a soft Italian roll stuffed with sliced tomatoes, black olives, onions, dill pickle, green peppers, provolone cheese, and Moe's own mild salami, all doused with a bit of olive oil.

Vegetarians needn't go hungry: Just ask for a Moe's without the meat.

Mombo, 66 Marcy St., Portsmouth; (603) 433-2340; www.mombo restaurant.com; $$$. New American cooking meets Olde American surroundings at this lively contemporary restaurant amid the historic houses of Strawbery Banke. One of the highlights of the dining week here are the inexpensive "Taste of Mombo" plates offered on Thursday night. They capture the eclectic cooking style with everything from seared tuna with crispy wontons to chicken sausage and biscuits or a fried green tomato BLT. Regional favorites also shine, like the classic lobster bisque and pan-seared sea scallops served with the decidedly untraditional pork belly cured with five-spice powder and maple syrup. It's a noisy room, but that's almost by design. Mombo treats the dining experience as a kind of boisterous party.

Newick's Lobster House, 431 Dover Point Rd., Dover; (603) 742-3205; www.newicks.com; $$. No one is ever going to accuse Newick's of being trendy, but we sleep better knowing that places like this not only exist, but continue to thrive. This setting on Great Bay is working waterfront, but only a few tables in the cavernous dining room actually have views of the lobstermen unloading their catch at the dock out back. The kitchen turns out all the coastal classics—baked, boiled, broiled, and steamed. So one member in the party can order steamed lobster while another has broiled swordfish and yet another a plate of fried flounder. Prices are about as good as you'll find on super-fresh fish. Newick's has another location in Concord (see p. 289) and even one in Portland, Maine, but this is the 1948 original.

Petey's Summertime Seafood & Bar, 1323 Ocean Blvd., Rye; (603) 433-1937; www.peteys.com; $$. The name tells almost everything you need to know about this small eatery precariously perched roadside between Rye's pounding surf and rocks and the wetlands of the back-marsh estuary. Enormously popular as a bar that offers shelter from an afternoon sunburn, Petey's can be a hard place to score an indoor dining table. But given that most of the fish is fried (clams, haddock, shrimp, calamari, etc.), it's more fun to eat outdoors at the picnic tables next to the unnamed stream that connects marsh and ocean. Between the cold beer, the fresh seafood, and the scent of hot fryolators, this is summer on the coast at its best.

Ristorante Massimo, 59 Penhallow St., Portsmouth; (603) 436-4000; www.ristorantemassimo.com; $$$. Long known as Anthony Alberto's, this bastion of authentic Italian fine dining took its current name in 2007, when Massimo Morgia bought out his partner and refocused on Italian fresh-cuisine classics using a lot of local products. The lobster preparation is a classic Italian interpretation that uses the whole lobster for several components: You get a grilled lobster tail with rosemary infused butter, a lobster risotto with flecks of body meat topped with butter-poached lobster claws, and a small side of arugula salad sprinkled with truffle oil as a counterpoint to all that unctuous lobster meat. Yes, there are some pastas, but they tend to be chef's pastas, not nonna's—like little cracked-pepper gnocchi tossed with braised tenderloin and a dollop of crème fraîche. The wine list is strong on Piemontese and Napa reds, and offers some hard-to-find white gems from Alto Adige and Friuli. Oh, and did we mention that the subterranean dining room veritably drips with romance?

Rocky's Famous Burgers, 171 Main St., Newmarket; (603) 292-3393; www.rockysfamousburgers.com; $. The first time we visited Rocky's, a local woman had brought a couple of Thai friends to taste a "real American burger." As they stood at the counter and read the menu, they were overwhelmed by the choices. The 8-ounce burgers are available with Black Angus beef, bison, chicken breast, or a black bean–based veggie patty—and a myriad of toppings. They wisely settled on beef versions of "The Rocky," with lettuce, tomato, onion, and American cheese. It's an elegant American classic. The shop's best seller, the "Bat Man," piles lettuce, tomato, bacon, cheddar cheese, onion rings, and barbecue sauce onto the burger for a two-fisted treat.

Street Food 360, 801 Islington St., Portsmouth; (603) 436-0860; www.streetfood360.com; $$. Portsmouth's West End is only starting to emerge as a dining and entertainment district, but if it can score a few more places with the panache of Street, the sky is the limit.

Don't let the industrial mini-park surroundings dissuade you. Once you're safely in the door, the post-industrial decor kicks everything up a notch. The food concept is simple: the best street food from around the world. "We wanted to create good food in a casual setting," says Chef-Owner Josh Lanahan. He's a big fan of breakfast ("I don't think enough people put their heart and soul into breakfast," he says) so the menu has great dishes like Korean bibimbap. You choose either barbecued beef or seitan (wheat protein) on a bed of sticky rice. Piled on top are sesame-sautéed carrot, mushroom, zucchini, spinach, and bean sprouts. The pièce de résistance is a sunny-side-up egg and a generous dollop of Korean hot pepper paste. "It's great, but so simple," says Lanahan. Just don't forget to stir up the bowl before eating. You can get lunch and dinner daily, but, as you might guess, Sunday brunch is a really big deal.

UNH Dairy Bar, Durham/UNH Station, 3 Depot Rd., Durham; (603) 862-1006; www.unh.edu/dairy-bar; $. We feel sorry for commuters on the Boston to Portland, Maine, Downeaster rail line because they don't have time to jump off the train for breakfast or lunch in Durham's cute little cafe in the Beaux Arts–style yellow-brick train station. It's operated by the University of New Hampshire, with a menu that emphasizes fresh and local products in a range of breakfast and lunch sandwiches, along with salads, soups, and ice cream desserts. All sandwiches—from chocolate peanut butter with sliced bananas to chicken with tomatoes, olive tapenade, and feta cheese—are available in half sizes so that diners can save room for a scoop of **Blake's** ice cream (p. 296).

Specialty Stores, Markets & Producers

Annabelle's Natural Ice Cream, 49 Ceres St., Portsmouth; (603) 436-3400; www.annabellesicecream.com. Although Annabelle's makes about 30 flavors of ice cream, along with frozen yogurt and fruit sorbet, a lot of adults opt for the classic French vanilla or Dutch chocolate. The more adventurous often gravitate to Mint Summer Night's Dream (mint chocolate ice cream with white and dark chocolate chunks) or Yellow Brick Road (golden vanilla ice cream with roasted pecans, praline pecans, and caramel swirls). For the kids? Chocolate Chip Cookie Dough. You might find Annabelle's served at other Granite State establishments, but it's freshest right here at the source.

Breaking New Grounds, 14 Market Sq., Portsmouth; (603) 436-9555. Although a franchise of the ubiquitous Seattle coffee giant manages to hold on by its fingernails across the street from the Portsmouth location, most locals favor Breaking New Grounds for their drip coffee and espresso drinks. The roasts are fairly light with no burnt flavors and pair well with the good selection of baked goods. The **Durham location's** (50 Main St., Durham;

603-868-6869) version of BNG has a more modest selection of sweets.

British Aisles, 1634 Greenland Rd., Greenland; (603) 881-9511; www.britishaisles.com. British-born Denise and Gerry Pressinger started British Aisles more than 20 years ago so that they and their friends could stock up on the food they missed from home. "Silly things, really," says Denise, "like HP sauce and Heinz beans, all the biscuits, and the pickled onions like they sell in every fish-and-chips shop in London." What began almost as a hobby is now a full-fledged business and the Pressingers ship jams and pickles, cookies and teas, sauces and condiments to gourmet shops around the country. Since their relocation in 2011 from Nashua to Greenland, individuals can actually shop a real retail store instead of wandering the warehouse to fill their shopping baskets with Indian cooking sauces and chutneys, mustards, custard powder, relishes, and marmalades. A temperature-controlled room is devoted to sweets. "They have a real sweet tooth in Britain," says Gerry. "That's why there are so many biscuits—what we call cookies over here—and candy." British Aisles is especially busy at Christmas when expats stock up on colorful tins of cookies and cardboard "stockings" covered with candy bars. There's always a holiday-time run on plum pudding, which the Pressingers have even shipped to Alaska, Guam, and Hawaii.

Byrne & Carlson, 121 State St., Portsmouth; (888) 559-9778; www.byrneandcarlson.com. These boutique chocolates are hand-made across the Piscataqua River in Kittery, Maine, but we won't be sticklers for geography when the product is so scrumptious. Regulars at this cozy shop in a brick town house in downtown Portsmouth are partial to the caramels in dark chocolate sprinkled with *fleur de sel* and the dark and crunchy cacao nibs (with or without chipotle peppers). The shop's fruit jellies are made only with fresh fruits, juices, and zests and are so intensely flavored that they hold their own against the more decadent chocolates.

The Chocolatier, 27 Water St., Exeter; (603) 772-5253; www.the-chocolatier .com. The Chocolatier creates a full range of sophisticated chocolate-covered caramels, creams, and jellies. But customers can't seem to get enough of its popcorn mix with caramel, white, dark, and milk chocolates, marshmallows, and almonds. The shop also offers about 100 molded chocolate items and is the go-to place for party favors and stocking stuffers.

Flag Hill Winery & Distillery, 297 N. River Rd. (Rte. 155), Lee; (603) 659-2949; www.flaghill.com. This hugely popular pioneer New Hampshire winery (the first vineyards were planted in 1990) focuses on a mixture of fruit wines and wines produced from winter-hardy hybrid and American grapes. Mild, unassuming Cayuga and tangy Niagara form the backbone of the white-grape wines, while the reds are fashioned from such first-generation hybrids as De Chaunac and Marechal Foch—both grapes that favor the American rather than the French sides of their heritage. The fruit wines can be notably good. The tangy apple-cranberry goes well with food, while the deeply colored and flavored raspberry is perfect for sipping on a summer afternoon sitting in the shade of a tree. The real surprises lie among the distilled spirits. The grappa distilled from the pomace left over from making wine is very smooth and rich, while the barrel-aged apple brandy is done in the classic American applejack style—more apple than barrel. Flag Hill's General John Stark vodka, triple-distilled from apples, is a terrific neutral spirit—smooth and sultry. The facilities are thoroughly modern, but the tasting room occupies a picturesque circa-1796 post-and-beam barn.

Hickory Nut Farm, 21 York Lane, Lee; (603) 659-6885; www.hickorynutfarm.com. A little out of the way and a little out of the mainstream when it comes to their cheeses, Hickory Nut makes several styles of firm goat cheeses and a bunch of specialty flavored cheeses. Tops among the conventional cheeses is Terrene, which is rolled in vegetable ash and aged at least two months. Maybe the most unusual cheese is called Hot Chocolate. Very hot little japones chiles are infused in the cheese, which is then rolled in cacao and aged for several months. The self-service store in a small shed is open at all hours.

Jewell Towne Vineyards, 65 Jewell St., South Hampton; (603) 394-0600; www.jewelltownevineyards.com. When you pull up to the tasting room, the first thing you'll notice is the vineyard of surprisingly mature vines. Jewell Towne's plantings are a virtual roster of French-American hybrids and American varietals, and some are nearly 20 years old. In all, they grow 25 grape varieties. The winery also purchases juice from traditional European wine grapes (Riesling, Chardonnay, Pinot Grigio, Cabernet Sauvignon) to make more conventional, non-estate wines. In nice weather, many visitors come for a tasting, pick a bottle or two, and spend the afternoon enjoying their new finds at picnic tables by the vineyards.

Kitchen & Company, 45 Gosling Rd., Newington; (603) 433-2100; www.thekitchenstore.com. This cavernous shop located in the Fox Run Crossing mall is overwhelming at first and serious cooks will definitely feel as if they are kids in a candy store. Get your bearings by perusing the 120-foot wall of kitchen gadgets, helpfully arranged by categories such as Eggs and Breakfast; Slice, Grate and Chop; Measure; or Whisks and Tongs. The shop claims the largest K-Cup coffee selection in the area and has equally impressive offerings of glassware, white bistro ware, Ball canning jars, barbecue grills and accessories, and high-end cookware. There's still room for novelty items including turkey fryer kits, commercial-grade juicers, and crème brûlée sets.

Leroux Kitchen, 23 Market St., Portsmouth; (603) 430-7665; www.lerouxkitchen.com. Leroux stocks all the gadgets and basics to equip a serious kitchen, including Le Creuset cookware and Vic Firth salt and pepper mills, both in a rainbow of colors. (Firth, a former timpanist for the Boston Symphony Orchestra and renowned manufacturer of drumsticks, has turned his attention to gourmet mills.) But this charming Portsmouth shop exudes a strong sense of place with a display of just about every lobster and crab cracker and fork imaginable and a full line of speckled enamel Granite-Ware, including corn and lobster pots and a clam steamer with a faucet for broth.

Philbrick's Fresh Market, 69 Lafayette Rd. (Rte. 1), North Hampton; (603) 379-2500; and 775 Lafayette Rd. (Rte.1), Portsmouth; (603) 422-6758; www.philbricksfreshmarket.com. Philbrick's is a hybrid food store—one part traditional chain grocery, one part natural foods store, and one part gourmet shop. Its aisles carry brand name plastic wrap, coffee filters, and even breakfast cereal, but they also have a case of artisan cheeses (including many local ones), organic produce and meats from nearby farms, and fresh breads from area bakeries. We like Philbrick's for its democratic approach to wholesome food and for its ready-to-eat case filled with freshly made salads and sushi. The North Hampton store also has an in-house coffee shop.

Popovers on the Square, 8 Congress St., Portsmouth; (603) 431-1119; www.popoversonthesquare.com. Portsmouth has no shortage of convivial cafes. To set itself apart, Popovers has revived its namesake retro classic and made it a mainstay of the menu. Diners can opt for a popover with maple butter for breakfast or a bowl of soup (tomato bisque, New England clam chowder) with a mini popover for lunch. The kitchen even stuffs its popovers with salads (Caesar or pear and Gorgonzola, for example) or smoked salmon and pairs mini popovers with hummus and vegetables. Unlike some Portsmouth cafes, Popovers also serves beer, wine, and cocktails. Relaxing with a glass of wine and an elegant dessert (chocolate mousse cake, apricot almond torte) has become a favorite way for locals to end the day. In case you were wondering, there is also a popover ice cream sundae for dessert.

Portsmouth Baking Company, 121 Congress St., Portsmouth; (603) 319-8841; www.portsmouthbakingcompany.com. Portsmouth Baking Company builds its menu around a range of artisan breads that are baked on the second level of this sleekly stylish storefront eatery. In fact, diners can watch the bakers at work behind big glass windows or follow them on large screen video monitors hung on the walls. Quality and efficiency go hand-in-hand here as breakfast baked goods and lunch sandwiches and salads are laid out cafeteria style. Some of the more unusual breakfast offerings include french toast bread pudding made with the bakery's brioche and a roasted tomato and cheddar cheese strata. Sandwiches are all made on French-style baguettes and include turkey breast, brie, and citrus-infused cranberry sauce or roast beef, aged cheddar, arugula, and Dijon mustard. Signature cupcakes are big enough to split, though you may not want to.

Red Hook Brewery/Cataqua Public House, 35 Corporate Dr., Portsmouth; (603) 431-8600; www.redhook.com. The international brewing giant, InBev, owns about a third of this craft brewery, established in 1982 in Washington State. That means that Red Hook gets distributed all over the lower 48. Even though they ride on the same trucks with Budweiser and Stella Artois, Red Hook's beers retain their original Pacific Northwest character, especially the signature IPA. This location is the only Red Hook brewery on the East Coast, and it offers afternoon tours for a nominal fee. Predictably, the shop is full of T-shirts, coasters, and beer. The adjoining Cataqua pub is a nifty bar with decent beer food (pulled pork, burgers, chicken strips, pot stickers, ribs, etc.).

Sanborn's Fine Candies, 293 Lafayette Rd. (Rte. 1), Hampton; (603) 926-5061; www.sanbornscandies.com. Befitting its seacoast location, Sanborn's stocks saltwater taffy in a multitude of flavors during the summer. But the house-made chocolates are the shop's stock in trade. "People love anything with a nut in it," says Bob Cooper, who runs the shop with his wife Billie. Nut offerings include walnut, cashew, pecan, or almond turtles, barks or nut clusters, and a thin peanut brittle. Sanborn's also makes a retro "snowflake" of coconut and fondant dipped in dark or milk chocolate and old-fashioned molasses honeycomb sponge candy. "We can't make it in the summer," says Cooper "because it absorbs the moisture in the air and shrinks to nothing." During the winter months the sponge is packaged in 12-ounce bags that quickly disappear off the shelves.

Sanders Fish Market, 367 Marcy St., Portsmouth; (603) 436-4568; www.sandersfish.com. Sanders carries its share of flying fish—i.e., fish from distant waters that have to arrive by air—but when the season permits, the cases overflow with the local catch. We especially like the fact that the farmed Atlantic salmon comes from ecologically sensitive aquaculture farms on the Faroe Islands between Scotland and Iceland. The Sanders folk prepare a lot of food as well. Stop by for smoked bluefish and ready-to-cook crab cakes, stuffed scallops, and codfish cakes. If you get hungry, have a bowl of hot chowder or a lobster roll. The shop also sells bait for salt-water anglers. You can arrange to have lobster shipped almost anywhere in the country.

Smuttynose Brewing Co., 225 Heritage Ave., Portsmouth; (603) 436-4026; www.smuttynose.com. We've been partial to Smuttynose ever since we first tasted the company's Old Brown Dog in the mid-1990s. Apparently we're not the only ones, as Smuttynose ales are now distributed all up and down the East Coast. Fans of malt beverages that verge on barley wines should note that Smuttynose releases a new "big beer" about every 6 weeks. Stop at the brewery on weekdays to buy beer and souvenir paraphernalia. A 1-hour brewery tour and tasting is offered on Friday and Saturday.

Stonewall Kitchen Warehouse Store, 7 Amarosa Dr., Unit 1, Rochester; (603) 994-1110; www.stonewallkitchen.com. Jonathan King and Jim Stott's jars of jams, jellies, condiments, sauces, dips, marinades, and more are easily recognizable by Stott's hand-lettered labels. Though now mass-produced, they recall the company's origins as a table at the Portsmouth farmers' market. The products are available in shops throughout New Hampshire and Vermont, as well as in Stonewall's free-standing stores. This Rochester outlet is the only warehouse store and offers discounts of 50 percent or more on seconds and discontinued or sale items. As in all Stonewall stores, sampling is encouraged.

Sweet Dreams Bakery, 100 Portsmouth Ave., Stratham; (603) 772-8432; www.sweetdreamsbakery.net. David Italiano's parents opened this bakery in 1988. "I learned everything here," he says "and we still use some of my mom's and my grandmother's recipes." Celebration-worthy cakes such as a rich chocolate torte topped with chocolate whipped cream, strawberries, and shaved dark and white chocolates, are specialties. But the bakery also excels in the homier side of baking with cookies, brownies, fig squares, lattice-topped fruit pies, and old-fashioned carrot cake. "Scones are one of our

CALL IT SODA, CALL IT TONIC, CALL IT POP

It's hard to believe, but the Granite State has lost some of its original fizz. "There used to be 54 independent bottlers in New Hampshire, but we're the last one," says Dan Conner. He represents the fifth generation of family-run Squamscot Old Fashioned Beverages, a business established in 1863 to bottle beer. Over time, the company branched out into its own "tonics," and stuck with the nonalcoholic beverages after Prohibition. Stop in the gray-shingled original bottling plant most weekday afternoons between 2 and 4 p.m. and you'll probably see the old capping machine in operation. "My great-grandfather bought her new in 1938," says Conner. "Her name is Dixie," he says fondly of the machine that handles 18 bottles per minute. "It's a long day," he admits, "and very loud." Conner makes the syrups fresh every morning and has seen annual production jump from 2,000 cases in 1997 to about 30,000. Of more than 25 flavors, Root Beer and Cream are the most popular, though many people favor the Golden Ginger Ale. In the summer, Raspberry Lemonade and Orange Cream (which tastes a bit like a Creamsicle®) are among the most refreshing. Buy a mixed case and you can conduct your own taste test. **Squamscot Old Fashioned Beverages,** 120 Exeter Rd., Newfields; (603) 772-3376; www.nhsoda.com.

most popular items," says Italiano. "We make two or three different flavors a day." Soups, quiche, and sandwiches on fresh-baked bread are available for lunchtime take-out and there are a few picnic tables on the lawn for warm-weather dining.

White Heron Tea, 3 Front St., Lower Mill #210, Rollinsford; (877) 501-6266; www.white herontea.com. Jonathan Blakeslee nurtured his childhood taste for tea during a Coast Guard posting in Japan and a stint in tea shops on the West Coast. The end result is his fair-trade tea import business and small tea shop in an old redbrick mill building. Blakeslee offers about 70 organic and fair-trade black, green, herbal, and white teas, along with a line of chai concentrate. He can advise about proper brewing of everything from African Rooibos to Ginger Mate Chai. A small selection of iced tea brew bags is also available.

Farmstands & Pick Your Own

Applecrest Farm Orchards, 133 Exeter Rd., Hampton Falls; (603) 926-3721; www.applecrest.com. Applecrest claims to have the largest apple orchard in New Hampshire but still finds room to grow peaches, nectarines, strawberries, blueberries, raspberries, corn, pumpkins, and just about any summer vegetable that will thrive in this climate. You can opt to pick your own fruit or grab a pre-picked basket in the farmstand, along with an apple, peach, blueberry or five-fruit pie. Better yet, from May through October stop in at the Creamery in an 1804 barn building next to the farmstand and savor a slice of pie with a scoop of ice cream. Farmstand open May through Dec.

Heron Pond Farm, 299 Main Ave., South Hampton; (603) 591-8720; www.heronpondfarm.com. The farm grows more than 250 varieties of 35 fruits and vegetables—from Lancelot leeks to Rosa Bianca eggplants, sweet candy onions to fiery cayenne peppers. Much of the produce is reserved for CSA members, but visitors will find a nice assortment in the tiny farmstand. In August, staff sort the tomatoes by day picked so that customers can select by ripeness. For sauce-making, 5-pound bags of damaged tomatoes are often available at a bargain price. Open May through early Nov.

Rawson's Farmstand, 5 College Rd., Stratham; (603) 686-0303; www.rawsonsfarmstand.com. Ed and Mary Rawson are friendly with a lot of Seacoast chefs who depend on them for outstanding heirloom tomatoes and for greens and herbs throughout the growing season. The roadside stand is a marvelously old-fashioned shed piled high with whatever is currently being harvested from the rich alluvial soils of the New Hampshire outwash plain. Even out of season you can pick up maple syrup, popping corn, firewood, and fresh eggs.

Tuttle Farm, Dover Point Rd., Dover; (603) 742-4313. Under cultivation since 1632, Tuttle's is probably America's oldest family farm. The 11th generation finally threw in the towel and put the farm up for sale in 2010, but it's unclear whether it will remain an agricultural enterprise or not, since there were no takers by early 2012. We put it into this guide with the fervent hope that a white knight will ride to the rescue and preserve this key piece of the American story. For the last several decades, the farm has sold tomatoes, corn, pumpkins, and other produce from its red barn on the Dover Point Road side of the 135-acre property.

Farmers' Markets

Dover Farmers' Market, 1 W. Broadway, Dover. Wed from 3 to 7 p.m., early July to late October.

Durham Farmers' Market, Mill Road Plaza, Durham. Mon from 2:15 to 5:30 p.m., early June to early October.

Exeter Farmers' Market, Swasey Parkway, downtown Exeter. Thurs from 2:15 to 6 p.m., mid-May through late October.

Hampton Falls Farmers' Market, Town Common, Hampton Falls. Mon from 2 to 6 p.m., May through October.

Hampton Farmers' Market, 289 Lafayette Rd. (Rte. 1), Hampton; Tues from 3 to 6 p.m., early June to mid-October.

Herbal Path Community Marketplace, 835 Central Ave., Dover. Fri from 3 to 6 p.m., June through September.

Lee Farmers' Market, Old Fire Station, Rte. 155, Lee. Thurs from 3 to 6 p.m., May through September.

Newmarket Farmers' Market, 220 S. Main St., Newmarket. Sat from 9 a.m. to 1 p.m., June through September.

Plaistow Recreation Farmers' Market, 145 Main St., Plaistow. Thurs from 2 to 6 p.m., Aug through October.

Portsmouth Farmers' Market, 1 Junkins Ave., Portsmouth. Sat from 8 a.m. to 1 p.m., early May through November.

Portsmouth Open Market, Strawbery Banke, Portsmouth; www.portsmouthopenmarket.org. Farmers' market occupies a corner of the open-air artisan market. Sun from 10 a.m. to 4 p.m., early June through October.

Rye Farmers' Market, Rye Center. Wed from 2:30 to 5:30 p.m., June through September.

Wentworth Greenhouses Farmers' Market, 141 Rollinsford Rd., Rollinsford. Sat from 10 a.m. to 2 p.m., mid-June to late October.

Apple Harvest Day, www.dovernh.org. More than 300 vendors line the streets of downtown Dover for this popular early October event that also features a 5K road race, pancake breakfast, and apple pie baking contests.

Hampton Beach Seafood Festival, www.hamptonbeachsea foodfestival.com. About 60 restaurants serve lobster, fried clams, shrimp, and more at this early September beachfront party that marks the end of the summer season. The 3-day event also features cooking demonstrations by local chefs and a lobster roll eating contest.

Hampton Historical Society Southern Style Pig Roast, www .hamptonhistoricalsociety.org. Hampton's historic Tuck Museum hosts this early September event that features roast pork, home-made baked beans, applesauce, salads, and an array of desserts.

Portsmouth Restaurant Week, www.portsmouthchamber.org/restaurantweek.cfm. About 40 restaurants in the city and surrounding seacoast area offer bargain priced 3-course prix-fixe menus at lunch and dinner. Diners eagerly await the March and November events.

Rochester Fair, www.rochesterfair.com. Although Rochester sits at the edge of the increasingly developed Seacoast region, the mid-September fair retains its strong agricultural roots with a special emphasis on youth showing livestock and even judging of hay, silage, and grain.

St. Nicholas Greek Festival, www.portsmouthgreekfestival.com. St. Nicholas Greek Orthodox Church in Portsmouth is the site of this mid-July festival that features music and dancing, along with Greek food specialties such as moussaka, spanakopita, pastitsio, souvlaki, and lots of pastries.

Stratham Fair, www.strathamfair.com. Although only established in 1967, the Stratham Fair adheres to the old time country fair traditions, including 4-H competitions, pie-eating contests, and lots of food. Highlights of the mid-July event might include Texas roadhouse-style steak, barbecued ribs, or even a lobster bake.

Taste of the Nation, www.strength.org. Portsmouth is one of many cities around the country that participate in the Share Our Strength effort to end childhood hunger. This late-June fundraising event generally features about 70 restaurants and other food makers, along with wine and beer and entertainment.

Vintage & Vine Wine Tasting & Sale, www.strawberybanke .org. At this September event at Strawbery Banke museum in Portsmouth, guests can select from hundreds of wines to sample and enjoy food offerings from some of the top chefs and restaurants in Portsmouth and the Seacoast Area.

Recipes

We always find that re-creating local recipes in our own kitchen is a good way to bring the taste of travel back home. So we are grateful to the chefs and growers who provided these recipes that highlight local flavors and reflect local traditions of New Hampshire and Vermont. We have adapted the recipes for home kitchens and standardized their presentation. Any errors are our inadvertent introductions rather than the fault of our sources.

Beth's Baked Oatmeal

Beth Kennett at Liberty Hill Farm serves a big farm breakfast of pancakes, eggs, homemade sausage, coffeecake, and muffins for guests who stay in the B&B in the farmhouse. But the dish that wins the most raves is this simple and filling baked oatmeal. For best flavor and nutrition, Beth recommends using whole milk.

Serves 2–4

- 1⅓ cups oats (must use old-fashioned, steel cut; never use quick oats)
- ¼ cup brown sugar or maple sugar
- 1 apple, peeled, cored, and diced
- ⅓ cup dried cranberries
- ½ teaspoon cinnamon
- ¼ teaspoon salt
- 2 tablespoons melted butter
- 2 cups milk

Stir all ingredients together in large ovenproof bowl or 8 x 8-inch pan. Bake at 375°F for 45 minutes. Serve in bowls with milk.

Adapted recipe courtesy of Beth Kennett
at Liberty Hill Farm, Rochester, VT (p. 138).

Crowley & Bacon Scones

This variant of old-fashioned bacon and cheddar scones adds an upcountry touch by including maple syrup. If you can't find Crowley cheese, use a sharp Colby cheese or, in a pinch, medium sharp cheddar.

Makes 20 scones

¾ cup well-shaken buttermilk

¼ cup pure Vermont maple syrup

½ cup plus 2 tablespoons heavy cream

3½ cups all-purpose flour

¾ cup sugar

1 teaspoon salt

1 teaspoon baking powder

½ teaspoon baking soda

1½ cups unsalted butter, cut into ½-inch cubes

1 cup shredded Crowley Medium Sharp cheese

5 slices cooked bacon, crumbled

2 large egg yolks

Preheat oven to 400°F.

Put buttermilk, maple syrup, and ½ cup cream in a small bowl and whisk together.

Mix flour, sugar, salt, baking powder, and baking soda in a separate large bowl and whisk to combine. Add butter cubes and blend by hand or pastry blender until mixture resembles coarse meal with some small (roughly pea-size) butter lumps.

Mix in cheese and bacon, then add buttermilk mixture and stir until just combined.

Turn out mixture onto parchment paper and pull together any unmixed flour. Gently pat dough into 1-inch thickness. Cut scones into 20 rough-hewn triangles or use biscuit cutter. Place on lined baking sheet.

Whisk together yolks and remaining 2 tablespoons cream, then brush over tops of scones (use all of egg wash).

Bake 20 minutes or until puffy and golden brown.

Adapted recipe courtesy of cheesemaker Ken Hart
of Crowley Cheese, Healdville, VT (p. 128).

Pumpkin Bread

Theodora Damaskos makes the pumpkin bread she sells at Trap Door Bakehouse & Cafe with organic sugar pumpkins from Cedar Circle Farm (p. 88). Ever practical, she notes that canned pumpkin can also be substituted for fresh.

Makes 2 loaves

1 cup softened unsalted butter
3 cups sugar
4 eggs
2 cups pumpkin puree (see below)
¼ cup water

3 cups flour, sifted
2 teaspoons baking soda
1 teaspoon nutmeg
1 teaspoon cinnamon
1 cup chopped dates and/or walnuts

Glaze:

1 cup maple syrup
Juice of ½ orange

Zest of ½ orange

Preheat oven to 325°F.

Cream the softened butter in a mixer with a paddle attachment and add sugar, eggs, and the pumpkin puree. Combine well on medium speed. Reduce the speed to low and add the water. Sift together the flour, baking soda, nutmeg, and cinnamon. Add the dry ingredients to the mixer on low speed and continue to mix for 2 minutes. Add the dates and/or walnuts.

Grease 9 x 5-inch (8 cups) loaf pans and line with parchment paper. Fill each pan ¾ full.

Bake for 1¼ to 1½ hours. Remove the breads from the pans when finished baking and cool on a rack.

To make the glaze:

Combine the maple syrup, orange juice, and zest in a pan and bring to a boil. Brush the top of each cooled loaf with the glaze.

To prepare puree:

Slice two pie pumpkins in half, scoop out the seeds, and place pumpkins cut side down on a greased pan. Cover with foil and bake for about 30 minutes at 350°F until tender. Cool and scoop out flesh and mash. If you want a finer puree, process pumpkin in a food processor. Excess puree can be frozen for future use.

Courtesy of Theodora Damaskos,
Chef-Owner of Trap Door Bakehouse & Cafe, Quechee, VT (p. 135).

Carrot Apple Thyme Soup

This all-time favorite at Miller's Cafe & Bakery relies on the extra flavor that comes from leaving the skins on the fruit and vegetables.

Serves 8–12

1 small onion, diced

2 tablespoons olive oil

1 pound carrots, scrubbed but not peeled, then diced

2 red or green apples, cored but unpeeled, diced

1 red potato, unpeeled, diced

1 vegetable or chicken bouillon cube

1 teaspoon fresh or ½ teaspoon dried thyme leaves

¼ cup parsley, chopped

¼ teaspoon curry powder

1 teaspoon garlic powder (not garlic salt)

1 tablespoon kosher salt or to taste

½ teaspoon ground black pepper or to taste

¼ cup honey

8 cups water

2 cups heavy cream

Sauté onion in olive oil until tender. Add all remaining ingredients except heavy cream. Bring to a boil, then reduce heat and simmer covered on low heat until carrots are cooked thoroughly, about 1 hour.

Puree soup with an immersion blender until smooth, or puree in batches in a stand blender and return to the pot. Add heavy cream and stir in gently. Reseason soup as needed.

Adapted recipe courtesy of David Eyler,
Chef/Owner Miller's Cafe & Bakery, Littleton, NH (p. 206).

Vermont Farmhouse Potato Chowder

The Vermont Department of Agriculture asked Sugarbush Executive Chef Gerry Nooney to create a dish that would help farmers by highlighting the flavor and versatility of local potatoes. With input from a number of eager tasters, he developed this hearty soup that is perfect after a day on the slopes.

Serves 4–6

- 12 ounces Vermont potatoes, peeled
- 1 quart chicken stock
- ¾ cup Vermont cider
- 1 link hot Italian sausage
- 1 small Spanish onion, small dice
- 2 stalks celery, small dice
- 2 tablespoons vegetable oil
- 1 teaspoon smoked paprika
- ½ cup heavy cream
- ½ pound Vermont potatoes, large dice
- 1 teaspoon whole leaf dried marjoram
- 1 teaspoon whole leaf dried basil
- 1 teaspoon kosher salt
- Fresh ground black pepper, to taste

Simmer potatoes in chicken stock and cider until very tender. Puree potatoes with stock/cider mixture in blender.

Slow roast sausage until cooked through by placing in a 300°F oven for about 25 minutes. Chill, pulse in food processor until coarsely chopped. Add sausage to pureed soup mixture

Sweat onion and celery in vegetable oil until translucent. Add smoked paprika and cook additional 3 minutes, stirring often. Add vegetable/paprika mixture to pureed soup.

Add cream to soup mixture.

Simmer the ½ pound of large-dice potato in enough salted water to cover, until tender. Drain and rinse under cold water. Add to soup mixture. Add marjoram, basil, salt, and pepper to soup. Bring soup back to simmer before serving.

Recipe courtesy of Gerry Nooney,
Executive Chef at Sugarbush Resort, Warren, VT (p. 70).

Bison Chili

This recipe is a favorite at local chili cookoff events, although previously published versions omit the secret ingredient of Hershey's semisweet chocolate chips. Bison meat is so much leaner than beef that the recipe can handle the extra calories. Keep in mind that because bison is so lean, it should be cooked slowly at low to medium heat.

Serves 4

- **1 pound ground bison**
- **1 medium onion, chopped**
- **1 (15-ounce) can pinto beans, rinsed and drained**
- **2 (16-ounce) cans peeled tomatoes**
- **½ cup water**
- **½ cup Hershey's semisweet chocolate chips**
- **2 teaspoons chili powder**
- **½ teaspoon ground cumin**
- **½ teaspoon salt**
- **½ teaspoon ground pepper**
- **¼ cup chopped fresh cilantro**
- **Grated cheese or jalapeño peppers for garnish**

In a nonstick skillet, slowly sauté the ground bison and onion until the meat is browned and onion is tender. Add the pinto beans, tomatoes, water, chocolate, and spices. Cover and simmer for 1 hour, adding more water if the chili becomes too thick. Stir occasionally to keep chili from sticking to the pot.

Add chopped cilantro and simmer an additional 10 minutes. Spoon into bowls and garnish with grated cheese or diced jalapeño peppers.

Adapted recipe courtesy of Yankee Farmer's Market, Warner, NH (p. 251).

Chilled Curry-Scented Cauliflower Puree

This appetizer dish turns cauliflower haters into fans of the crucifer, which happens to grow especially well in the cool climate of New Hampshire and Vermont. The key is to place the warm puree into martini glasses and chill. Assemble just before serving.

Serves 6

1 head cauliflower, cleaned and cut into florets
1 teaspoon minced garlic
1½ teaspoons curry powder
1 quart heavy cream
½ cup chopped white onion
Kosher salt and ground black pepper to taste
¼ cup olive oil, divided

1 cup cleaned, diced portobello mushrooms
¼ cup diced red bell pepper
¼ cup diced red onion
¼ cup white balsamic vinegar
2 teaspoons chopped fresh basil
3 ounces radish sprouts

Place the cauliflower, garlic, curry, cream, and white onion into a sauce pot and cook on low heat until the volume of cream is reduced by 75 percent. Place into a blender and blend on high until smooth. Add salt and pepper to taste. While still warm, halfway fill 6 martini glasses. Chill until ready to serve.

Place 3 tablespoons olive oil in sauté pan over medium heat. Add mushrooms, bell pepper, and red onion and sauté until *mushrooms are soft. Add the balsamic vinegar, basil, and salt and pepper to taste. Chill until ready to serve.*

Toss the radish sprouts with remaining tablespoon of olive oil, salt and pepper. Set aside.

To assemble, place a teaspoon of the mushroom relish on top of the chilled cauliflower puree. Place the radish sprouts on top of the mushroom relish and serve.

Adapted recipe from Ed Swetz,
Executive Chef at Omni Mount Washington Resort, Bretton Woods, NH (p. 196).

Chilled Brandywine Heirloom Tomato & Cilantro Cooler

This is just what the doctor ordered when you have a glut of heirloom tomatoes. Brian Aspell of the Mountain View Grand Resort & Spa likes to offer this chilled cocktail as a tastebud awakener. He serves it in clear double shot glasses to highlight the wonderful colors and textures. It could also be served as a soup course—or even by itself as lunch.

Makes about 10 cups

- **4 cups peeled, seeded, and diced overripe Brandywine tomatoes**
- **2 cups seeded, peeled, diced cucumber**
- **6 large shallots, minced**
- **1 teaspoon minced garlic**
- **2 serrano peppers, seeded and minced**
- **2 teaspoons extra-virgin olive oil**
- **10 drops Tabasco sauce**

- **Juice of 2 limes**
- **3 cups V-8 juice**
- **⅛ cup aged sherry wine vinegar (more if needed to increase tartness)**
- **2 teaspoons finely chopped cilantro**
- **1½ cups diced yellow bell peppers**
- **Kosher salt and white pepper to taste**
- **¼ cup minced scallions**

In a blender combine the tomatoes, cucumbers, shallots, garlic, serrano peppers, olive oil, Tabasco sauce, lime juice, V-8 juice, and sherry wine vinegar. Puree for 30 seconds or long enough to achieve a slightly thickened juice.

Fold in the cilantro and bell peppers and season with salt and pepper. Refrigerate overnight and serve with minced scallions on top.

Adapted recipe courtesy of Brian Aspell,
Executive Chef at Mountain View Grand Resort & Spa, Whitefield, NH (p. 195).

Garden-Fresh Peach Salsa

To enjoy the freshest flavors of just-picked fruit, Diane Souther, who owns Apple Hill Farm with her husband Chuck, likes to serve this salsa on the day that she makes it. But it can be stored in the refrigerator for 2 days. We like it all by itself—just scooped up on a tortilla chip, but it's also a perfect complement to charcoal-grilled chicken. For a less coarse salsa, peel the peaches, tomatoes, and bell peppers by quickly blanching, then removing skin.

Makes about 4 cups

- 3 medium yellow peaches, pitted, and cut into small pieces
- 5 medium firm fresh tomatoes, stems removed, and cut into small pieces
- 1½ cups fresh corn kernels (from about 2 ears)
- 2 medium bell peppers, one green and one red or yellow, seeded and cut into small dice

- 1 jalapeño pepper, seeded and finely diced
- 1 small white onion, finely diced
- 2 teaspoons chopped cilantro leaves
- 2 teaspoons chopped parsley leaves
- 1 tablespoon balsamic vinegar
- 1 tablespoon olive oil
- ½ teaspoon salt
- ¼ teaspoon black pepper

Put the ingredients into large bowl and toss gently to mix together. Let stand for 30–60 minutes to allow flavors to blend together before serving.

Adapted recipe courtesy of Diane Souther,
co-owner of Apple Hill Farm, Concord, NH (p. 306).

Pork Loin Stuffed with Blue Cheese & Caramelized Apples

Chef John Lumbra's cooking classes at The Kitchen at The Store in Waitsfield, VT, range from comfort food to special occasion fare to classics of international cuisine. For this recipe, he adds a taste of Vermont with tart apples and artisanal blue cheese. While Lumbra's students will certainly know how to butterfly the pork loin, the rest of us can ask our butchers to do it for us.

Serves 6

1 (2½ pound) center-cut
    boneless pork loin, trimmed
    and butterflied

3 tablespoons olive oil
1 cup diced sweet onion
1 tablespoon minced garlic
1 tablespoon finely chopped
    fresh rosemary
1 tablespoon chopped fresh
    thyme leaves
1 teaspoon kosher salt
1 teaspoon black pepper

Stuffing:

6 tablespoons unsalted butter,
    divided
1½ cups panko bread crumbs
2 tart apples, peeled, cored,
    and sliced thinly
2 cups chicken stock, divided
1 cup Vermont artisan blue
    cheese, crumbled
2 tablespoons olive oil (for
    browning)

Pan Sauce:

1 cup chicken stock
1 tablespoon balsamic vinegar
4 tablespoons unsalted butter

Salt to taste
Black pepper to taste

Heat a large skillet over medium heat. Add the oil and onions, and sauté, stirring, until translucent, about 7 minutes. Add the garlic and seasonings; cook for another 2 minutes. Transfer to a bowl and set aside to cool.

Reheat the skillet over medium heat. Melt half of the butter and add the panko crumbs. Lightly toast the crumbs, stirring continuously until lightly browned. Transfer the crumbs to a large bowl and set aside.

In the same skillet, add the remaining butter and apples, and sauté over medium-high heat, continuously stirring, until the apples start to caramelize and turn a light brown. Once the apples have caramelized, add them to the bowl with the bread crumbs. Add the onion mixture, 1 cup chicken stock, and blue cheese to the bowl and mix until well combined and the bread crumbs have absorbed the chicken stock. DO NOT CLEAN SKILLET YET!

Preheat the oven to 400°F. Position the oven rack in the lower third of the oven.

Season the loin with salt and pepper. Spread an even layer of stuffing on top, to give the finished product a nice spiral pattern when it is sliced. Roll the pork loin gently so as not to displace the stuffing. Tie it securely with kitchen twine, but not so tight that you squeeze out the filling.

In your skillet, heat the olive oil over medium-high heat. Season the outside of the loin with salt and pepper. When the oil is hot, brown the pork loin on all sides, for 6–8 minutes. Place the pork loin in a flameproof roasting pan. Deglaze the skillet with 1 cup chicken stock, scraping the brown bits off the bottom with *a wooden spatula. Pour the deglazing liquid over the loin and place the roasting pan in the oven.*

Roast about 25–30 minutes until an instant-read thermometer registers 145°F when inserted into the thickest part of the meat. Remove the meat to a cutting board; cover loosely with foil and let rest for 15 minutes. Remove any loose stuffing from the pan. Skim off and discard any fat in the pan.

To make the pan sauce, place the roasting pan over medium-high heat and add the cup of stock and vinegar; bring to a boil and reduce the liquid by a third while scraping the bits on the bottom of the pan into the sauce. Swirl in the butter and season with salt and pepper.

To serve, remove the strings. Carve the roast into ¾-inch thick slices. Drizzle the meat with some pan sauce.

Adapted recipe courtesy of Chef John Lumbra
of The Kitchen at The Store, Waitsfield, VT (p. 81).

Brookford Farm Braised Country-Style Ribs with Star Anise & Whiskey

Brookford Farm pasture-raises all its animals, resulting in very lean cuts of meat. This braising technique develops intense flavor while making the meat nearly fall off the bone.

Serves 4

3 or 4 pounds country-style spare ribs

1 cup whiskey, divided

4 whole star anise

2 cups crushed, pureed tomatoes

½ cup red wine vinegar

½ cup balsamic vinegar

1 tablespoon peanut oil

1–2 dashes soy sauce (or more)

¾ cup blackstrap molasses

Quartered rind of 1 organic lemon

To brown the meat, pat the ribs dry and place them in a single layer in the bottom of a heavy, nonreactive pan with a tight-fitting lid. Slowly heat the pan on the stove top until the ribs begin to render out a little of their fat. Then turn the heat up to medium-high and brown the meat on both sides. It's fine to do this in batches if your pan is not large enough to do it all at once.

Deglaze the pan with ½ cup whiskey, then return

any meat you might have removed to the pan. Add the star anise and remaining whiskey, shut the lid, and leave the ribs alone on low heat to braise for a couple of hours. Try to refrain from peeking too much, as you want to keep the vapors in with the ribs.

To make barbecue sauce, combine remaining ingredients in a 2-quart saucepan, and let simmer for a couple of hours, until thickened. Add the sauce to the ribs for the last hour of cooking. If it suits you, drain some or all of the fat from the meat before you add the sauce. At this point, it's better to take the lid off until your sauce is thick and you have coated the ribs.

Serve with rice or crusty rolls.

Recipe provided by Mary Brower
of Brookford Farm, Canterbury, NH (p. 307).

Orange Polenta Cake

This is one of the many popular gluten-free desserts that nutritionist and baker Audrey Pellegrino developed for Cornucopia Bakery Cafe in Bristol, NH.

Serves 8–10

For Caramel Sauce:

2 tablespoons water
½ cup sugar

2 tablespoons butter, cut into bits
2 navel oranges

For Cake:

1¾ sticks butter, softened
1 cup sugar
3 large eggs
2 teaspoons orange flower water
½ cup millet

1 teaspoon baking powder
½ teaspoon salt
2 cups ground almonds
⅔ cup quick-cooking polenta or corn flour

For Glaze:

¼ cup orange marmalade

1–4 tablespoons water

For the caramel layer, melt water and sugar together in a large, flat-bottomed pan over medium heat. Do not stir but swirl until it is a dark amber color. Remove from heat and add butter, swirling until melted.

Peel, pith, and slice oranges. Place them in a 9-inch springform pan that has been well greased and lined with parchment paper. Pour caramel layer over the oranges.

Preheat oven to 350°F (325°F for a convection oven). Mix all cake ingredients and stir very well with spoon or with mixer on lowest speed. Place cake mixture carefully over the caramel layer. Bake 50 minutes or until a wooden pick comes out clean from the center. Invert onto cake stand. Stir water into marmalade and brush this glaze over the top of the cake.

Adapted recipe courtesy of Audrey Pellegrino,
baker and owner of Cornucopia, Bristol, NH (p. 224).

Berry Creek Farm's Chocolate Strawberry Tarte

Rosemary Croizet created this recipe (with love) for her chocoholic French husband. The strawberries from their farm are so delicious that we imagine folks all over the Northeast Kingdom enjoy this delicious dessert in June.

Serves 8

For the shell

4 tablespoons butter
¼ teaspoon cinnamon

½ package chocolate wafers (20–30), crushed

For the ganache:

1 cup heavy cream
½ cup whole milk

10 ounces bittersweet chocolate, chopped
1 large egg

For the topping:

1 quart organic strawberries, washed, hulled, and dried
½ cup honey, or fine clear jelly such as gooseberry or currant for glaze

Whipped cream, to serve

Preheat oven to 325°F.

Melt butter, add cinnamon and crushed wafers, then place in 9-inch springform pan and press evenly to form a crust, as you would for a cheesecake. Refrigerate while making the rest of the tarte.

Heat cream and milk in a double boiler over medium-high heat until just begin-ning to boil. Add the chocolate and reduce to simmer while whisking the mixture until smooth. Turn off heat and let stand for 10 minutes. Whisk in the egg. Pour mixture into the shell and bake until set, about 25 minutes. Cool completely. Arrange berries pointed side up on top of the ganache. Using a pastry brush, paint on warmed honey or jelly for a glaze. Serve with whipped cream.

Adapted recipe courtesy of Rosemary Croizet
of Berry Creek Farm, Westfield, VT (p. 108).

Appendices

Appendix A: Eateries by Cuisine

Buffalo Mountain Food Coop and Cafe, Hardwick, VT (NEK), 103

Capitol Grounds, Montpelier, VT (HOV), 77

Front Porch Cafe, Putney, VT (SV), 152

La Brioche Bakery & Cafe, Montpelier, VT (HOV), 66

Mirabelle's Cafe & Bakery, Burlington, VT (CHAMP), 46

On the Rise Bakery, Richmond, VT (CHAMP), 29

Otter Creek Bakery, Middlebury, VT (CHAMP), 48

Rainbow Sweets, Marshfield, VT (NEK), 106

Trap Door Bakehouse & Cafe, Quechee, VT (CV), 135

Trapp Family Lodge, Stowe, VT (HOV), 71

Vergennes Laundry, Vergennes, VT (CHAMP), 50

Barbecue

Curtis' All American BBQ, Putney, VT (SV), 149

Casual American

Al's French Frys, South Burlington, VT (CHAMP), 16

American Flatbread/Hearth, Burlington, VT (CHAMP), 17

American Flatbread/Hearth, Middlebury, VT (CHAMP), 17

Basin Harbor Club, Vergennes, VT (CHAMP), 17

The Bee's Knees, Morrisville, VT (HOV), 63

Birdseye Diner, Castleton, VT (CV), 116

Blue Paddle Bistro, South Hero, VT (CHAMP), 19

Bob's Diner, Manchester, VT (SV), 148

Burger Barn, Cambridge, VT (HOV), 64

Chelsea Royal Diner, West Brattleboro, VT (SV), 149

Cliff House, Stowe, VT (HOV), 64

Daily Planet, Burlington, VT (CHAMP), 22

Dutch Pancake House, Stowe, VT (HOV), 65

Eaton's Sugarhouse, South
Royalton, VT (HOV), 77
Farmers Diner, Quechee, VT
(CV), 118
Flatbread Kitchen, Waitsfield, VT
(HOV), 65
Harpoon Brewery, Windsor, VT
(CV), 118
Kitchen Door Cafe, Grand Isle, VT
(CHAMP), 24
Libby's Blue Line Diner,
Colchester, VT (CHAMP), 26
Little Rooster Cafe, Manchester
Center, VT (SV), 153
Mountain Creamery Restaurant,
Woodstock, VT (CV), 121
Norwich Inn, Norwich, VT (CV), 122
Parker Pie Co., West Glover, VT
(NEK), 99
Penny Cluse, Burlington, VT
(CHAMP), 29
Perfect Pear Cafe & Vermont
Beer Company, Bradford, VT
(HOV), 69
Putney Diner, Putney, VT (SV), 157
Red Hen Baking Co., Middlesex, VT
(HOV), 83

The Skinny Pancake, Burlington,
VT (CHAMP), 30, Montpelier, VT
(HOV), 70
Sonny's Blue Benn Diner,
Bennington, VT (SV), 158
Sugar & Spice, Mendon, VT
(CV), 124

Delicatessen
Harrington's of Vermont,
Shelburne, VT (CHAMP), 39
Vermont Country Deli, Brattleboro,
VT (SV), 173

French
Black Sheep Bistro, Vergennes, VT
(CHAMP), 19
Cafe Provence, Brandon, VT (CV),
116
Cafe Shelburne, Shelburne, VT
(CHAMP), 21
Chantecleer, East Dorset, VT (SV),
148
Leunig's Bistro & Old World Cafe,
Burlington, VT (CHAMP), 26
Tourterelle, New Haven, VT
(CHAMP), 32

German/Austrian/Swiss

Asta's Swiss Restaurant, Jamaica, VT (SV), 146

Cliff House, Stowe, VT (HOV), 64

Countryman's Pleasure, Mendon, VT (CV), 117

Das Bierhaus, Burlington, VT (CHAMP), 22

Trapp Family Lodge, Stowe, VT (HOV), 71

International/Continental

Le Belvedere, Newport, VT (NEK), 98

Reluctant Panther Inn & Restaurant, Manchester Village, VT (SV), 157

Windham Hill Inn, West Townshend, VT (SV), 162

Irish

Inn at Long Trail, Killington, VT (CV), 119

Italian

Allegro, Bennington, VT (SV), 146

Bove's Cafe, Burlington, VT (CHAMP), 20

Fireworks Restaurant, Brattleboro, VT (SV), 151

Lago Trattoria & Catering, Newport, VT (NEK), 98

Leonardo's Pizza, Burlington, South Burlington, VT (CHAMP), 25

Osteria Pane e Salute, Woodstock, VT (CV), 122

Trattoria Delia, Burlington, VT (CHAMP), 33

Mediterranean

Bistro Henry, Manchester, VT (SV), 147

New American

Basin Harbor Club, Vergennes, VT (CHAMP), 17

Belted Cow Bistro, Essex, VT (CHAMP), 18

Cafe Provence, Brandon, VT (CV), 116

Church & Main, Burlington, VT (CHAMP), 21

Claire's Restaurant & Bar, Hardwick, VT (NEK), 96

Dorset Inn on the Green, Dorset, VT (SV), 150

Elements Food and Spirit, St. Johnsbury, VT (NEK), 97

The Essex, Vermont's Culinary Resort & Spa, Essex, VT (CHAMP), 23

Farmhouse Tap & Grill, Burlington, VT (CHAMP), 24

Four Columns Inn, Newfane, VT (SV), 151

Hen of the Wood, Waterbury, VT (HOV), 66

The Hermitage, West Dover, VT (SV), 152

Inn at Weathersfield, Perkinsville, VT (CV), 119

Inn at Weston, Weston, VT (SV), 153

Kitchen Table Bistro, Richmond, VT (CHAMP), 25

Mangowood Restaurant, Woodstock, VT (CV), 120

Mary's Restaurant, Bristol, VT (CHAMP), 27

Michael's on the Hill, Waterbury Center, VT (HOV), 67

Monty's Old Brick Tavern, Williston, VT (CHAMP), 27

Mountain Top Inn & Resort, Chittenden, VT (CV), 121

NECI on Main, Montpelier, VT (HOV), 67

Norma's, Stowe, VT (HOV), 68

North Hero House, North Hero, VT (CHAMP), 28

Pangea Fine Dining, North Bennington, VT (SV), 155

The Perfect Wife Restaurant & Tavern, Manchester, VT (SV), 156

Putney Inn, Putney, VT (SV), 157

Rabbit Hill Inn, Lower Waterford, VT (NEK), 99

Red Rooster, Woodstock, VT (CV), 123

Salt Cafe, Montpelier, VT (HOV), 69

Shelburne Farms, Shelburne, VT (CHAMP), 38

Simon Pearce Restaurant, Quechee, VT (CV), 124

Solstice, Stowe, VT (HOV), 70

Sonoma Station, Richmond, VT (CHAMP), 31

Stuart & John's Sugar House,
Westmoreland, NH (MON), 262
Sunny Day Diner, Lincoln, NH
(WM), 193
Tilt'n Diner, Laconia, NH (LR), 220
UNH Dairy Bar, Durham, NH (P&S),
325
Union Diner, Laconia, NH (LR),
220
Waterwheel Breakfast House,
Jefferson, NH (WM), 194

Delicatessen
Butternuts Good Dishes,
Wolfeboro, NH (LR), 223
Moe's Italian Sandwich,
Portsmouth, NH (P&S), 321
Wendle's Delicatessen, Cafe, and
Then Some!, Franconia, NH
(WM), 208

French
L.A. Burdick Cafe, Walpole, NH
(MON), 257
Le Rendezvous, Colebrook, NH
(WM), 203

German/Austrian/Swiss
Bavaria German Restaurant,
Hooksett, NH (MV), 280

International/Continental
Mile Away Restaurant, Milford, NH
(MON), 259
Street Food 360, Portsmouth, NH
(P&S), 324

Irish
Holy Grail, Epping, NH (P&S), 320
Peddler's Daughter, Nashua, NH
(MV), 289
Seven Barrel Brewery, West
Lebanon, NH (SUN), 242

Italian
Angela's Pasta and Cheese Shop,
Manchester, NH (MV), 295
The Colosseum, Salem, NH
(MV), 283
Lago, Meredith, NH (LR), 217
900 Degrees, Manchester, NH
(MV), 289
Tuscan Kitchen, Salem, NH
(MV), 293

Traditional American

Common Man Ashland, Ashland, NH (LR), 215

Common Man, Claremont, NH (SUN), 238

Greenwood's at Canterbury Shaker Village, Canterbury, NH (MV), 285

Hart's Turkey Farm Restaurant, Meredith, NH (LR), 216

Inn on Newfound Lake, Bridgewater, NH (LR), 216

O Steaks & Seafood, Lakeport, NH (LR), 219

Rainbow Grille and Tavern, Pittsburg, NH (WM), 192

Sugar Hill Inn, Sugar Hill, NH (WM), 193

Vegetarian Friendly

Blue Moon Evolution, Exeter, NH (P&S), 318

Half Baked and Fully Brewed, Lincoln, NH (WM), 201

Maia Papaya, Bethlehem, NH (WM), 205

Pickity Place, Mason, NH (MON), 261

Rocky's Famous Burgers, Newmarket, NH (P&S), 324

Stella Blu, Nashua, NH (MV), 292

Street Food 360, Portsmouth, NH (P&S), 326

Appendix B: Dishes, Specialties & Purveyors

Breakfast/Brunch

Maple Grove Farms of Vermont, St.
Johnsbury, VT (NEK), 105
Morse Farm, Montpelier, VT
(HOV), 82
New England Maple Museum,
Pittsford, VT (CV), 132
Sugarbush Farm, Woodstock, VT
(CV), 134
Vermont Maple Outlet,
Jeffersonville, VT (HOV), 87

Markets & Co-ops

The Baker's Store, Norwich, VT
(CV), 126
Buffalo Mountain Food Coop and
Cafe, Hardwick, VT (NEK), 103
Cabot Annex Store, Waterbury, VT
(HOV), 76
Cabot Quechee Store, Quechee, VT
(CV), 127
Castleton Village Store, Castleton,
VT (CV), 128
City Market, Burlington, VT
(CHAMP), 37
Cold Hollow Cider Mill, Waterbury,
VT (HOV), 77

F. H. Gillingham & Sons General
Store, Woodstock, VT (CV), 129
Harvest Market, Stowe, VT
(HOV), 80
Healthy Living Natural Foods
Market, South Burlington, VT
(CHAMP), 40
Middlebury Natural Foods Coop,
Middlebury, VT (CHAMP), 46
Misty Knoll Farms, New Haven, VT
(CHAMP), 47
Mountain Cheese & Wine, Stowe,
VT (HOV), 83
Powers Market, North Bennington,
VT (SV), 171
Singleton's General Store,
Proctorsville, VT (CV), 134
Taftsville Country Store, Taftsville,
VT (CV), 135
Upper Valley Food Coop, White
River Junction, VT (CV), 136
Vermont Country Store, Weston &
Rockingham, VT (SV), 174
Village Butcher, Woodstock, VT
(CV), 174
Warren Store, Warren, VT
(HOV), 88

Smokehouses

Dakin Farm, Ferrisburgh, VT
(CHAMP), 38
Green Mountain Smokehouse,
Windsor, VT (CV), 131
Harrington's of Vermont,
Shelburne, VT (CHAMP), 39
Lawrence's Smoke Shop,
Townshend, VT (SV), 170

Tea

Dobra Tea, Burlington, VT
(CHAMP), 39
Twilight Tea Lounge, Brattleboro,
VT (SV), 173
Vermont Liberty Tea, Waterbury,
VT (HOV), 87

Wine

Artesano Meadery, Groton, VT
(NEK), 101
Boyden Valley Winery, Cambridge,
VT (HOV), 74
Caledonia Spirits & Winery,
Hardwick, VT (NEK), 104

Charlotte Village Winery,
Charlotte, VT (CHAMP), 37
Grand View Winery, East Calais, VT
(NEK), 105
Grand View Winery Tasting Room,
Waterbury Center, VT (HOV), 79
Honora Winery, Jacksonville, VT
(SV), 168
Lincoln Peak Vineyard, New Haven,
VT (CHAMP), 44
Neshobe River Winery, Brandon,
VT (CV), 131
Otter Valley Winery, Brandon, VT
(CV), 132
Putney Mountain Winery Tasting
Room, Putney, VT (SV), 172
Shelburne Vineyard, Shelburne, VT
(CHAMP), 48
Snow Farm Vineyard, South Hero,
VT (CHAMP), 48
Snow Farm Vineyard Tasting Room,
Waterbury, VT (HOV), 84
Tastes of the Valley, Brandon, VT
(CV), 131

New Hampshire

Breweries

Anheuser-Busch Brewery, Merrimack, NH (MV), 297

Elm City Brewing, Keene, NH (MON), 256

Flying Goose Brewpub and Grille, New London, NH (SUN), 238

Martha's Exchange Restaurant & Brewing Co., Nashua, NH (MV), 287

Milly's Tavern, Manchester, NH (MV), 288

Moat Mountain Smoke House & Brewing Co., North Conway, NH (WM), 191

Red Hook Brewery/Cataqua Public House, Portsmouth, NH (P&S), 333

Seven Barrel Brewery, West Lebanon, NH (SUN), 242

Smuttynose Brewing Co., Portsmouth, NH (P&S), 334

Tuckerman Brewing Co., Conway, NH (WM), 207

White Birch Brewing, Hooksett, NH (MV), 305

Woodstock Inn Station & Brewery, North Woodstock, NH (WM), 194

Burgers

Arnie's Place, Concord, NH (MV), 279

Barley House Restaurant & Tavern, Concord, NH (MV), 279

Flying Goose Brewpub and Grille, New London, NH (SUN), 238

Rocky's Famous Burgers, Newmarket, NH (P&S), 324

Beer-Making Supplies

Granite Cask, Whitefield, NH (WM), 200

Mount Washington Homebrew Supply, Littleton, NH (WM), 206

Candy & Chocolatiers

Ava Marie Chocolates, Peterborough, NH (MON), 263

Byrne & Carlson, Portsmouth, NH (P&S), 328

The Chocolatier, Exeter, NH (P&S), 328

Chutters, Littleton, NH (WM), 198

Granite State Candy Shoppe & Ice Cream, Concord, NH (MV), 300

Jacques Fine European Pastries, Suncook, NH (MV), 301

Kellerhaus, Weirs Beach, NH
(LR), 225

L.A. Burdick Chocolate Shop,
Walpole, NH (MON), 266

Lee's Candy Kitchen, Meredith, NH
(LR), 226

The Mill Fudge Factory & Ice
Cream Cafe, Bristol, NH
(LR), 226

Sanborn's Fine Candies, Hampton,
NH (P&S), 333

Stella's Fine Chocolates, Bedford,
NH (MV), 303

Van Otis Chocolates, Manchester,
NH (MV), 305

Winnipesaukee Chocolates,
Wolfeboro, NH (LR), 228

Ye Goodie Shoppe, Keene, NH
(MON), 269

Cheese

Agape Homestead Farm, Ossipee,
NH (LR), 222

Boggy Meadow Farm, Walpole, NH
(MON), 264

Brookford Farm, Canterbury, NH
(MV), 307

Harman's Cheese & Country Store,
Sugar Hill, NH (WM), 201

Hickory Nut Farm, Lee, NH (P&S),
329

Landaff Creamery, Landaff, NH
(WM), 202

Robie Farm & Store, Piermont, NH
(SUN), 246

Sandwich Creamery, North
Sandwich, NH (LR), 227

Taylor Brothers Sugarhouse &
Creamery, Meriden, NH
(SUN), 247

Via Lactea, Brookfield, NH
(LR), 228

Coffee

A&E Roastery, Amherst, NH
(MV), 294

Breaking New Grounds, Portsmouth
& Durham, NH (P&S), 326

The Met Coffee House, North
Conway, NH (WM), 205

White Mountain Gourmet Coffee,
Concord, NH (MV), 306

Black Forest Cafe & Bakery, Amherst, NH (MV), 282

Cornucopia Bakery, Bristol, NH (LR), 224

Frederick's Pastries, Amherst & Bedford, NH (MV), 299

German John's Bakery, Hillsborough, NH (MON), 265

Jacques Fine European Pastries, Suncook, NH (MV), 301

Le Rendezvous, Colebrook, NH (WM), 203

Madeleines, Concord, NH (MV), 302

Miller's Cafe & Bakery, Littleton, NH (WM), 206

Portsmouth Baking Company, Portsmouth, NH (P&S), 332

Sweet Dreams Bakery, Stratham, NH (P&S), 335

Sweet Retreat, Manchester, NH (MV), 304

Pizza

900 Degrees, Manchester, NH (MV), 289

Smokehouses

Fox Country Smoke House, Canterbury, NH (MV), 298

Garfields Smokehouse, Meriden, NH (SUN), 244

North Country Smokehouse, Claremont, NH (SUN), 245

Tea

White Heron Tea, Rollinsford, NH (P&S), 337

Wine

Candia Vineyards, Hooksett, NH (MV), 298

Flag Hill Winery & Distillery, Lee, NH (P&S), 328

Fulchino Vineyard, Hollis, NH (MV), 300

Haunting Whisper Vineyards, Danbury, NH (SUN), 244

Hermit Woods Winery, Sanbornton, NH (LR), 225

Jewell Towne Vineyards, South Hampton, NH (P&S), 330

Moonlight Meadery, Londonderry, NH (MV), 303

Appendix C: Food Events

Regional Codes for Corresponding Vermont Chapters:

(CHAMP)   Burlington & the Champlain Valley, 15
(HOV)   Montpelier, Stowe & the Heart of Vermont, 61
(NEK)   St. Johnsbury & the Northeast Kingdom, 95
(CV)   Rutland, Woodstock & Central Vermont, 115
(SV)   Bennington, Brattleboro & Southern Vermont, 145

STATEWIDE

Maple Weekend, www.vtmaple.org. The last full weekend in March is open house at sugarhouses around the state, offering a chance to see syrup being made. Most offer samples of syrup and other maple products.

Vermont Vineyard and Winery Open House Weekend, www.vermontgrapeandwinecouncil.com. Vineyards and wineries host open houses in late August as the harvest is about to begin. Activities vary by site, but generally include wine tastings.

Champlain Valley Fair, Essex
  Junction, VT (CHAMP), 58
Deerfield Valley Blueberry Festival,
  Wilmington, Whitingham &
  Dover, VT (SV), 182
Deerfield Valley Farmers' Day Fair,
  Wilmington, VT (SV), 182
Franklin County Field Days,
  Highgate, VT (CHAMP), 59
Orleans County Fair, Barton, VT
  (NEK), 113
Quechee Scottish Festival and
  Celtic Fair, Quechee, VT (CV),
  142
Taste of Woodstock, Woodstock,
  VT (CV), 143
Vermont State Fair, Rutland, VT
  (CV), 143
Vermont State Zucchini Festival,
  Ludlow, VT (CV), 143
Washington County Fair & Field
  Days, Waitsfield, VT (HOV), 93

September
Guilford Fair, Guilford, VT
  (SV), 182
Plymouth Cheese & Harvest
  Festival, Plymouth, VT (CV), 142

Shelburne Farms Harvest Festival,
  Shelburne, VT (CHAMP), 59
Southern Vermont Garlic & Herb
  Festival, Bennington, VT
  (SV), 182
Tour de Farms, Addison County, VT
  (CHAMP), 59
Tunbridge World's Fair, Tunbridge,
  VT (HOV), 92
Vermont Life Wine & Harvest
  Festival, Dover & Wilmington,
  VT (SV), 183
Vermont State Fair, Rutland, VT
  (CV), 143

October
Apple Pie Festival, Cabot, VT
  (NEK), 112
Famous Apple Pie Festival,
  Dummerston, VT (SV), 182
Stowe Oktoberfest, Stowe, VT
  (HOV), 92

November
Bradford Wild Game Supper,
  Bradford, VT (HOV), 92

New Hampshire

Regional Codes for Corresponding New Hampshire Chapters:

(WM)	White Mountains & the Great North Woods, 187
(LR)	Lakes Region, 213
(SUN)	Sunapee & the Upper Connecticut River Valley, 235
(MON)	Keene & the Monadnock Region, 255
(MV)	Concord, Manchester, Nashua, & the Merrimack Valley, 277
(P&S)	Portsmouth & the Seacoast, 315

STATEWIDE

New Hampshire Maple Weekend, www.nhmapleproducers.com. One weekend in late March is open house at sugarhouses around the state, offering a chance to see syrup being made. Most offer samples of syrup and other maple products.

INDEX BY MONTH

February

Annual Chocolate Festival, Mount Washington Valley, NH (WM), 211

March

Portsmouth Restaurant Week, Portsmouth, NH (P&S), 341

April

Taste of the Nation Manchester, Manchester, NH (MV), 314

May

Chowderfest, Waterville Valley, NH (WM), 212

June

New England Brewfest, Lincoln, NH (WM), 212

Taste of the Nation, Portsmouth, NH (P&S), 342

Index